CONTEMPORARY
MUSIC
AND
MUSIC
CULTURES

CONTEMPORARY MUSIC AND MUSIC CULTURES

Charles Hamm
Bruno Nettl
Ronald Byrnside

School of Music
University of Illinois

PRENTICE-HALL, INC., Englewood Cliffs, New Jersey

Library of Congress Cataloging in Publication Data

HAMM, CHARLES E
    Contemporary music and music cultures.

    Includes bibliographies.
        1. Music—History and criticism—20th century.
    2. Ethnomusicology. I. Nettl, Bruno, 1930–
    joint author. II. Byrnside, Ronald, 1933– joint
    author. III. Title.
    ML197.H245C6   780′.904   74–4427
    ISBN 0–13–170175–4

780.904
H18c
94342
aug 1975

© 1975 by Prentice-Hall, Inc.
Englewood Cliffs, New Jersey

Printed in the United States of America

10   9   8   7   6   5   4   3   2   1

PRENTICE-HALL INTERNATIONAL, INC., *London*
PRENTICE-HALL OF AUSTRALIA, PTY. LTD., *Sydney*
PRENTICE-HALL OF CANADA, LTD., *Toronto*
PRENTICE-HALL OF INDIA PRIVATE LIMITED, *New Delhi*
PRENTICE-HALL OF JAPAN, INC., *Tokyo*

Dedicated to
BECKY
BRUCE
CHRIS
CHRISTOPHER
GLORIA
RACHEL
STUART

Contents

Preface

The purpose of this book of essays is to provide a novel sort of introduction to music. Struck by the fact that most introductions to the art are oriented toward an historical approach or, on the other hand, cover the field of music systematically by giving attention to selected parameters such as melody, rhythm, and harmony, or to genres of music such as symphony, opera, and song, we were impressed by the attractiveness of an approach that focuses on music in the contemporary world, and particularly on the way in which it interacts with those social, political, and cultural processes that distinguish the twentieth century. We have therefore attempted to produce a group of original essays, each of which is devoted to an approach to the study of music and musical culture, and which has one repertory or culture as its main topic of discussion. We view the contemporary world as consisting of the industrialized nations of the West and the developing countries of the Third World; we include among contemporary musics all sorts of musical styles that have come into existence in the twentieth century, whether their background is part and parcel of the twentieth century or whether it is to be ultimately sought in the distant past. We feel also that the reader will be interested in musics of the educated and elite as well as those of the broad masses of urban and rural population.

Music can be studied and appreciated in many ways. It can be approached as an art that comprises great exemplars and masterworks; or it can be viewed as the entire musical product of a whole people. It can be studied as a chain of history in which each event causes another; or it can be considered a group of processes that reflect in sound what is happening in life. It can be regarded as a group of techniques, a craft in which structural relationships are translated into patterns of sound. We have tried to provide insights into a number of these approaches.

The first essay, dealing with concepts and terminology, enables the reader to consider music as the craft of the composer. This chapter is in some ways exceptional in the book, for it draws together a number of different kinds of music to show some of the basic principles and elements of musical structure. We then proceed to the main body of the book, which consists of more specialized studies. Chapter 2 focuses on the relationship between the recent political and social history of the United States and the American music of that period, illustrating the typical development of music in industrial society. Chapter 3 attempts to do essentially the same thing but in a very different venue, the rapidly developing but still essentially traditional musical culture of Iran, with comparative notes on India and Japan. Chapter 4 is, like the previous two chapters, essentially a study of historical processes in the twentieth century; it assesses the impact of Western music on two non-Western cultures, Africa and the American Indians, which reacted quite differently to this influence. History is also the basic point of reference of Chapters 5 and 6, the first showing the way in which a number of musical styles from diverse sources have come together to form the popular music of the present, and the second dealing with the formation of a new musical style—early rock'n'roll. In Chapter 6 we approach, from the standpoint of a genre popular music, a question that has been studied many times by music historians dealing with the classical music of periods as diverse as the early Baroque, the Ars Nova, the pre-classical, and the early twelve-tone movement. Thus, while we are writing about the twentieth century, several of our chapters indicate that history and its processes is one of our major concerns.

Chapters 7, 8, and 9 discuss issues that are frequently neglected in introductory treatments, but which are particularly important to a general understanding of music from a twentieth-century viewpoint. In Chapter 7 the relationship between words and music in song is explored with the use of English folk music as it exists in the United States, in the earlier rural culture as well as its current urban and campus environment. The importance of the performer is rarely discussed, even in scholarly studies of music, and Chapter 8, which concerns the concept of improvisation, particularly in jazz, introduces this important issue. And finally, while the impact of technology has always been great in music, and although the available technology of a culture has always been a great factor in the development of its musical identity, at no time has technology been as pervasive an influence as in the last several decades. The last chapter therefore deals with an aspect of this technology, the development of sound recording and its role in music.

We have tried to consider a variety of problems. We have tried to balance historical considerations from a twentieth-century viewpoint with analytical and systematic approaches. We look at both Western and non-Western music, and we deal with several strata of musical culture—folk, popular, and classical. We discuss the music itself, though as much as possible in nontechnical language accessible to the non-musician. And we are particularly concerned with interactions among musics, among peoples, and between music and its cultural context. In some respects the reader may feel that this is an essentially ethnomusicological approach. Be that as it may, we feel that it is also the basic stuff of musicology, a discipline whose aim is, after all, the understanding of music as an art, in its cultural and historical context. Many scholars maintain that an understanding of the past is basic to an understanding of the present. We have no quarrel with this approach, but we feel that it should be balanced by its opposite, that is, that an understanding of the whole, including the past, can best be formed by first comprehending that part which is closest, the present. We have by no means tried to deal with all aspects of the current state of music in the world; instead, we have concentrated on a small number of approaches and repertories. We therefore offer nine separate studies, each presented in some degree of intensity, and together they represent a sampling of the many things that music does for man, and the many things that music is. We have not tried to formally interrelate our essays, but we assume that the reader, with the help of this preface, will be easily able to see how they fit together.

We conceived of this book as a possible text for a course introducing students to music, though we are aware that there are few courses now taught in which this book would be truly suitable. But we would like to stimulate the development of general courses on music that use the twentieth century in all its ramifications as a point of departure. We also conceive of this volume a source of supplementary reading in a wide range of courses—twentieth-century music, American music, ethnomusicology, music and society, and, of course, general introductions to and appreciations of music. It is not a book particularly directed to the specialist in music, but we feel that our approach is sufficiently novel to merit his occasional attention as well. The order of chapters should not be regarded as organic; readings can easily be assigned in any decided order. The three of us wrote our essays independently, and the author of each essay is identified.

We are grateful to many individuals for their help, and we would like to single out only the most prominent. The bulk of the research and organization of Chapter 9 is the work of Dale Cockrell, whose contribution is gratefully acknowledged. We would like to thank Stephen Blum for permission to use material from his thesis on the music of Northeastern Iran in Chapter 3, and William Amoaku for providing information on West African drumming in Chapter 4. Finally, we should like to thank Mrs. Pat Madsen and Mrs. Jean Mitchack for a great deal of patient secretarial help.

R.B.
C.H.
B.N.

CONTEMPORARY
MUSIC
AND
MUSIC
CULTURES

1

Introduction:
Concepts and Terminology

RONALD BYRNSIDE

There are many musics in the world, and they are as
different as the cultures in which they are found. The individuality of a music
may be traced to many things: the composers and the society which gave
birth to the music; the acoustical materials used to perform the music; and
the specific manner and medium of performance. Some of these factors will
be examined elsewhere in this book, but this chapter will focus attention on a
few elements and concepts basic to all musics. The terminology introduced
here will be used in subsequent chapters of the book; most of these terms
originated in the field of Western art music, but with certain modifications
they can and will be used in discussions of non-Western, popular, and folk
musics. The few technical terms used will be interpreted broadly and flexibly.

Listening to Music

All musics are a combination of sound and silence, and all musics exist in
time, but they don't all use the same sounds and they don't all measure time
in the same way. Every music can be analyzed in terms of what we may call
its rhetoric: how it forms itself. The basic elements of this rhetoric, the very

1

elements with which we shall be concerned in this chapter, are a part of all music. But as we move from music to music we discover that the uses of these elements are many and varied, so that something that is a part of the personality of one music may not even exist in the same form in an other music.

For example, a certain arrangement of sounds—a certain harmony—is part of the rhetoric of rock music. In part, our grasp of this music depends upon our ability and willingness to accept harmony as a delineator of formal structure. However, an audience conditioned to *depend* upon harmony for the creation of formal sense in music may find Indian classical music (and several other musics around the world) void of harmony; the music seems formless and, hence, senseless to them. This misconception remains unless and until that audience discovers that Indian music develops its own rhetoric—that it uses and arranges sound, silence, and time in its own way.

Music does more than simply form itself in a particular way; it seems to focus sharply on some things, and less sharply on other things. The result is what we might call a set of signals. For example, the repetition of a given fragment, theme, sound, or word tends to elevate the importance of that thing in our mind. Repetition is one of several devices used in music to create such signals. As we summarize in our mind a given moment or passage of music, the signal(s) within it are what the composer is "saying."

Music simultaneously develops, in addition to a rhetoric and a set of signals, a much more amorphous entity called mood, which comprises the aesthetic impact and psychological effect of a given music or piece of music. Mood leads us to consider what a piece of music "means." Probably no one, including the composer, can fully determine this meaning for any other person. A group of people might generally agree that a given composition establishes a certain mood or has a particular impact; to varying degrees these people might become involved in this mood. But the nature of this involvement and the associations that arise therein are personal. Beyond a general level, the meaning of a piece of music varies from person to person.

We have spoken of music as a phenomenon that does something, says something, and means something. We have spoken of these as three facets of music, suggesting that what music does can be analyzed in terms of its rhetoric, that what it says can be perceived as a set of signals, and that what it means and the effect it has on the listener is determined largely by the individual. We separate these three strands only to examine them independently, as one might examine the smell, texture, and taste of an orange. But in music these three strands are one—we do not separately experience form, substance, and meaning.

Analyses and discussions of music, and comparisons among them, are of value only when they positively affect one's experience of music. Music can be experienced on several levels, and one's capacity to experience music in general and musics in particular can be broadened and deepened. This process is personal, not competitive. It does not dictate, for example, that we try to experience a Beethoven symphony in exactly the same way that a famous conductor does; that would be neither possible nor desirable. Nevertheless, that conductor's understanding, involvement, and experience with the symphony may be a means by which we discover something that to us is meaningful in the piece.

Music tells us something about ourselves, for from it we learn something about our capacity to experience; the meaning that each of us derives from a musical composition may tell us something about ourselves that we might not otherwise have realized. Similarly, a music that is new to us can, if we deal with it intelligently, tell us something about those to whom the music is native.

Music and Time

Formal Structure

It is in the nature of a piece of music that it cannot be heard all at once. A musical composition is dispersed over a span of time. To make sense out of a piece of music, one must listen to each moment of music in the span, listen to each succeeding moment, and, simultaneously, recall and relate previous moments in the span to the present one. It is this process by which we grasp the formal structure of a piece of music.

Form is unavoidable in music. The form of a piece may satisfy us or displease us. If the latter, perhaps the form is too redundant and, hence, monotonous, or it may strike us as too complicated or chaotic and, hence, difficult or impossible to follow. It seems to be in our nature to try to make some kind of formal sense out of music. If the music does not shape itself into some obvious form or pattern, then we, consciously or unconsciously, try to shape it ourselves. And if, for some reason, we cannot do this, we become bored by the music. The blame for this can be assigned in some cases to the composer, sometimes to a performer who poorly re-creates the composition, or to us, the audience.

If it is true that we are uncomfortable when faced with something that is virtually unknown to us, then it is true that many pieces of music make us feel this way when we listen to them for the first time. But if there is a psychological rapport between the music and the audience, discomfort can become interesting. The composer who attempts such a relationship incorporates, very early in the piece, something that he believes will draw the audience into his music. This something can be fairly sophisticated, but more often it is simple and basic.

The *Brandenburg* Concerto No. 2, by Johann Sebastian Bach (1685–1750), attracts us by appealing to a basic musical urge, that of tapping our foot or in some other way keeping time with the music. Whatever else this piece does, and however complicated it may be in certain respects, it pulls us into itself through its irresistible rhythmic drive—it has a constant, regular, uncluttered pulsation. We are willing to listen to the piece because from the very beginning there is a reward: the toe-tapping sensation. We are willing to endure and eventually to explore the unknowns of the piece because on this basic level we are "in the music."

Once the composer "has us," so to speak, we are not so uncomfortable with the unknowns and complexities of what he is doing. On the contrary, we are likely to be intrigued by them. As the unknowns become known and understandable to us, we begin to piece together the music in our minds, and the composition becomes meaningful to us. Ultimately, we make a value judgment: we do or we do not like the piece. This judgment is based not simply on a gut reaction, but on an understanding of what the piece does, says, and means.

Musics throughout the world exhibit a great diversity of formal characteristics. What makes a particular form satisfying depends in large measure upon the intentions of the composer and the aesthetic and intellectual disposition of the audience. It is therefore not possible to specify the ingredients of a satisfying musical form. But despite this great formal diversity among the world's musics, there appear to be some fundamental components of musical form.

The first and probably the most frequently encountered of these elements is *repetition:* the recurrence within the time span of some musical event or events. Repetition may be literal (the event in question recurs in its original state) or non-literal (the event recurs as a variation of itself). A composer utilizes repetition for a number of reasons, the most basic of which is the potential for repetition for unifying a piece of music, to establish a thread that connects what might otherwise be a conglomeration of musical events.

One kind of repetition, utilized in the old song, "My Bonnie Lies Over the Ocean," is called phrase repetition. We can call each unit of music in this song a phrase, and for purposes of analysis we can assign a letter name to each. Phrases that sound exactly the same (literal repetitions) will have the same letter name. A phrase that sounds similar to but is not the same as an earlier phrase will have the same letter name as the earlier phrase, plus the mark "(1)" (an indication that the repetition is non-literal). By listening to or singing the song (for now, just the first half of it), we discover that the phrase structure is as follows:

Phrase	a	$a^{(1)}$	a	b
	(My bonnie lies over the ocean)	(My bonnie lies over the sea)	(My bonnie lies over the ocean)	(Oh, bring back my bonnie to me)

Notice as you listen that the first and third phrases are exactly the same; the second phrase begins like the first but has a slightly different ending; and the last phrase is different from the three preceding ones.

Repetition is an element in the song, "I Had a King," by Joni Mitchell (Reprise R 6293, part one, band 1). In this song several phrases, and not just one, are repeated, some literally and some non-literally. Of special interest in the phraseology of this song is the fact that the phrases are not all the same length. Below is a diagram of the phrase structure of this piece. The number under each phrase letter indicates the length of the phrase in measures. (We shall deal with measures on pp. 12–14.)

$$a \quad a^{(1)} \quad b \quad c \quad c^{(1)} \quad d \quad d \quad d \quad e$$
$$2 \quad 4 \quad 2 \quad 4 \quad 5 \quad \dot{2} \quad 2 \quad 2 \quad 4$$

Phrase repetition in its simplest form is illustrated in the next example, a song consisting of just four short phrases of equal length, which alternate in a kind of question and answer pattern. The piece is "Bulu Song" (from *Africa South of the Sahara,* Ethnic Folkways Library FE 4503, band 28). The phrase structure is:

$$a \quad b \quad a \quad b^{(1)}$$

Somewhat more elaborate is the call and response pattern of the "Mbuti (Pygmy) song" (band 20 on the above recording). Here, one singer is clearly the leader, and repetitions of his phrase alternate with repetitions of the responding phrase of the chorus. This call and response or responsorial kind of singing is characteristic of much African music, though this technique is by no means limited to that continent.

Phrase repetition is an important factor in the Mazurka in C-sharp minor, Op. 63, No. 3, by Frédéric Chopin (1810–1849). Here, the repeated element has a more complicated setting. Several different phrases are repeated, but probably the most memorable of these is the very first one—it seems to be the principal signal of the piece. The repeats are always welcome, but they are not evenly spaced and, thus, are somewhat unpredictable. We shall return to this piece on p. 10, and examine it in a different way.

Phrase repetition figures prominently in the short piano piece "Gymno-pedies No. 1," from *Trois Gymnopedies* by Erik Satie (1866–1925). The phrase structure is as follows:

$$a \quad a^{(1)} \quad b \quad b^{(1)} \quad c \quad a \quad a^{(1)} \quad b \quad b^{(1)} \quad c^{(1)}$$
$$12 \quad 9 \quad 5 \quad 5 \quad 8 \quad 12 \quad 9 \quad 5 \quad 5 \quad 8$$

Again, notice that the phrases are not all the same length. Notice, too, that some phrases are repeated literally, while others are not.

Another kind of phrase repetition is found in *The Unanswered Question* (1908), by Charles Ives (1874–1954). The orchestra is divided into three separate bodies of sound: strings; four flutes; and a solo trumpet (in some versions, a woodwind instrument is substituted for the trumpet). The sound of the strings is sustained throughout. The flutes and the solo trumpet enter alternately, though sporadically. Each repetition of the trumpet phrase is literal, but each repetition of the flute phrase is varied. (Recording: *Charles Ives Orchestral Works,* Vanguard VCS 10013)

A second repetitive element that may be heard in some music is the ostinato, a short musical fragment that, in its purest form, is repeated without interruption throughout a composition, or a large section thereof. Ostinato is used in a musical fabric in which there are other, changing elements to play off against it. In the example below the ostinato is in the lowest part of the musical texture, and the rest of the piece is built on top of it.

Ex. 1. *Sumer is icumen in* (c. 1300); (Recorded in *The History of Music in Sound,* Vol. 2, side 3, last 1/4″ of band 5). Used by permission of Harvard University Press.

Des pas sur la neige, by Claude Debussy (1862–1918), has an ostinato consisting of four notes. Sometimes the ostinato is in the lowest voice of the musical fabric, and at other times it is heard above other voices.

Ex. 2. Debussy: *Des pas sur la neige.*

The following example of ostinato is much more aurally complex. But with patience and careful listening one can discover that it, too, has a number of sections built on top of, in this case, multiple ostinatos. The solo voices (the highest and loudest voices) enter sporadically and sing the dominant melodic lines. A short rhythmic ostinato is supplied by a native instrument called split sticks, while two melodic ostinatos are chanted by other members of the chorus.

Ex. 3. Recording: *Music of the Rain Forest Pygmies,* Lyrichord 157, side 1, band 1 Quoted with permission of Lyrichord Records.

A kind of ostinato called a *riff* is characteristic of certain kinds of jazz. A riff is usually played by the ensemble or a section thereof, and often functions as a kind of melodic and rhythmic basis, upon which a solo or a series of solos is played. In "Flying Home" (recorded by Lionel Hampton and his band on *Encyclopedia of Jazz Records,* Decca DL 8386, Vol. III—"Jazz of the Forties"—side 2, band 5), there are three riff sections. First, the saxophone section plays a riff under the vibraphone solo; later, the trombone section plays a different riff under the tenor saxophone solo; finally, the brass section plays a riff and the saxophones play a different riff against it.

Another kind of ostinato is found in the aria "When I Am Laid in Earth," from the opera *Dido and Aeneas,* by Henry Purcell (1659–1695). Here, the ostinato, again the lowest voice in the texture, is fairly extended, spanning eleven notes:

Ex. 4. Purcell: from *Dido and Aeneas.*

The song is built upon eleven successive statements of this ostinato. This kind of ostinato, sometimes called a *ground bass,* was especially popular among composers in the baroque era of Western art music.

Repetition, on one or more levels, is a common element in all the musics of the world. The ostinato has been employed in both vocal and instrumental compositions, ranging from simple children's songs to exceedingly complicated drum music from central Africa. Its use extends far back into the history of music, and it has been a standard technique in Western art music, both sacred and secular, since the Middle Ages. The ostinato and phrase repetition are two basic kinds of repetition found in music.

A second fundamental of form is the use of certain kinds of punctuation in a composition. The most basic kind of punctuation in music is the *cadence,* which marks off one phrase or section (*section* will be discussed below) of music from the next; this keeps the phrases or sections from running together. The word cadence is derived from the Latin *cadere,* meaning "to fall," and a cadence or closing formula represents a falling off of musical activity. Cadences accomplish for music what periods, question marks, and commas do for spoken or written phrases and sentences. There is a variety of cadences— some are more emphatic than others, and some are longer in unfolding. As an example of the former, note in the short excerpt below the two cadences, each clearly marking off a phrase of music.

Ex. 5. Beethoven: Piano Sonata, Op. 2, No. 1, first movement, opening bars.

But this is not the whole piece, and for that reason the ends of these phrases are not designed to sound final. Below is the ending of the piece. Note how much more emphatic and final-sounding the cadence is here, and note as well that the sonority of this ending sound is repeated (for emphasis) several times.

Ex. 6. Beethoven: Piano Sonata, Op. 2, No. 1, first movement, closing bars.

A final cadence need not have this particular configuration; in many musics this configuration doesn't even exist. But in any music there is a distinction between internal and final cadences.

In "My Bonnie Lies Over the Ocean" each of the phrases, *a*, *a*[(1)], *a*, and *b*, is marked with a cadence. In this song the formula of the cadence is simple: the last sound in each phrase is followed by a rest (cessation of sound). This cadence clearly marks off the end of one phrase from the beginning of the next.

The *section* is a larger unit of the musical time span than the phrase, and a more general formal analysis of music may be undertaken on this level. The phrase structure of the second half of "My Bonnie Lies Over the Ocean" may be diagrammed as follows:

Phrase	*c*	*d*	*c*	*d*[(1)]
	(Bring back, bring back)	(Oh, bring back my Bonnie to me)	(Bring back, bring back)	(Oh, bring back my Bonnie to me)

Combining the two halves of our analysis of this song, we discover its phrase and sectional structure to be as follows:

Form according to phrase: *a* *a*[(1)]   *a*   *b*   *c*   *d*   *c*   *d*[(1)]
Form according to section: A   B

In terms of section this is a two-part, AB formal structure. A and B are noticeably different from each other, yet they have some melodic, rhythmic, and textual similarities that make them sound as if they are part of the same composition. By careful listening we can discover that the same kind of unity exists in the formal structures of longer and more complicated pieces of music.

Several clear-cut sectional designs, such as AB, ABA, and ABACA, have been utilized over the years. Thus, we can analyze the form of music on both a lowercase (phrase) and an uppercase (section) level. Listening to, understanding, and gaining meaning from a musical composition frequently requires us to perceive these two levels simultaneously.

As we examine music on the sectional level we discover that a musical form follows one of two basic courses: repetitive or non-repetitive. Once a composer creates a section of music, call it A, he can continue the composition in one of two ways: he can repeat the first section (A or $A^{(1)}$), or he can create something different—B (B meaning anything that is not A). Once he has done this, he still has but two choices as he continues his composition: he can repeat a previous section (A or B), or he can compose C—something different from A or B. Regardless of the length and complexity of his composition, his choices at every step will be those just described. Thus, depending upon the choices a composer makes, the form of his composition is one of two basic kinds: returning (or repetitive), and non-returning (or non-repetitive).

The Chopin Mazurka discussed earlier is an example of a returning form, for, on the most general level, it is constructed of three large sections: A, B, and $A^{(1)}$. With repeated listenings we discover that each of these sections consists of at least two clear-cut subsections, as shown below:

$$\underline{\text{A}} \qquad\qquad \underline{\text{B}} \qquad \underline{A^{(1)}}$$
$$\overline{\text{A} \quad A^{(1)} \quad \text{B} \quad B^{(1)}} \quad \overline{\text{C} \quad C^{(1)}} \quad \overline{\text{A} \quad A^{(2)}* \quad A^{(3)}}$$

(The asterisk—*—denotes a variation of A different from $A^{(1)}$). On a still more particular level, each subsection comprises several individual phrases. Illustrated below is the structure of this piece on three levels: the section (indicated by underscored capital letters); the subsection (capital letters); and the phrase (lowercase letters).

$$\underline{\text{A}}$$

*	A	*	*	$A^{(1)}$	*	*	B	*	*	$B^{(1)}$	*
a	$a^{(1)}$	$a^{(2)}$	$a^{(3)}$	a	$a^{(4)}$	$a^{(5)}$	$a^{(6)}$	b	$b^{(1)}$	b	$b^{(2)}$

$$\underline{\text{B}}$$

C		C	
c	$c^{(1)}$	$c^{(2)}$	$c^{(3)}$

$$\underline{\text{A}}$$

$A^{(2)}$				$A^{(3)}$				$A^{(4)}$					
$a^{(7)}$	$a^{(8)}$	$a^{(2)}$	$a^{(3)}$	$a^{(9)}$	$a^{(10)}$	$a^{(11)}$	$a^{(12)}$	$a^{(13)}$	$a^{(14)}$	$a^{(15)}$	$a^{(16)}$	$a^{(17)}$	$a^{(18)}$

Clearly, the most important signal of this short composition and the element on which Chopin seems to focus most sharply, is the phrase *a*. It and its eighteen variants dominate the piece. The three-part structure is, and for centuries has been, a basic formal pattern in many of the world's musics; in Western art and popular music it has been one of the dominating forms.

Another much-used design is the rondo, a kind of multi-sectional returning form in which a primary section (A) recurs two or more times and is played off against other, diversionary sections of music. The lineage of the rondo extends back to the Middle Ages, but it was particularly favored by composers of the classical era of Western art music. An example of rondo from the classical literature is found in the last movement of the String Quartet, Op. 33, No. 2 ("The Joke"), by Joseph Haydn (1732–1809). A rondo from a later period of Western art music is found in the *Pavane pour une Infante défunte* (1899) by Maurice Ravel (1875–1937). The sectional form of Ravel's composition is illustrated below:

A   B   A   C   A

The rondo and rondo-like forms have also been used by twentieth-century composers such as Igor Stravinsky (1882–1971), in the third movement ("Rondoletto") of his *Serenade en la.*

A composition in non-returning form does not return to or repeat a previously stated section. In effect, every section of such a composition offers new material. The problem of unifying instrumental music written in this manner is often solved by maintaining rhythmic, textural, harmonic, melodic, and intervallic correspondences among the various sections. Thus, a non-returning form is not one in which nothing is repeated or in which there is no constant element; it is a form in which there are no sectional repeats.

The term *through-composed* is the common label for vocal music that has non-returning form. In such music the text is frequently the principal unifier, but the accompaniment may also serve this role. "Kriegers Ahnung" (from the *Schwanengesang*) and "Erlkönig," by Franz Schubert (1797–1828), are good examples of through-composed songs.

Rhythmic Structure

So far we have examined time in music, as it manifests itself in formal structure. We shall now consider time in music on another level, namely, the rhythmic level. In the broadest sense, the term rhythm is applicable to all temporal aspects of a piece of music; but we shall use it in a more restricted sense here, encompassing the smaller units of temporal measure such as beat, meter, and a few other terms. All musics in some way measure time at this level, but they do not all measure it in the same way. A music that measures time in a way with which we are unfamiliar may sound chaotic to us until we discover how its time is organized and, thus, how to empathize with the music rhythmically.

The temporal organization with which we are most familiar is metrical. The smallest unit of meter is the beat. We may think of a series of beats or pulses as a series of durations, the beginnings of which are articulated by small attacks—like heartbeats or clock tickings. In metrical music these beats are organized into various patterns by, at regular intervals, giving a beat more stress, or emphasis, than its neighbors. Thus, a regular four-beat pattern calls for a stress or accent on every fourth beat: ONE-two-three-four/ONE-two-three-four/, and so on. A regular three-beat pattern calls for: ONE-two-three/ONE-two-three/, and so on. Each repetition of the pattern is called a *measure* (or bar).

The beat in music measured in this way is a fixed value, and all other units of time that may be used are either multiples or divisions of it. All of these units can be translated into a notational system in which various durations are represented by symbols such as: o (whole note), 𝅗𝅥 (half note), 𝅘𝅥 (quarter note), 𝅘𝅥𝅮 (eighth note), 𝅘𝅥𝅯 (sixteenth note), and so on. For each of these values there is a symbol for its equivalent in silence, called a rest: ▬ (whole rest), ▬ (half rest), 𝄽 (quarter rest), 𝄾 (eighth rest), 𝄿 (sixteenth rest), and so forth. Each of the note values in metrical music is normally divisible by two and by three. For example, the note value 𝅘𝅥 may be divided into two eighth notes 𝅘𝅥𝅮𝅘𝅥𝅮 (or into higher duple divisions, such as four sixteenths 𝅘𝅥𝅯𝅘𝅥𝅯𝅘𝅥𝅯𝅘𝅥𝅯 , eight thirty-seconds 𝅘𝅥𝅰𝅘𝅥𝅰𝅘𝅥𝅰𝅘𝅥𝅰𝅘𝅥𝅰𝅘𝅥𝅰𝅘𝅥𝅰𝅘𝅥𝅰 , and so forth) ; or the 𝅘𝅥 may be divided into triplets 𝅘𝅥𝅮𝅘𝅥𝅮𝅘𝅥𝅮 , each member of the triplet having one-third the durational value of 𝅘𝅥 . A dot placed immediately behind a note increases the duration of that note by half its normal value.

Theoretically, this system of measurement is strict, in that the durations of the notes and rests are invariable. But in practice, composers and performers do not always adhere doggedly to this mathematical strictness. Although performers may play some passages of music in this strict manner, they may prefer to play others with a certain amount of rhythmic flexibility—that is, they may occasionally speed up (sometimes indicated in the musical score by the word *accelerando*) or slow down (*ritardando*) their performance. Different styles of metrical music allow for different degrees of rhythmic strictness or flexibility. Most modern performers tend to play Bach in the strict manner except when they play his more rhapsodic compositions, where rhythmic flexibility is better suited. The music of Chopin, on the other hand, calls for considerable flexibility, and a performer who is sensitive to Chopin's style knows when and how to exercise this flexibility. The careful listener can detect fairly easily the give and take between strictness and laxity by playing any good recording of, for instance, the Chopin Prelude No. 4, and tapping along.

The rate of speed at which metrical music is played is called *tempo*. A piece may be played at tempos ranging from very slow to very fast. Some composers dictate precisely the tempo at which they wish a given piece to be performed: instead of indicating the desired tempo by a word such as "fast,"

they may use a sign such as ♩ = 120. This means that the piece should be played at a speed at which there would be 120 quarter notes per minute if the music were played with no variation in tempo. Accelerando and ritardando affect individual notes by causing them to be played faster or slower than they would in strict time; thus, they simultaneously and necessarily affect tempo. These speedings up and slowings down are themselves not strictly regulated and are, in fact, open to a range of interpretations. The careful listener can detect this relativity by listening to two or more recorded versions of the same piece, for example, the Chopin Prelude No. 4, as performed by (1) Artur Rubenstein (RCA Victor LM-1163); (2) Jeanne-Marie Darré (Vanguard VRS-1151); and (3) Géza Anda (Deutsche Grammophon Gesellschaft LPM 18604).

A meter signature signifies two things: the number of basic beats in a measure (usually, the number of toe taps); and the note value equivalent to the basic beat of the piece. For example, in the meter signature 3/4 the upper number indicates a three-beat pattern, implying a stress on every third beat. The lower number signifies that the basic beat of the piece is the quarter note.

By far, the most commonly used meters in Western music are fractions of two equal parts, such as:

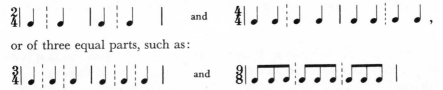

or of three equal parts, such as:

Western metrical music incorporates downbeat and upbeat. A downbeat receives more stress than the other beats in the bar. It is a beat that actively submits to the pull of musical gravity, in the sense that our footfalls submit to the pull of physical gravity. An upbeat is lightest among its neighbors, in the sense that it is farthest from the center of gravity, as is a foot at the top of a footstep. In a meter it is often the case that the first beat of every measure is a downbeat, and the last beat of every measure an upbeat. These are called metrical downbeat and metrical upbeat, respectively. Some meters, such as

4/4, also include a secondary downbeat and secondary upbeat. Normally, the distribution of beat weight in a measure of 4/4 is as follows:

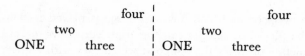

Beat ONE is the metrical downbeat, and beat three the secondary downbeat; beat four is the metrical upbeat, and beat two the secondary upbeat.

Downbeat and upbeat can be created in a variety of ways, and a composer can, if he wishes, circumvent the force of the metrical downbeat by stressing another beat in the measure, thereby creating a downbeat on that beat.

"My Bonnie Lies Over the Ocean" is a metrical song composed of groups of three quarter-note beats. We notice, if the song is played or sung at a moderate tempo, that the quarter note is the basic beat to which we tap our foot (three taps per measure). The metrical scheme and the formal structure of this song are illustrated below. Note that each of the four phrases in section A begins with an upbeat, but that, in contrast, the first and third phrases of section B begin on a metrical downbeat.

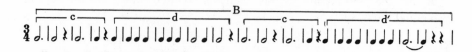

Some musics are similar to Western metrical music in that the beat is a fixed durational value and all other values are multiples or divisions of it, but are different in that they do not make use of the regular accent patterns discussed above. Much recent Western art music is of this type. The composer may or may not use meter signatures, but even if he does, he does not think of metrical downbeats and upbeats as measures of time in his music. The beat itself is the unit of temporal measure. In this recent music the composer creates the sense of downbeats and upbeats, but, unlike conventional metrical music, these downbeats and upbeats occur irregularly. In the example below, the bar lines do not mark off the ends of repetitions of metrical patterns; rather, they merely mark off groups of notes.

Ex. 7. Pierre Boulez: *Première Sonate*, first movement, bars 1–3. Quoted with permission of Belwin-Mills Publishing Corp.

Other musics around the world are metrical, but not in the Western sense. In Indian classical music the basic temporal element is the *tala,* a time pattern or cycle composed of internal groups called *angās* which in turn may consist of a variable number of "beats" or *màtras.* The temporal unit of this music is thus the whole cyle—the *tala*—and not merely a subdivision of it. Herein lies the basic difference between Western and Indian rhythm. Each *tala* has a name; illustrated below is the *Adi tala.*

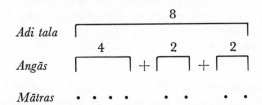

Unlike Western meters, the *tala* is not divisible into two or three equal parts, for the *angās* within a *tala* are not all equal in size.

Western musicians interpret 8/8 as measures of eight equal durations, the pattern of which is articulated by stressing the first duration of the eight in each measure. At a fast tempo, we might feel only two toe taps instead of eight in every measure. We would therefore divide each measure into two groups of four beats each, with a downbeat beginning the first group and an upbeat beginning the second. In other words, we divided the measure as follows:

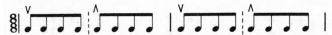

In Indian music a *tala* consisting of eight eighth notes would be grouped not in this symmetrical fashion but, rather, as follows: 4 + 2 + 2 (*Adi tala*). The following are groupings of some other *talas*: 2 + 4 (= 6)—*rúpaka tala;* 3 + 2 + 3 (= 8)—*tiśra jāti matya tala;* 7 + 1 + 2 (= 10)—*Jhampa tala.*

As mentioned above, we understand a measure of beats by dividing it into two or three equal groups, and, perhaps, by subdividing these into smaller symmetrical groups. In this sense, our metrical system is divisive. The Indian system is sometimes called additive, meaning that a time span of beats is perceived through a process of adding.

Ex. 8.

Western divisive system
(8÷2=4)

Indian additive system
(3+2+3=8)

Instructive examples of various *talas* are contained in the following recordings:

Reflets d'Indie (Phonodisc: Barklay XBLY 86120 S)

Additive or unsymmetrical rhythm is typical of many musics of the Far and Near East. Additive rhythms are also found in certain eastern European folk musics. The Hungarian composer Béla Bartók (1881–1945) used such rhythms in several of his compositions. Hear, for example, the "Scherzo" of his String Quartet No. 5 (1935), which begins:

Ex. 9. Bartók: String Quartet No. 5, "Scherzo," bars 1–5. Copyright 1936 by Universal Edition; Renewed 1963. Copyright and Renewal assigned to Boosey & Hawkes, Inc., for the U.S.A. Reprinted by permission.

Another example of this kind of rhythm is found even closer to home, in the song "America" from *West Side Story,* by Leonard Bernstein.

Ex. 10. Bernstein: "America." Used by permission of G. Schirmer & Chappell.

There are still other ways of organizing musical time on the level that we have been discussing. Some twentieth-century experimental music measures time not in beats, meters, or patterns, but in seconds. Instead of a certain number of equal beats per second or per minute, composers of such music utilize seconds and minutes themselves as the basic units of temporal measure. Their directions to the performer(s) might be something like this: "Make 4 seconds of sound A (whatever it might be); followed by 20 seconds of sound B; followed by 8½ seconds of sounds A and B together."

Such an approach to the concept of time in music has abetted a musical and aesthetic split between many contemporary composers of Western art music. The crux of this dichotomy may in part be understood by considering this question: Can a performer accurately execute music measured in clock time? It is doubtful that any performer can, over any length of time, consistently and precisely gauge the actual seconds and minutes allotted him to perform a composition of this type. Furthermore if such a composition called for more than one performer, the already remote possibility of a truly accurate performance would be further diminished since there would likely be multiple discrepancies between performers and clock. This is true because humans are the medium of performance. However, certain kinds of electronic equipment are capable of the precision necessary in performing music measured in clock time. Some composers have turned to electronic equipment because it affords them absolute control over all parameters of their music, and guarantees them performances that are always the same and always free from human error and idiosyncracy.

Other composers of non-metrical music recognize the fallibility of human performers and capitalize on it. For instance, many have opted to allow the performer as much interpretive freedom as is possible within the framework of a given composition. In a sense, the performers become co-composers. Many compositions by such composers are designed never to sound the same twice. In such music the composer's directions to the performers might consist of something like the following: "Play this passage as fast as you can; hold this note for as long as possible; don't begin your next sound until you hear the trumpet sound fade; play these four pitches for as long you like."

Such music is not measured by meter, beat, or real time, but by each performer's interpretation of the composer's general directions governing time. We might refer to this as "free time" music. Below is a set of instructions and a page of the score from a composition called *For 1, 2 or 3 People* (1964), by Christian Wolff, which illustrates the use of free time.

Ex. 11. Christian Wolff: *For 1, 2 or 3 People.* Copyright © 1964 by C. F. Peters Corporation, 373 Park Ave. South, New York, New York 10016. Reprint permission granted by the publisher.

INSTRUCTIONS

There are ten parts, one to a page. A performance can be made of any number of them, repeating none, or of any one, repeated no more than ten times.

Each part, or page, is a score, and each player should have his copy of it.

Play all that is notated on a page, in any convenient sequence, not repeating anything; except in IX, where any of the events can be played or omitted any number of times.

Black notes are variously short, up to about one second. With stems as sixteenth notes (e.g. in III, etc.) they are very short. White notes are of any length, sometimes determined by the requirements of coordination (see further on).

A dynamic indication may stand by itself (as at left top of I): assume a note to go with it or apply it to any note given on the page. However, $\Longrightarrow$ or $\Longleftarrow$, standing by themselves, should always be applied to a note (any one) already given.

A diagonal line towards a note = play that note directly after a preceding one. A diagonal line away from a note = that note must be followed directly by another.

A vertical line down from a note = play simultaneously with the next sound (both attack and release).

A small number at the end of a line (e.g. at left top of I) = coordinate with the second (if the number is 2; third, if 3; etc.) sound, preceding (if diagonal line towards note), following after one has begun one's note (if diagonal line away from it), or play simultaneously with the second next sound (if the line is vertical).

If a line to a note is broken by a number followed, after a colon, by a zero (—2:0—) (e.g. top middle of III), that number of seconds of silence intervene before the required coordination.

An α at the end of a line (e.g. middle left in I) = coordination must be with a sound made by another player. If only one person is playing, he must coordinate either with a sound he hears in the environment or with a sound he has himself made unintentionally.

$\smallint$ = play after a previous sound has begun, hold till it stops.

$\smallint$ = start anytime, hold till another sound starts, finish with it.

$\smallint$ = start at the same time (or as soon as you are aware of it) as the next sound, but stop before it does.

$\smallint$ = start anytime, hold till another sound starts, continue holding anytime after that sound has stopped.

Horizontal lines joining two notes = a legato from the one to the other (both played by the same person).

If no line leads to a note or drops vertically from it, one can start to play at any time. If no line leads away from a white note, it can last as long or as short as you like.

One, two, or three people can play. If one plays alone, he must realize all "open" coordinations (lines with notes at only one end) himself, that is, he must use other notes given on a page, as he can to provide something to coordinate with; or, sometimes, he may use sounds from the environment (as he must when there is an α at the end of a line). (He may in some cases have to rearrange the material on a page and consider a disposition of it which will ensure that all the required coordinations can be managed.) All the material on a page can be freely superimposed, so long as the requirements of coordination are met.

If two or three play, the material on a page should be distributed between them, in any way (in VII a distribution for two players is indicated); but no material marked off for one player should be played by another (note: this holds for IX too). Coordination, then, for each player can be either with his own material (as if he were playing alone)—unless there is an α—or with whatever sound(s) he hears next from another player (or both).

Players can use any ways of making sounds, allowing for the following specifications:

Some notes are on staves: play the indicated pitch (reading either bass or treble clef; sound at pitch; if pitch not available in range, transpose at least two octaves; short lines off a pitch at an angle = fraction of a tone less than half up where line angles up, down where down).

Where no pitches specified, they are free (recognizable or not).

Larger numbers directly over a note: if black = that number of tones (not necessarily played together unless bracketed, [2]); if red number = that number of timbres. No number = one (e.g. $\frac{2}{0}$ = two tones, one timbre; $\frac{2}{0}^{(red)}$ = one tone, two timbres).

Larger numbers on a line between notes: if black = that number of changes of some aspect(s) of the sound before reaching the next note; in red = that number of changes of the timbre of the first note before reaching the next one.

A red number 1 over a note = use a different timbre from the one immediately preceding.

X = anything

= a high in some aspect

△, ▲ = a sound in some respect dissonant with what immediately precedes

= a sound as far away as possible, in some aspect, from what immediately precedes it

= a noise

= a low in some aspect

◇ = a harmonic

= change the direction in space of a sound

= a sound in a middle place, in some respect, of the sounds around it

asp. = as possible

met = a sound using metal (generally of low resonance; met^2 = a higher resonance)

wd = a sound using wood (generally of low resonance; wd^2 = a higher resonance)

t = a sound made by tapping or touching or tracing or the like

b = a sound made by breathing or blowing or the like (but not singing)

fr = a sound involving friction

pl = a sound involving plucking or pulling

sn = a sound involving snapping

stret = a sound involving stretched material

In parts V-X notations such as the following not standing by a note are to be applied to any sound on that page, whether produced by oneself or another player.

= a slight alteration of a sound

Λ = cut off a sound

⟶ = extend a sound

= raise a sound in some respect

= lower it in some respect

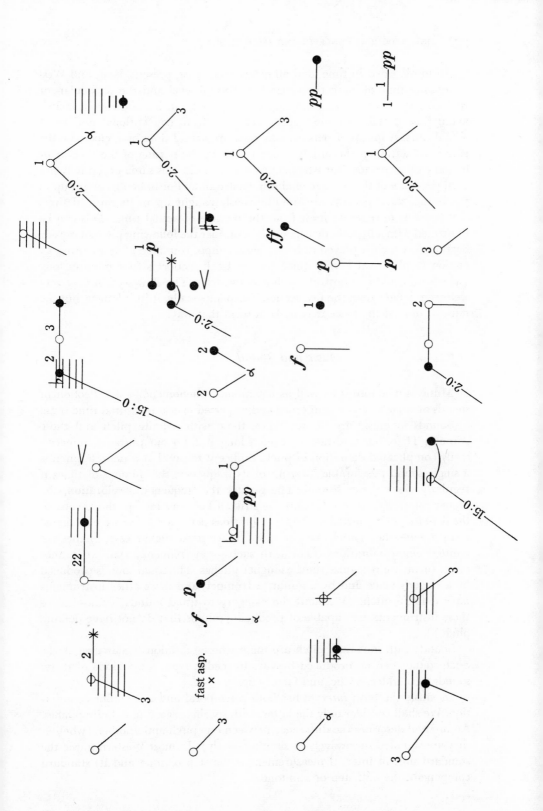

All music exists in time, and all composers—past, present, East, and West —organize time on both the general, or formal level and the particular, or rhythmic level. In so doing a composer can create in his audience a feeling about time that is in some respects different from conventional notions of actual time. A group of persons may measure actual time by a clock, by the rising and setting of the sun, by moon cycles, by the passing of the seasons, or by some other means. But when engrossed in music, this same group may not even be aware of the passage of chronological time. For in being caught up in the music, these persons are simultaneously caught up in its musical time, which seems to separate itself from the passage of actual time. This can be illustrated with a hypothetical example. Consider the following piece of music: Section A, which is played at a very slow tempo, is immediately followed by section B, played at a very quick tempo. Each section is four minutes long (which we could demonstrate with a stopwatch). The slow section may very well seem longer than the fast section. Chronologically, it isn't longer, but the musical time of the piece may make it seem that way.

Music and Sound

Music is a sonorous as well as a temporal phenomenon—a collection of sounds arranged in a certain order and dispersed over a measured time span.

Sounds in music are of two types, those with definite pitch and those without. There has traditionally been a long and, for our purposes, unnecessarily complicated definition of pitch. Suffice it to say that a definite pitch is a single sound measurable in terms of its frequency, the number of times it regularly vibrates per second. The greater the frequency of vibration, the higher the sound. If, on a piano, we strike a key very low on the keyboard, the definite pitch emitted has so few vibrations per second that we can almost count them—they sound like pulsations. If we strike higher keys, pitches are emitted whose vibrations occur with such great frequency that we cannot count them; we recognize these as higher pitches. The usual sounds produced by a singer's voice and by a guitar, a trumpet, and most other instruments have definite pitch. (We limit the category to usual sounds because all of these instruments are capable of producing sounds that do not have definite pitch.)

Sounds with indefinite pitch are those whose vibrations occur irregularly. Such sounds can be produced by various media, from some kinds of drum sounds to thunder, traffic, and factory noises.

In music the term *interval* has both a temporal and a sonorous connotation. We shall consider only the latter, with specific regard to definite pitches. An interval describes the difference between one pitch and another (whether they are sounded successively or simultaneously). In most Western music the standard unit of interval measurement is the step or tone and its standard component, the half step or semitone.

Intervals larger than a whole step have individual names, according to the number of whole steps and half steps they span. For example, the interval called the major third spans a distance of two whole steps:

Major third = one whole step + another whole step.

The minor third is a slightly smaller interval, spanning one whole step and one half step:

Minor third = one whole step + one half step.

The same procedure is used to describe the span of other intervals, such as the major and minor 6th, major and minor 7th, major and minor 9th, and so forth. For reasons that need not trouble us here, the intervals called the 4th, 5th, and 8th (octave) are called perfect or imperfect, depending upon the specific number of whole and half steps they span.

Some musics make use of intervals that are smaller than the Western half step (quarter tones and microtones) or larger than the Western whole step (but not as large as the Western minor third). This is particularly true of several Far Eastern and a lesser number of Near Eastern musics. An excellent introduction to one of these musics is contained in *Indonesia* (Columbia Masterworks KL 210), edited and narrated by Jaap Kunst, who provides some valuable explanatory remarks.

Several Western composers in this century have written music containing quarter tones and microtones. Charles Ives used quarter tones in a number of his compositions, especially the *Three Quarter-tone Pieces for Two Pianos,* in which the two pianos are tuned one quarter tone apart. Harry Partch (born 1901) has devoted much of his career to working with non-Western tunings. To accommodate the tunings of many of his compositions, he has invented new musical instruments. Hear, for example, his *Windsong* and other pieces on *The Music of Harry Partch* (Composers Recordings CRI 193B). Benjamin Johnston (born 1926), a former pupil of Partch's, has also worked extensively with various tuning systems. Johnston's String Quartet No. 2 (1969—recorded on Nonesuch H 71224) is based on a system of tuning known as *just intonation,* which utilizes intervals different from those found in traditional Western music.

Sounds may be dispersed one at a time or more than one at a time, creating, respectively, a one-voiced or monophonic music, or a many-voiced or polyphonic music. Below is an example of monophonic music. The melody consists of a fairly small number of pitches (six), and is restricted to a rather small range. (*Range* is the difference between the highest and lowest pitches in a composition.) Notice that the melody consists for the most part of whole-step and half-step intervals, with some occasional larger intervals. In addition to examining the intervallic structure of this piece, study its phrase structure and cadential formulas.

Ex. 12. "Qui me sanum fecit," Antiphon 1 at Vespers, first week of Lent, transcribed from *Liber Usualis*, Tournai, 1956, p. 1084.

Note the number and variety of intervals in the monophonic piece below, and note also the nature and variety of the phrases and cadences.

Ex. 13. "Victimae paschali laudes," in *Historical Anthology of Music*, Vol. I (Cambridge, Mass.: Harvard University Press, 1950), p. 13.

There are two general types of many-voiced (polyphonic) music: homophonic and contrapuntal. A homophonic composition contains a dominant melody and some accompanimental sounds. This may be observed in the following excerpt from an opera by the Italian composer Giuseppe Verdi (1813–1901).

Ex. 14. Verdi: "Tacea la notte," from *Il Trovatore*, Act I.

There is a clear distinction in this song between melody and accompaniment. The latter is fairly inactive, consisting of conglomerate sounds (chords) that succeed one another at a moderate pace: the first chord occupies the first two bars; the third bar contains two different chords; and the fourth bar returns to the chord of bars 1 and 2. Chord changes produce a rhythm of their own—a harmonic rhythm. The harmonic rhythm of this particular song is moderately slow.

Harmony is a term used in discussing the multiple voices of polyphonic music; it may be described as the simultaneous sounding of two or more different pitches. There are many different kinds of harmony, each organizing sounds in its own way and usually emphasizing some pitches more than others.

The kind of harmony used in the Verdi song is known as functional harmony. Functional harmony utilizes a body of chords, all of which are constructed in a similar way, but among which is a variety of chord colors: major chords, minor chords, diminished chords, and augmented chords. These chords are selected and arranged by the composer in such a way that a hierarchy emerges, in which some chords are more important than others to the establishment of what we shall call tonal direction and tonal finality. For example, most Western listeners are conditioned to regard the last chord in the example below as an ending sound. The chords preceding it seem to lead to it, as if it were a goal.

Ex. 15.

But hear what happens if we end the piece on the penultimate chord. Don't we feel that this chord should proceed to a different chord? And not to just any other chord, but to one chord in particular? This series of chords seems to us to have a destiny, a goal toward which it directs itself, and the series sounds complete only when that goal is reached. Functional harmony is goal-directed—it persuades us that the music is proceeding somewhere. Possibly, we may even have a physical response to this harmonic progression; it is as if on the penultimate chord we are raised from our chairs, and as we progress to the final chord, we are lowered back into them. The penultimate chord creates a tension that is dissipated as we reach the last chord. To recognize this is to recognize the separate functions of these two elements in the system of functional harmony. The tonic chord (the last chord) is the ending sound. The dominant chord (the second to the last chord in Ex. 15) creates a tension that can be resolved in the tonic; thus, its function is both to oppose (by creating tension) and to lead to the tonic. A third element in functional harmony is the subdominant chord, whose primary function it is to lead to the dominant. All other chords used in functional harmony are either orna-mentations of or substitutes for one of these three basic elements.

The harmony in the example below strikes us as being noticeably different from that in the Verdi song.

Ex. 16. "Organum," from the *Musica Enchiriadis*, paraphrased from the example in *Historical Anthology of Music*, Vol. 1 (Cambridge, Mass.: Harvard University Press, 1950), p. 22.

The difference results from the fact that the chords in the two pieces are constructed in different ways. Those in the "Organum" are built of 4ths and 5ths; that is, the intervals between the individual notes of each chord are 4ths and 5ths, and these sounds dominate the piece. Another basic difference between this piece and the Verdi song is that in this piece the harmony seems much less goal-directed. There is considerably less urgency for one chord to move to another particular chord. The functions of the individual chords in this piece seem much less critical than in the Verdi song. To return briefly to the Verdi song, which, as we have determined, utilizes functional harmony, we notice that its chords are constructed of superimposed thirds; we call this tertian harmony. The individual notes of such chords are stacked atop one another. The lowest note in the stack is the root of the chord, the only note in the chord upon which the stack of 3rds may be built. In Ex. 17 we can see that other members of the chord also have names, and that the color of a triad is determined by the placement of major and minor 3rds within the stack.

Ex. 17.

5th of the chord — major triad   minor triad   diminished   augmented
3rd of the chord —
root of the chord —

When a major or minor triad is sounded together with another pitch that is not a duplication of a member of the triad, a dissonance is created. The non-triad member of the sonority is dissonant and requires resolution. Some dissonances are more pronounced than others. Broadly speaking, the more strident the dissonance within a given musical context, the more urgently we sense the need for a resolution to consonance or at least to a milder dissonance.

Thus far, we have discovered that functional harmony is one way of organizing conglomerate sounds that have definite pitch. The sounds being organized are major and minor triads and a variety of dissonances that may be played off against them. These sounds, by dint of the way they are organized, create a sense of direction and goal, to which three particular chords are indispensable: the tonic, dominant, and subdominant chords. Functional harmony creates the sense of tonal or key center. This "centerness" is not unlike the center of the gravitational system, in the sense that everything ultimately falls to the center.

Not all music written in the functional harmony system sounds alike, even though it is all based on the same fundamental principles. Some music is more tonally centered than other music. The most direct path to a tonal center is through chords whose roots are related to one another by 4ths and 5ths. The tonic chord root is a 4th apart from the subdominant chord root and a 5th apart from the dominant chord root. Speaking as broadly as possible, we may say that Western art music of the so-called classical era (roughly, the last half of the eighteenth century) is dominated by these strong, unequivocal chord progressions, as in the excerpt below.

Ex. 18. Joseph Haydn: Piano Sonata in C major (No. 5 in the Peter's edition), second movement, mm. 1–5.

Notice how much more circuitous the path to a tonal center is in the example below. This music utilizes root progressions other than 4ths and 5ths. Again, in the broadest possible terms we may say that Western art music of the romantic era (the nineteenth century) is dominated by these less direct root progressions and by chromaticism.

Ex. 19. Edvard Grieg: "Solvejg's Song," from the *Peer Gynt* Suite, mm. 18–24.

The other branch of polyphony is contrapuntal music, the texture of which contains two or more melodic lines of equal significance, which are sounded simultaneously. Of necessity, these coexisting lines form harmonies, but our attention, though it may be drawn to these harmonies, is focused primarily on the individual lines. Thus, we may perceive of homophonic music as being essentially vertical, and contrapuntal music as being essentially horizontal.

The world's musics utilize several kinds of counterpoint. Readily accessible to Western listeners is a kind of contrapuntal music called a *round,* of which "Row, Row, Row Your Boat" is an example. In a round there is only one melodic line, but because of the way in which a round is performed, the illusion of several short independent lines is created. Four people or four groups of people can perform "Row, Row, Row Your Boat" as a *round* by staggering their entrances in this way:

1. Row row row your boat gently down the stream merrily merrily merrily
2.   Row row row your boat gently down the stream
3.   Row row row your boat
4.   Row

The focus of our attention is not on the harmonies created in the course of performance but, rather, on the four individual voice lines. Similar to this is *Sumer is icumen in,* mentioned earlier, which combines a round (in the upper voices) with an ostinato (in the two lower voices).

Dixieland jazz mixes homophonic sections with contrapuntal sections. The basic dixieland group usually features three front-line or solo instruments—trumpet, trombone, and clarinet—which, in the contrapuntal sections, interweave three individual melodic lines. These lines have melodic independence, but are all anchored to a common set of chords. The individual *timbres* (characteristic sounds) of the trumpet, trombone, and clarinet make the contrapuntal nature of dixeland jazz especially easy to grasp. In the following recording notice how attention is drawn primarily to the activities of these three lines and only incidentally to the harmonies they create when they sound together: "Tin Roof Blues," played by the New Orleans Rhythm Kings, in *Encyclopedia of Jazz on Records* (Decca DL 8386, MG 5082).

A special kind of counterpoint called imitative counterpoint has been a feature of much Western art mustic since the Renaissance. Imitative counterpoint is the basis of the *fugue,* a type of musical composition in which an initially stated theme or melodic fragment is echoed (imitated) in one or more other voices. Once the following voices have imitated the theme stated by the lead voice, the imitation stops, and the several voices of the texture go their independent ways. This is different from the round, in which the following voices, in their turn, duplicate throughout, everything that is stated by the lead voice. The fugue is a process that was favored by many composers in the baroque era. An important collection of fugues is contained in Bach's *Well-Tempered Clavier.* Hear, for example, the Fugue in C minor from Book I of this collection.

Numerous composers of art music in the twentieth century have also been attracted to the fugue. Hear, for example the last movement of Piano Sonata No. 3, by Paul Hindemith (1895–1963); the first movement of Symphony No. 4, by William Schuman (born 1910); the first movement of *Music for Strings, Percussion and Celesta,* by Bartók; the "Sinfonia" from Octet for Wind Instruments, by Stravinsky; and the Piano Prelude No. 4, by Dimitri Shostakovich (born 1906).

The term *texture,* as it applies to musical compositions, incorporates several factors. The term was casually introduced earlier; it is now time to deal more formally with it. Basic to a description of a musical texture is an acknowledgement of both its density and its activity. The density of a musical texture is determined by: (1) the number and kinds of voices it contains; and (2) the dynamic and articulative means of sound production. Activity simply involves a determination of whether the texture is chordal or contrapuntal. For example, a quartet of trombones playing four different parts, but all within a fairly constricted range and all fairly loud, would likely produce a thick or dense texture. If, in addition, the parts are four autonomous (contrapuntal) lines, the whole might be described as a thick, contrapuntal texture.

Texture is a term to which descriptive words such as dense, light, active, static, and heavy can be meaningfully added, despite their lack of precision. To an extent, the description of a given musical texture is a personal and, hence, a relative matter. The reader can surely find his own words sufficient to describe the texture of music he hears, as long as he is careful to describe both its density and its activity.

Variation

Central to music is the process of *variation*. Indeed, from a certain point of view, all music may be regarded as variational, in the sense that any musical composition might be understood as a series of variational extensions of an initially stated cell of music. For example, the melody below may be understood as eight individual phrases: *a b c d e f g h*. But the activity and shape of phrases *b, c, d, e, f, g* and *h* may be perceived merely as adjuncts or variations of phrase *a*. In a sense, the size and shape of phrase *a* forms the basis of all the subsequent phrases. From this point of view, everything that occurs in this song is derived from phrase *a* and is, thus, a variation of *a*.

Ex. 20. Leonard Bernstein: "America." Used by permission of G. Schirmer & Chappell.

One can sense the process of variation on a more rarefied level. For example, the opening melody from the Symphony No. 40 in G minor (K. 550), by Wolfgang Mozart (1756–1791), may be reduced to a series of variations on the first two pitches—E♭ and D—and on their metrical arrangement.

Ex. 21. Mozart: Symphony No. 40, first movement, bars 1–8.

The large melodic leap in bar 2 would, under this kind of analysis, be understood as a variation of the small, germinal interval E♭—D. The downward drift of the melody through bars 3 and 4 would be understood as a variation and extension of the descent of the opening E♭—D.

The entire first movement of the String Quartet, Op. 3 (1909), by Alban Berg (1885–1935), seems to grow out of the opening motive of the piece:

Ex. 22. Berg: String Quartet, Op. 3, first movement, opening. Copyright 1925, Universal Edition, Vienna. Used by permission of the Publisher. Theodore Presser Company, sole representative, United States, Canada and Mexico.

Notice as you listen to this movement that almost everything seems to be a variation of the shape of this motive, an exploitation of one of the intervals of the motive, or, by some other means, a reminiscence of some aspect of this motive. (This composition has been recorded by the Juilliard String Quartet on Columbia ML 4737.)

To summarize, the analytical view discussed above suggests that everything in a piece of music is interconnected, and that every piece is ultimately reducible to a germinal idea, which is the piece in microcosmic form.

Most of us probably perceive and experience music not on the microcosmic level, but on a more general level. And most of us probably group the interconnection within a composition on a broader level—that is, we may begin to sense that a given event or section is more a contrast to than a variation of some other event or section in the piece. In other words, we begin to focus on the differences rather than the similarities between the two events or sections. The result is that we may unconsciously hold the notion that *a* and *b* represent unity, for we sense that *b* is some kind of variation of *a*, but we may consciously and simultaneously perceive that *a* and *b* represent variety, for we perceive that *b* is in some respects different from *a*. It is a paradox in music, and perhaps elsewhere, that unity and variety can be conceived of as phenomena that occur simultaneously as well as consecutively. A review of the examples discussed earlier in connection with formal structure in music may now reveal this paradox.

As one surveys the history and the kinds of music, one discovers that the process of variation takes many forms. The so-called theme with variations has been a staple of Western art music since the seventeenth century. Notice in the composition from which the example below is taken that the intially stated melody is subjected to a series of changes in each succeeding section of the music. But throughout the constant process of variation, we never lose track of the original melody.

Ex. 23. Mozart: theme from Variations in C major on "Ah, vous dirai-je, Maman" (K. 265). (Recording: Deutsche Grammophon Gesellschaft, SL PM 138, 949, [1967]).

Notice in the next example that the initially stated melody is a constant throughout the movement, and that each of the several sections of the piece is a variation not of the melody, but of the melody's environment. That is, as the environment is changed from section to section, the melody, even though its pitches remain the same, seems to vary in what we could call its personality. These variations in both the environment and the personality of the theme result from the composer's varied use of harmony, counterpoint, texture, and dynamics.

Ex. 24. Joseph Haydn: theme from second movement of String Quartet, Op. 76, No. 3.

Conclusion

We have spoken of music and of musics, suggesting that while certain elements and procedures are common to all music, the full benefit, pleasure, and understanding of musics is dependent upon our willingness and capacity to accept every music as unique. Music is useful to different people in different ways, but whatever its uses and meanings, it is inextricably bound with the human condition. We cannot fully understand other peoples and their environments merely by superimposing upon them our understanding of ourselves. Similarly, we cannot fully grasp the nature, meaning, and essence of all musics by interpreting them in terms of one music.

The elements and concepts with which we have been working in this chapter might well be regarded as the unity among all musics. The unique qualities and the manifold uses of these elements and concepts constitute a convincing, effective, and intriguing variety among the musics of the world.

BIBLIOGRAPHY

Of the several available English language dictionaries of music, the most comprehensive and perhaps most readily available is the *Harvard Dictionary of Music,* 2nd ed., edited by Willi Apel (Cambridge, Mass.: Harvard University Press, 1969). Another useful source, which deals with basic musical terminology and includes brief biographies of major Western composers, is *Everyman's Dictionary of Music,* ed. Eric Blom, rev. Sir Jack Westrup (London: J. M. Dent, 1964).

There are innumerable books dealing with Western music theory. Of the many good ones, the following, which treat various aspects of music theory on an introductory level, are recommended: William Mitchell, *Elementary Harmony,* 3rd ed. (Englewood Cliffs, N.J.: Prentice-Hall, 1965); Howard Boatwright, *Introduction to the Theory of Music* (New York: Norton, 1956); Victor Zuckerkandl, *The Sense of Music* (Princeton: Princeton University Press, 1959).

Valuable sources that discuss Western music theory on a more advanced level include: Walter Piston, *Harmony* (New York: Norton, 1950); Richard Franco Goldman; *Harmony in Western Music* (New York: Norton, 1965); Roger Sessions, *Harmonic Practice* (New York: Harcourt, Brace, and World, 1951); Edward Cone, *Musical Form and Musical Performance* (New York: Norton, 1968); Wallace Berry, *Form in Music* (Englewood Cliffs, N. J.: Prentice-Hall, 1966); Alfred Mann, *The Study of Fugue* (Brunswick, N. J.: Rutgers University Press, 1958); Curt Sachs, *Rhythm and Tempo* (New York: Norton, 1953).

These books are valuable sources of information on the nature, theory, performance, instruments, and functions of various non-Western musics: William Malm, *Music Cultures of the Pacific, the Near East, and Asia* (Englewood Cliffs, N. J.: Prentice-Hall, 1967); Bruno Nettl, *Folk and Traditional Music of the Western Continents,* 2nd ed. (Englewood Cliffs, N. J.: Prentice-Hall, 1973).

Useful sources dealing with the musical experience, music criticism, and with aspects of musical aesthetics include: Oliver Strunk, ed., *Source Readings in Music History* (New York: Norton, 1950); Jacques Barzun, *Pleasures of Music* (New York: Viking, 1951); Paul Hindemith, *A Composer's World* (Garden City, N. Y.: Doubleday, Anchor Books, 1961); Leonard Meyer, *Emotion and Meaning in Music* (Chicago: University of Chicago Press, 1957); Suzanne Langer, *Philosophy in a New Key* (Cambridge, Mass.: Harvard University Press, 1942); Charles Ives, "Essays Before a Sonata," in *Three Classics in the Aesthetic of Music* (New York: Dover, 1962), pp. 103–185.

2

Changing Patterns in Society and Music: The U.S. Since World War II

CHARLES HAMM

"The times they are a-changing'," sings Bob Dylan in one of his most popular and widely quoted songs. The times were changing in 1963, when the song was written. But the times have always been changing. And so has music. Anyone can hear, listening to a piece of music from 50 or 500 years ago, that it doesn't sound like music of today. The question to be investigated here is what relationship there is between changes in the times and changes in music.

One view is that since music is an abstraction—a series of marks on paper that are transformed into patterns of sound in time when the piece is performed—there can be no connection between it and such things as political events, wars, spiritual crises, labor movements, revolutions, natural disasters, and religious upheavals. Since music is an abstraction, goes this argument, it can only be understood as an abstraction—studied, talked about, described, and analyzed as a succession of sounds obeying their own rules, related only to themselves, and following certain laws of musical structure and logic. Music is something to be understood only its own terms. The proper study of it leads to an understanding of the rules, procedures, and laws governing the organization of the various notes making up a given composition; the best analysis shows how certain pieces of music observe these rules and procedures.

An alternate view holds that there *is* a relationship between a piece of music and what was happening in the world when it was written. While there can be no direct connection between the notes in a musical score and a political campaign, an anti-war demonstration, or a discovery in the chemical laboratory, there is a possible link between such events and music written at the time they are taking place. The link is the person who writes the music. As a human being, he may be aware of, responsive to—and in the case of an exceptional person, perhaps even partially responsible for—what is happening in the world around him. As a composer of a piece of music, he consciously chooses the notes he will write down. He may be concerned with the questions of why he is selecting certain notes, who he hopes will listen to his music when it is performed, and what effect he would like his music to have on his audience. To the extent that he is aware of, and wishes to participate in, the world in which he lives, any conscious action that he takes—including the writing of a piece of music—will be affected by this world.

This is the question to be dealt with in this chapter. The procedure will be to take a given period in history—in this case the post-World War II period in America—examine it, characterize it, summarize the most important events that took place in it, attempt to sketch a "personality" of this particular time, and then to examine some of the music written and played during this period to see if the character of the times is reflected in this music. On the basis of this investigation of a specific time in history, some generalizations will be drawn regarding relationships between music and the world surrounding the composer when he writes this music.

World War II was one of the great turning points in the history of the United States. Although the country had been steadily growing in population, wealth, and influence in the nineteenth and early twentieth centuries, and although it had made certain contributions in science and even in several of the arts, until the Second World War it was regarded as an isolated, young, and relatively unimportant country by the major European powers that had shaped the destiny of the world, or at least western Europe, for some centuries. America's intervention in World War I was late, and from the European point of view, relatively insignificant; its refusal to participate in the League of Nations minimized its role in international politics and economic and cultural exchange; severe internal problems, centered in the Great Depression, helped to maintain a low level of participation in international affairs. Europeans tended to regard Americans as naive, crude, unsophisticated, and often vaguely comic people with little history and culture. This view was shared by many Americans, particularly musicians and other artists. Generations of American composers and performers went to Europe to study, and writers and intellectuals fled the country for such "true" centers of culture (and life) as Paris. When a truly original creative genius such as the composer Charles Ives did emerge, he was often misunderstood and ignored.

Things began changing in the late 1930s and early '40s, when American economic life was revitalized. Many world-famous scientists, scholars, and artists fled Europe for the United States, finding here the security, freedom, support, and encouragement they needed to continue their activities. Their integration into the sciences and arts of the country provided a tremendous spark to American life. World War II changed the whole image of the United States. Threatened with isolation from the rest of the world and eventual annihilation, the country mobilized its military and industrial resources to a degree unprecedented in its history. At the end of the war, American troops were in almost every part of the world, having played a major role in the eventual defeat of the Germans and Japanese, and American industry was churning out an incredible flood of weapons and supplies of every sort.

When the war ended, there was no turning back. There was no denying the critical role American arms, men, and supplies had performed in defeating the Germans and the Japanese; neither could the dominant position the U.S. had attained in the world be argued. American troops occupied defeated countries and supported allied ones. American money and goods continued to pour into countries all over the world. American diplomats and statesmen, even American presidents, took part in conferences and meetings to try to determine the future of the postwar world. America was a charter member of the United Nations, one of the 29 nations that ratified the U.N. charter in October, 1945; the permanent headquarters of the U.N. were established in New York City. Its industry undamaged by the war, its casualties small in comparison with those of most European nations, its national pride in its military victories and industrial output high, the U.S.A. was undeniably one of the two most powerful nations in the world, the other being Russia.

It was assumed by the leaders of the country, apparently without question, that this new political, military, and economic strength would be sustained at a high level. Though the majority of non-career military personnel was discharged rather quickly when the war ended, the strength of the armed services was kept at a much higher level than was ever maintained in peacetime. Occupational forces remained in defeated countries, troops and military bases were maintained in countries that had been our allies, and bargains were made to establish new bases in countries such as Spain that had remained neutral during the war. Food, money, and supplies of all sorts were sent to countries wrecked by the war; billions of dollars were made available under the Marshall Plan to various European countries, playing a critical role in their amazing recovery. It was not just allies who were helped; Japan, Germany, and Italy were given major portions of American aid for rebuilding—physically, economically, and eventually militarily.

Just as our money and goods were everywhere, so was our political influence. American isolationism was dead. The Truman Doctrine, announced in

1947, stated that "it must be the policy of the United States to support free peoples who are resisting attempted subjugation by armed minorities or by outside pressures." Under this doctrine additional billions of dollars were sent to such countries as Greece and Turkey. Direct military intervention in Korea in 1950 made clear America's determination to play an active role in Asian affairs. The Eisenhower Doctrine announced that the U.S. would supply economic and military aid to countries in the Middle East that were determined to "stop Communist aggression." Countless other less dramatic and less publicized decisions and actions reinforced the image of a new America very much concerned with political, economic, even social affairs in practically every part of the world.

American economic and military victories during World War II were possible in large part because of the unity of the country during this period. There had been widespread discontent with many internal policies of the government in the 1930s and strong support for the notion that the United States should not become involved in European affairs; but in the several years preceding our entry into the war there was increasing sympathy for the Allies, and after the Japanese attack on Pearl Harbor there was almost unanimous support for a policy of total mobilization for victory. A smattering of pacifists and political dissenters were isolated, potentially troublesome aliens were segregated, and almost all Americans settled down to doing what they could, through military service or otherwise, to see that the country prevailed against a common foe. The hardships and dangers of military duty, separation of families, and restrictions on normal activities even in civilian life—censorship, rationing, severe shortages, overtime work, limitations on travel, priorities given to military needs—were accepted, and endured, as necessary conditions for victory. Most Americans recognized this period as a crisis in their lives, and endured conditions they might otherwise have rebelled against.

The end of the war did not bring about much change in the mood of the country. After several tentative and confusing years, Americans were once again asked to mobilize against an enemy, and conditions that most people expected to change, once the war was won, were still part of American life. This time the enemy was Communism—international Communism. The American government took the view that there was an international Communist conspiracy to overthrow or conquer the United States and the entire world, and this conspiracy had to be fought as vigorously at home and abroad as the totalitarian governments of Japan and Germany had been fought during the war.

Secretary of State James Byrnes announced a new "get tough with Russia" policy early in 1946. An advisory committee recommended to President Truman in 1947 that compulsory military training for all 18-year-old Americans be instituted; consequently, the Selective Service Act went into effect in 1948, requiring all males in the 18–25 age bracket to register for a minimum of 18 months' service. This was only the second peacetime draft in American history, the first having been that ordered by President Roosevelt shortly before our entry into World War II.

The war against Communism was conducted as vigorously within the country as it was in the area of international politics. President Truman ordered loyalty investigations of all federal employees in March, 1947, and by the following year more than two million persons had been investigated— 526 resigned and 98 others were dismissed for supporting or sympathizing with Communist causes and ideas. The search for Communist influence broadened. The House Committee on Un-American Activities began hearings in 1947 on Communist sympathizers in the motion picture industry; writers, actors, and technicians were blacklisted by the industry as a result. In 1949 the New York State legislature ordered the dismissal of public school employees who were Communists; in 1950 the Board of Regents of the University of California dismissed 157 staff members who refused to sign statements disclaiming membership in the Communist party; the Supreme Court ruled in 1952 that "subversives" could legally be barred from teaching in public schools. Millions of Americans were asked to sign "loyalty oaths" to the effect that they did not belong to or sympathize with organizations attempting to overthrow the government. General Electric announced in 1953 that all Communists on their payroll would be fired. The government pursued legal warfare: 11 top Communists were convicted late in 1949 of conspiring to overthrow the United States government, and, finally, in 1954 the Communist Party itself was outlawed in America. By this time the country was again in armed conflict. In the summer of 1950 Truman ordered American troops to Korea to help resist the invading (Communist) forces from the north; an additional ten billion dollars was immediately requested to augment the military budget; and a state of emergency was declared in the country on December 16, 1950, when it became apparent that a major effort would be needed to pursue this new war.

One must not necessarily conclude that this continuing state of confrontation, conflict, and emergency was the result of a deliberate military-political scheme to keep the coutry on a wartime basis. The unity and single-mindedness of purpose in the country during the war had been a very real thing, sensed, understood, and appreciated by most Americans. Pearl Harbor, D-Day, and V-Day had been profound emotional experiences. The war years had been difficult in many ways, but they were also good years. There had been a sense of common purpose, a sense of working with other people to attain a common goal, a feeling that everyone was in the same situation and, as a result, could understand and relate to everyone else. Complete strangers meeting on trains, groups of people brought together by chance, felt a comradeship and a closeness that had not been part of American life in prewar years. There was a genuine sense of national pride, a feeling that our involvement in the war was a humane thing, that we were truly fighting evil. There was genuine pride in the victories of our armed forces. The clarity of the situation during the war, when Americans identified themselves as a good and righteous people fighting to overthrow evil, appealed to and inspired many people; the role had been played with great success, and it was easy enough for America to continue the same role when the enemy was redefined as Communism.

It was not just the government that was attracted to the idea of a country united behind its policies and actions. Americans of all kinds understood how the unity of the country behind its leaders had contributed to the victories of the war years, and how the same kind of unity could help achieve economic and social victories in peacetime. Americans both in and out of military service had, during the war, sacrificed some of their traditional independence and freedoms for what was felt to be the common good. The success of this course of action persuaded many people that continued unity, even if it were brought about by outside pressures, was highly desirable. This desire for unity was buttressed by an important, Pulitzer Prize-winning book of 1948, *The Disruption of American Democracy* by Roy Franklin Nichols, who explored the causes of the American Civil War, and in doing so investigated a much more general (and quite pertinent) question: What conditions can cause a successfully functioning democratic government to become disrupted and inefficient and, perhaps, even disintegrate? The author summarized his conclusions in this way:

> Why a civil war? Most of the principal "causes"—ideological differences, institutional differences, moral differences, cultural differences, sectional differences, physiographic differences—have existed in other times and places, without necessarily causing a war. Then why should they set the people of the United States to killing one another in 1861?...
>
> People fight under the stress of hyperemotionalism. When some compelling drive, whether it be ambition, fear, anger, or hunger, becomes supercharged, violence and bloodletting, thus far in human history, seem "inevitable."...
>
> So rapid and uneven a rate of social growth was bound to inflict upon Americans this "confusion of a growing state." Characteristic of it and dominant in it were pervasive, divisive, and cohesive attitudes which, as Whitman put it, were "significant of a grand upheaval of ideas and reconstruction of many things on new bases." The social confusion in itself was the great problem confronting statesmen and politicians....
>
> This lack of understanding was accompanied by a deep-seated enjoyment of political activity by Americans which proved dangerous. They gave themselves so many opportunities to gratify their desire for this sport. There were so many elections and such constant agitation....
>
> A great disruptive fact was the baneful influence of elections almost continuously in progress, of campaigns never over, and of political uproar endlessly arousing emotions. The system of the fathers might possibly bear within itself the seeds of its own destruction.
>
> This constant agitation certainly furnishes one of the primary clues to why the war came. It raised to an ever higher pitch the passion-rousing oratory of

rivals. They egged one another on to make more and more exaggerated statements to a people pervasively romantic and protestant, isolated and confused. The men and women exhibiting these different attitudes were not isolated and separated by boundaries—they dwelt side by side, and the same person might be moved by more than one attitude at a time, or by different attitudes at different times. The emotional complex which was created by the variety of these attitudes, and the tension which their antagonisms bred, added confusion to that already provided by the chaotic electoral customs and poorly organized parties; the total precipitated a resort to arms. . . .

War broke out because no means had been devised to curb the extravagant use of the divisive forces. . . .

At certain times and in certain circumstances, cooperative behavior predominates; but competitive behavior is seldom if ever absent, and when too vigorously aroused leads to a strife which ranges from argument to war. Indeed argument is itself a form of conflict short of war, more or less, and if pressed without checks and restraints easily passes over into war.[1]

For many Americans it was scientific rather than military achievement that was most exciting and held the most promise for a better life in the future. It was our scientists, after all, who had devised the arsenal of weapons that made our armed forces so effective—the always-improving fighter planes and bombers, radar, rockets, flame throwers, proximity fuses, and eventually the atomic bomb—and who had perfected methods of treatment for the wounded and sick that kept the rate of fatalities much lower than it might have been. One of the most widely read books in the years just after the war was James Phinney Baxter's *Scientists Against Time* (1946), an account of the activities of the Office of Scientific Research and Development during the war. The foreword by Vannevar Bush, director of this office, explains the subject matter:

> It begins in 1940, when this country was still asleep under the delusion of isolation—when only a few realized that a supreme test was inevitable, to determine whether the democratic form of government could survive; when none could see clearly the full revolution in the art of war that impended.
>
> It recites the extraordinarily rapid evolution of weapons, as the accumulated backlog of scientific knowledge became directly applied to radar, amphibious warfare, aerial combat, the proximity fuze, and the atomic bomb.
>
> But it tells also of something that is more fundamental even than this diversion of the progress of science into methods of destruction. It shows how men of good will, under stress, can outperform all that dictatorship can bring to bear—as they collaborate effectively, and apply those qualities of character developed only under freedom. It demonstrates that democracy is strong and virile, and that free men can defend their ideals as ably in a highly complex world as when they left the plow in the furrow to grasp the smoothbore. This is the heartening fact which should give us renewed courage and assurance, even as we face a future in which war must be abolished, and in which that

[1] Roy Franklin Nichols, *The Disruption of American Democracy* (New York: The MacMillan Company, 1948), pp. 513–17. Reprinted by permission.

end can be reached only by resolution, patience, and resourcefulness of a whole people.[2]

And at the end of his history (which brought him a Pulitzer Prize) of the stirring accomplishments of American scientists during this tense and dramatic period, Mr. Baxter expresses his view of the present and future role of America and of its scientists—a view as widely held outside the political/military leadership of the country as within it:

> Until the world creates an international organization strong enough to control the genie who escaped from his bottle at Alamogordo, we must keep our powder dry. Only a strong United States can give sufficient support to the peace structure of the United Nations during the difficult period of transition in which the statesmen of the world must build more securely the foundations of international order. A generation ago some of our pacifists preached unilateral disarmament, in the belief that by setting other nations an example we should encourage them to decrease their own armaments. Such a course was dangerous then. It would be suicidal now. It would place in jeopardy both our national security and the contribution we must make to the enforcement of peace. If war comes again, it probably will come quickly, leaving us no opportunity for the lengthy preparations we made in World Wars I and II while associates and allies held the fronts.
>
> Our preparations must, therefore, provide for great offensive and defensive power from the outset of hostilities. Much of our strength will depend on the use we make of our scientists and engineers. It is not a question of scientific preparedness versus expenditures on ships, guns, and planes. We need big battalions, fleets, and air squadrons as well as factories, pilot plants, and laboratories. . . .[3]

Scientific research had been a key to military victory, and it held promise of winning other battles, those against disease, discomfort, death, and even the poor quality of life still afflicting so many Americans. The years after the war witnessed a series of scientific discoveries and developments so astonishing and so promising of a better life that reading a newspaper or listening to a news report on the radio became an exciting event, done in anticipation of hearing of yet another scientific marvel or miracle.

There were astonishing developments in transportation and communication, making the world an ever-shrinking globe. Pan American Airways began the first round-the-world passenger service in 1947. An experimental X-1 jet, piloted by Captain Yaeger, made the first supersonic flight during that same year. In 1949 an Air Force jet bomber flew across the continent in less than four hours. An Army missile reached the unheard of altitude of 259 miles the same year, arousing increased speculation that space flight might eventually be possible. Direct dial telephone service on a nationwide basis was

[2] James Phinney Baxter III, *Scientists Against Time* (Boston: Little, Brown and Company, 1946), vii.
[3] *Ibid.*, p. 449.

begun in 1951. A Bell X-1A plane reached a speed of 1600 miles per hour in 1953. A transatlantic telephone system began operation in 1956, replacing radio telephone circuits. Russia launched Sputnik 1, the first earth satellite, in 1957, and the United States took important steps toward manned space flight by launching its first satellite, Explorer 1, in 1958 and sending two monkeys on a suborbital flight (up to 350 miles) in 1959. In the same year (1959) radio beams were bounced off the moon and back to the earth, a major step toward direct radio and television communication over distances formerly prohibitive. It was clearly only a matter of time until man would be able to communicate instantaneously with any spot on earth, or journey to any city in the country, or even the world, in a matter of hours; it was equally certain that man would soon be exploring space.

Discoveries in medicine were just as exciting. "Miracle" drugs such as Aureomycin were being used by 1948, and cortisone was discovered the following year. Antihistamines were being widely used by 1950 to combat the symptoms of colds and other illnesses. Polio, the dread crippler of children, was conquered: Dr. Jonas E. Salk began a test program of inoculating school children in 1954 and reported the following year that the tests had been successful in the 44 states in which they had been given; within a few years almost everyone in the country had been protected by either his method or that of Dr. Sabin. The successful use of Thorazine and reserpine in mental illnesses was reported in 1955. Improved surgical techniques, news of progress in isolating the viruses known or suspected of causing other diseases—these and other developments gave Americans hope for longer and more healthful lives.

Science was also furnishing Americans with new uses for their leisure time. Commercial telecasts, beginning after the war, became the major amusement of millions of American families. Five million sets were owned by 1950, and in the following twenty-year period the number swelled to 93 million. The first commercial color telecast was a CBS show in June, 1951.

Science programs in colleges and universities expanded enormously in size and diversity and became financial mainstays of these institutions because of the federal government's willingness to grant large sums of money for research. Students entering college studied the sciences in ever-increasing numbers, many of them because of the promise of high salaries in these fields, but some because of a personal conviction that the most exciting and rewarding work was being done here. Respect and admiration for science and scientists cannot be demonstrated by statistics, but these feelings were dominant in postwar American life. As one illustration, the list of men elected to the Hall of Fame for Great Americans during this period is given below. Established in 1900 on the campus of New York University, the Hall of Fame holds elections every five years. The College of Electors is made up of approximately 100 eminent men and women from various professions. Americans with a wide range of accomplishments have been voted in: among those elected in 1900 were John Adams (statesman), John James Audubon (naturalist), Henry Ward Beecher (clergyman), Henry Clay (statesman), Peter Cooper (philanthropist), Ralph Waldo Emerson (author), Robert E. Lee (military officer), Henry W. Longfellow (poet), John Marshall (jurist), and Jefferson, Franklin, and Washington. But those elected in 1945, 1950, and 1955 were almost without exception men of science, politics, or war.

1945

Walter Reed (surgeon)
Booker T. Washington (educator)
Thomas Paine (author)

1950

Alexander Graham Bell (inventor)
Josiah Willard Gibbs (physicist)
William Crawford Gorgas (physician)
Theodore Roosevelt (statesman)
Woodrow Wilson (statesman)

1955

"Stonewall" Jackson (military officer)
Wilbur Wright (inventor)

An account of historical events or a recitation of facts and statistics cannot capture the mood, the feeling, of a given period of history. It is perhaps impossible for a person who did not live then to understand the attitude in the country toward science—the excitement over scientific achievements, the anticipation of continuing ones, the admiration accorded great scientists, the faith that science was leading mankind along the road to a peaceful, healthy, happy life. Much of this is summed up in a popular movie of the time, *Breaking the Sound Barrier* (1949), starring Ralph Richardson and Ann Todd. The plot involves attempts to perfect a test plane that will fly faster than the speed of sound. There is some belief that this is impossible, that a plane will disintegrate as it reaches this speed; in earlier flights there has been excessive vibration and malfunctioning of parts of the plane's mechanism as this speed is approached. Another attempt is made at the climax of the movie. It is successful, but the plane crashes, killing the pilot. The final scene includes a brief but dramatic statement by the scientist (Ralph Richardson) in charge of the operation: the pilot just killed was his son-in-law, and he is naturally shaken; but he says that the important thing is to continue this work until it is successful. Scientific achievement is more important than a human life. Audiences left movie houses excited and thrilled by this message.

Science is necessarily linked to education. Scientists must be educated more and more as their fields become increasingly complex. This period of great scientific achievement and promise was accompanied by an unprecedented expansion of higher education in America. A combination of two factors—a growing feeling that as much education as possible was a desirable and necessary thing in the postwar world, and the possibility of obtaining a college education (because of the GI Bill for veterans, the great availability of loans for education, and the generally higher level of family income) for many people who could not have afforded it before—filled colleges and universities to capacity, and encouraged and even forced a drastic increase in the enrollment at existing schools and the opening of new schools. Here, statistics are quite eloquent. Approximately 122,500 Americans were enrolled in colleges in the academic year 1929–30, representing 18 percent of the number of pupils in high school that year. By 1939–40 the number had risen to 186,500, but this increase reflected the population growth rather than any changing pattern; this figure was only 15 percent of the high school population that year. But by 1949–50 there were 432,000 college students, 36 percent of the number of high school students.

Musical life in America was rich and complex during this period. In some ways musical activity reached peaks rarely attained in the previous history of the country. Phonograph records sold in unprecedented numbers. Popular music on radio, television, and jukeboxes, in movies, and over public systems such as Muzak flooded the air to the extent that many people lived with music most of their waking hours. Classical music flourished likewise. The sales of phonograph records of this music soared to new highs, and occasionally a classical record rivaled the sale of a pop record. Live performance of classical music also prospered. School, community, and regional symphony orchestras were founded in unprecedented numbers, as were amateur and semiprofessional opera groups. The locus of music instruction shifted dramatically from private instruction and conservatory training to music schools and departments of music in colleges and universities. These campuses became chief centers of musical activity in the country; not only music majors, but other students (and faculty) as well, involved themselves in choral groups, school orchestras, various chamber ensembles, and opera, performing for large audiences drawn from the college community. The quality of performance in these schools steadily improved—as more and more talented young musicians chose college rather than conservatory or private training, and as professional musicians were attracted to the benefits and security of an academic position—until it sometimes equalled or even surpassed that of professional groups.

In a reversal of the situation in previous centuries, when musical life was built almost completely around contemporary music, a very large percentage of music performed during this period (excluding popular music) was from the past. Composition of new works continued to flourish, however, and it is to this body of music that we must look for parallels with what was happening in postwar American life, if indeed these exist.

It is difficult to characterize music during a period like this, when so many composers were writing music of quite different types. With popular music, it seems fair enough to select the songs that sold the most copies and that were listened to by the most people, and to say that a sampling of a certain number of these pieces gives a profile of popular music as a whole. It is not so easy with classical music, where individuality is more prized, where some composers make a deliberate effort to write music that does not sound like that of anyone else, and where measurement of popularity is not only difficult but perhaps meaningless. Music historians tend to approach this problem—that of selecting a small number of composers and compositions most representative of a given period—by resorting to the concept of "importance"; by assuming that the central figure at a given time is the man whose music and ideas seem most interesting, important, and influential to other musicians and composers, and who was most centrally involved in the important and characteristic currents flowing through the musical life of that time. Utilizing this approach to music in America during the several decades immediately after World War II, a strong case can be made for selecting Walter Piston and Milton Babbitt as two of the most important composers of the time.

Walter Piston was born in Rockland, Maine, in 1894. He was educated at Harvard and in Paris. Joining the music faculty at Harvard in 1926, he eventually became chairman of the department and held the Naumburg endowed chair of composition until his retirement from academic life in 1960. Though he composed diligently and with considerable success before World War II, the peak of his career came in the 1940s and '50s, and his success and influence as both a composer and a teacher reached new heights during that time.

As a professor at Harvard, he helped and influenced several generations of students, including the composers Arthur Berger, Irving Fine, Ellis Kohs, Leonard Bernstein, Harold Shapero, Daniel Pinkham, Billy Jim Layton, and Gordon Blinkerd. But his greatest impact on the training of musicians came after the publication of his three textbooks: *Harmony* (1941), *Counterpoint* (1947), and *Orchestration* (1955). These came out at just the right time, coinciding with the enormous increase in enrollment at colleges and universities, and the shift of musical training to these institutions. They became the most widely used music textbooks for some decades, adopted by teachers at hundreds of schools and used by tens of thousands of students. These books project Piston's basic belief about the study of music: it should be a rational thing; certain principles of music can and should be learned in a systematic, disciplined fashion; all musicians should learn these things. The introduction to his book on harmony states, with characteristic clarity and succinctness, his conviction regarding the importance and necessity of rational and systematic training in the fundamental elements of music:

> There are those who consider that studies in harmony, counterpoint, and fugue are the exclusive province of the intended composer. But if we reflect that theory must follow practice, rarely preceding it except by chance, we must realize that musical theory is not a set of directions for composing music. It is rather the collected and systematized deductions gathered by observing the practice of composers over a long time, and it attempts to set forth what is or has been their common practice. It tells not how music will be written in the future, but how music has been written in the past.
>
> The results of such a definition of the true nature of musical theory are many and important. First of all, it is clear that this knowledge is indispensable to musicians in all fields of the art, whether they be composers, performers, conductors, critics, teachers, or musicologists. Indeed, a secure grounding in theory is even more a necessity to the musical scholar than to the composer, since it forms the basis for any intelligent appraisal of individual styles of the past or present.
>
> On the other hand, the person gifted for creative musical composition is taking a serious risk in assuming that his genius is great enough to get along without a deep knowledge of the common practice of composers. Mastery of the technical or theoretical aspects of music should be carried out by him as a life's work, running parallel to his creative activity but quite separate from it. . . .[4]

The period 1945–60 was one of even greater activity, success, and acclaim for Piston the composer. He wrote merely two symphonies from the time he began composing in 1926 until the end of World War II, but after that time works began to pour from his pen. The Third Symphony was written in 1947, the Fourth in 1950, the Fifth in 1954, the Sixth the next year, and the Seventh in 1961. Other compositions were produced at a similar rate. For instance, the amount of chamber music he wrote in the 15 years after the end of the war was greater than what he had written before that time. Whatever the conditions were in the country and whatever Piston's own situation, they were clearly favorable to his creative work.

Recognition and performance of his music matched this impressive output. Piston was awarded two Pulitzer Prizes, one in 1948 for his Third Symphony, the other in 1961 for the Seventh. His music was performed by the major orchestras in the country as frequently as any contemporary American music. For example, his Second Symphony was premiered in 1944 by the National Symphony Orchestra of Washington, D.C., played the same year by the Boston Symphony Orchestra, done in New York in 1945 by the NBC Sym-

---

4 Reprinted from *Harmony* by Walter Piston, pp. 1–2. By permission of **W. W. Norton & Company, Inc.** Copyright 1941, 1948, © 1962 by **W. W. Norton & Company, Inc.**

phony, and played later the same year by the New York Philharmonic under the direction of Artur Rodzinski; it won the Music Critics' Circle Award as the best new composition of 1945. Other of his works have similar histories. Just as he was a central figure in music instruction, Piston was squarely in the center of activity in the performance of contemporary music by the major performing groups in the country.

His approach to composition was as rational and as historically oriented as his teaching and writing about music theory. He was familiar with the traditions, history, and style of Western European art music, and he saw his role as composer as one in which he studied, absorbed, and understood as much of this music as possible, borrowing whatever elements he chose for his own music. The formal structures, harmonies, melodies, instrumentation, and counterpoint of his compositions were his own and reflected his own musical taste and personality, but they were all firmly and obviously rooted in earlier music.

Piston had assimilated this earlier music by conscious study, intellectual examination, and a deliberate and rational dissection followed by an equally rational reassembling of their various elements. His symphonies are points in a line of symphonic history extending from Haydn to Beethoven to Schubert to Brahms to Dvořák to Sibelius to Piston to whatever composers after him who chose to continue this line. He understood his music this way; he had arrived at this point of view during his own academic work in music; other people could most readily understand his music and the assumptions behind it if they were exposed to the same sort of training. Piston was content to be a college professor. His ideas about music fit nicely into an intellectual atmosphere sympathetic to order, intellectual discipline, rational examination, and historical perspective. The composer Elliott Carter, a former student of his, says of Piston:

> The rather speculative enterprise of uniting the different styles of contemporary music into one common style and using this in an ordered and beautiful way needs the peacefulness and sense of long-term continuity nowadays more frequently found in a university than elsewhere. . . .
> His unique contribution is to have done this particular work with outstanding excellence in a country where few have ever made a name for themselves as thoroughly craftsman-like artists. In literature several names come to mind but in music there is hardly one to be found before our time.
> To have helped to establish a deep understanding of the value of craftsmanship and taste here and to have given such persuasive exemplification of these in his works is highly important for our future. For, not having as ingrained a respect and love for high artistic ideals as Europeans have had, we have often slipped into the trivial, chaotic, and transitory. Piston's work helps us to keep our mind on the durable and the most satisfying aspects of the art of music and by making them live gives us hope that the qualities of integrity and reason are still with us.[5]

[5] Elliott Carter, "Walter Piston," *The Musical Quarterly*, XXXII (1946), 354, 372–73. Reprinted by permission.

In a way Piston was a "popular" composer. The area of musical activity in which he worked, contemporary art music, was not a popular one in the sense that audiences and record sales matched those of pop music; but Piston had as many pieces performed, as many recordings made, and as large an audience as any other composer of this kind of music. The same cannot be said of Milton Babbitt, however. A discussion of his role in the music scene after World War II cannot stress the number of performances and recordings of his compositions (these were scarce), or the prizes and awards he won (such things were to come to him later), but must depend on the effect that his music and his ideas had on his contemporaries. Anyone involved in any serious way with contemporary music in the 1950s knew of Babbitt, knew at least something of his ideas, discussed them, felt it necessary to either agree or disagree with them, and in general was very much aware of his presence. In other words, he was an important figure.

Born in Philadelphia in 1916, Babbitt grew up in Jackson, Mississippi, was educated in Philadelphia and at New York University, and joined the faculty of Princeton University at the age of 22. He has taught at that institution ever since, eventually being appointed to an endowed chair in composition. Early in his career as a composer he combined a flair for mathematics with music. He has said:

> Some people say my music is "too cerebral." Actually, I believe in cerebral music—in the application of intellect to relevant matters. I never choose a note unless I know precisely why I want it there and can give several reasons why it and not another.[6]

He was attracted to twelve-tone (or serial) music, the system worked out by Arnold Schoenberg whereby the basis of a composition is a set series of the twelve tones of the chromatic scale. This row of notes may be used in its original form, transposed to any pitch level, inverted, or used backwards (retrograde); a single form of the row may be used, several forms may be combined, or vertical or horizontal combinations of the row—or both—may be used. Few if any listeners can follow the manipulations of the row, but it permeates the entire piece and, therefore, shapes the character of the composition regardless of whether or not it can be consciously perceived. Schoenberg's pupil Anton Webern utilized this system at another level in many of his compositions. Working in more conscious ways with symmetries, proportions, and other relationships, he fashioned a series of short but incredibly complex compositions that reveal, upon careful analysis, the amazing detail of a thoughtful, systematic, and imaginative organization.

Babbitt wrote several articles analyzing and describing Webern's methods of pitch organization; in his own compositions he went beyond Webern by organizing other elements of a composition, such as rhythm and dynamics, in

[6] *The Score*, XII (June, 1955), p. 53.

a similar way. The result has been called "totally organized" music, music in which every detail can be explained by reference to certain systematic compositional procedures planned and worked out before the piece is written.

By this time Babbitt's ideas and theories were so esoteric, so remote from usual musical experiences that very few people could follow or understand them. His articles and analyses were extremely difficult to comprehend, for musicians and even for theorists and other composers. No one, with the possible exception of a handful of other composers associated with him, could hear in his compositions what he was putting into them, the incredibly involved and complex relationships among notes and groups of notes that seemed so important, so basic to what he was doing. Rather than seeing this as an unfortunate situation, Babbitt regarded it as a natural and even desirable development. His article "Who Cares If You Listen," published in 1958, expressed his views of the relationship between the composer and the rest of the world with admirable clarity and eloquence:

> Why refuse to recognize the possibility that contemporary music has reached a stage long since attained by other forms of activity? The time has passed when the normally well-educated man without special preparation can understand the most advanced work in, for example, mathematics, philosophy, and physics. Advanced music, to the extent that it reflects the knowledge and originality of the informed composer, scarcely can be expected to appear more intelligible than these arts and sciences to the person whose musical education usually has been even less extensive than his background in other fields. But to this, a double standard is invoked, with the words "music is music," implying also that "music is *just* music." Why not, then, equate the activities of the radio repairman with those of the theoretical physicist, on the basis of the dictum that "physics is physics"? It is not difficut to find statements like the following from the New York *Times* of September 8, 1957: "The scientific level of the conference is so high...that there are in the world only 120 mathematicians specializing in the field who could contribute.."...
>
> ...I dare suggest that the composer would do himself and his music an immediate and eventual service by total, resolute, and voluntary withdrawal from this public world to one of private performance and electronic media, with its very real possibility of complete elimination of the public and social aspects of musical composition. By so doing, the separation between the domains would be defined beyond any possibility of confusion of categories, and the composer would be free to pursue a private life of professional achievement, as opposed to a public life of unprofessional compromise and exhibitionism....
>
> In E. T. Bell's *Men of Mathematics*, we read: "In the eighteenth century the universities were not the principal centers of research in Europe. They might have become such sooner than they did but for the classical tradition and its understandable hostility to science. Mathematics was close enough to antiquity to be respectable, but physics, being more recent, was suspect. Further, a mathematician in a university of the time would have been expected to put much of his effort on elementary teaching; his research, if any, would have been an unprofitable luxury...." A simple substitution of "musical composition" for "research," of "academic" for "classical," of "music" for

"physics," and of "composer" for "mathematician," provides a strikingly accurate picture of the current situation. . . .

Granting to music the position accorded other arts and sciences promises the sole substantial means of survival for the music I have been describing. . . .[7]

Pieces by Babbitt from this period are his *Composition for Four Instruments* (1948), *Composition for Viola and Piano* (1950), String Quartet No. 2 (1954), and *All Set* (1957, for jazz ensemble).

In the late 1950s he was attracted to the idea of creating electronic music. His precisely calculated rhythms and pitches were difficult for human performers to execute with absolute precision, but the most complex passages were matters of simple mathematics for an electronic instrument; and once fixed, they would stay that way forever, with not the slightest variation or imperfection in any performance. Babbitt served as a consultant in the planning of one of the largest and most complex electronic instruments in this country, RCA's Mark II Electronic Music Synthesizer, and has created on it such pieces as *Composition for Synthesizer* (1960–61) and *Ensembles for Synthesizer* (1961–63). The Synthesizer is housed in the Columbia-Princeton Electronic Music Center in New York, and is available to the students and faculty members of these schools.

As different from each other as their musics may seem to be, Piston and Babbitt share many ideas and attitudes. Both believe that music is something to be approached logically, rationally, analytically, systematically, and with historical perspective. Both regard music as an abstraction; neither has professed interest in music as a sociological phenomenon, neither sees music as reflecting historical, political, or even national trends. (Piston once said, "The self-conscious striving for nationalism gets in the way of the establishment of a strong school of composition and even of significant individual expression.") Both found an academic atmosphere most congenial to their careers and creative life.

Piston and Babbitt have been singled out as representative composers of this period. Their attitudes and approaches to music were shared by a large number of the other composers who enjoyed the most success at this time. Success was measured by performances of compositions, publications, prizes and awards received, and publicity, i.e., articles and criticisms in newspapers and journals. Success was rewarded by academic appointments and promotions. Other composers who were successful by these criteria were Roger Sessions, William Schuman, Quincy Porter, Elliott Carter, Peter Mennin, David Diamond, Leon Kirchner, George Rochberg, Ross Lee Finney, Vincent Persichetti, Halsey Stevens, Arthur Berger, and Harold Shapero. These men, with Piston and Babbitt, wrote the most widely performed music, won most

[7] Milton Babbitt, "Who Cares If You Listen?" *High Fidelity,* VIII, No. 2 (February 1958), 39–40, 126–27. Reprinted by permission.

of the major prizes and awards, and received the most attention in articles, essays, histories, and criticisms of contemporary music. Theirs was the music most often performed, most widely discussed, most praised, and most often used as models by younger composers. Almost all of these men share with Piston and Babbit a concern for music as a rational and intellectual thing, almost all were trained in colleges or universities, and almost all held academic positions.

A handful of composers did not fit into this pattern. Gian-Carlo Menotti wrote successful operas; Samuel Barber was able to live independently of any type of position; Roy Harris and Aaron Copland were still active, though their greatest successes had come in the period before the war, a time when composers had been more independent and more concerned with writing "American" music. Although these men enjoyed some success after World War II, they were a minority, and their music and artistic ideals were rarely taken as models by the younger generation of composers.

Other types of music changed in ways reflective of the moods and attitudes dominating American life and culture during this period. Early jazz was associated with Negro dance halls, bars, houses of prostitution, and other non-academic surroundings. Jazz musicians were largely untrained players who, usually, could not read music and had little knowledge of the Western musical tradition. Even when jazz became known to white audiences, it retained much of its original character, and for some generations most jazz musicians, black and white, continued to be individuals whose training was mostly informal and was based on the oral traditions of jazz.

The most popular, successful, and influential jazz group after World War II was the Modern Jazz Quartet. This group represented something quite different in the history of jazz: its founder and leader, pianist John Lewis, studied at the Manhattan School of Music, earning two degrees and in the process becoming familiar with a wide range of music and musical techniques; Milt Jackson, the quartet's vibraharp player, studied music at Michigan State University and was later a faculty member at the School of Jazz in Lenox, Massachusetts; bassist Percy Heath studied at the Granoff School of Music in Philadelphia. Shortly after the group was founded in 1951, John Lewis said: "I think that the audience for jazz can be widened if we strengthen our work with structure. If there is more of a reason for what is going on, there'll be more overall sense and therefore more interest for the listener."

Their stage dress and deportment accentuated the seriousness of their approach to music. They sought to lose their individual personalities through the complete integration of their talents in their music and by dressing and acting soberly; the impression they gave on stage was compared to that of a string quartet. Their music often borrows or is based on techniques or styles of classical music. Among their most popular pieces, *Vendome* and *Concorde* are fugues, and *The Queen's Fancy* was inspired by the Elizabethan composer

Giles Farnaby. Other pieces are based on more sophisticated and complex formal structures than had previously been usual in jazz. Their audiences listened quietly and seriously, rarely reacting to the rhythmic elements that appealed so much to listeners of earlier jazz, and discussions of their music were often quite intellectual. Nor was this approach to jazz unique to this group. Other important jazz musicians of this time, such as Dave Brubeck, had similar backgrounds and used similar techniques in their music.

Respect for scientific achievement, a profound belief that the best hope for the future lay with a rational and intellectual approach to the problems of man, a conviction that more and better education would bring this about, and a willingness to subjugate individual ambitions, desires, and even certain freedoms to what was felt to be the common good marked this period of American history. Music created at this time tended to be rational and logical; it would not be inappropriate to use the word "scientific" to characterize it. Musical training was undertaken primarily in academic institutions, and many musicians were convinced that more and better musical education was the key to a better musical future for America. Increasing uniformity in teaching methods and in general attitudes toward music did not seem too heavy a price to pay for this promising future.

Curious things began to happen in the early and mid-1950s. A number of seemingly isolated and unrelated events in the arts, in literature, and among scientists, had one important thing in common: they were inexplicable in terms of what had been happening in America since the end of World War II.

—In 1950–51 the artist Robert Rauschenberg did a series of all-white paintings. The viewer could see nothing but a white surface, sometimes with his shadow projected on it. Several all-black paintings followed, made of torn and crumpled newspapers covered with black enamel paint.

—John Cage's *Imaginary Landscape No. 4,* written in 1951, was performed by 24 players on 12 radios. One player manipulated the volume control on each radio, one the knob to change stations. The sound of the piece depended on what was being broadcast over various stations at the time of given performance, and, thus, no two performances were alike.

—In the summer of 1952, at Black Mountain College, Cage organized a "simultaneous presentation of unrelated events." Cage read a lecture; David Tudor played the piano; Merce Cunningham danced; Robert Rauschenberg played old phonograph records on a handcranked machine; M. C. Richards read poetry while perched on a ladder; various movies were projected on the ceiling. Each individual event was timed to the second, but the combination of them was unplanned, and left to chance. In a few years, such things would be called "happenings."

—The first issue of *Mad* magazine appeared in August, 1952. The early issues were devoted largely to wild parodies of popular TV shows, movies, and other comic books, but there were also satirical takeoffs on various aspects of American life and culture. From the beginning, the advertising world was attacked and ridiculed by a series of grossly parodied advertisements. Features in the first issues included "Is a Trip to the Moon Possible?" (no, because of comic inefficiency and the stupidity of scientists) ; a *Mad* award for outstanding commercials to Goldsmobile (showing highways impossibly cluttered with cars as a result of the effectiveness of automobile advertising) ; "How To Be Smart" (demonstrating how social acceptance and success of various sorts can be obtained by crude, anti-intellectual behavior) ; "Let's Go For A Ride" (to a picnic ground grotesquely crowded and cluttered with garbage, trash, and litter) ; and "Supermarkets" (inconvenient, expensive, tricking people into buying things they didn't want or need). *Mad* readers soon numbered in the millions, and subject matter expanded to parody and even ridicule of such American institutions as the government, schools, and military service.

—Jaspar Johns did a painting in 1954, entitled "Flag," that was an exact reproduction of an American flag—nothing more, nothing less. He also exhibited paintings of archery targets, and his "Painted Bronze," created several years later, consisted of two Ballantine Ale cans mounted on a base.

—A group of scientists who had been awarded the Nobel Prize met at Lake Constance in the summer of 1955 and issued a declaration reading in part: "With pleasure we have devoted our lives to the service of science. It is, we believe, a path to a happier life for people. We see with horror that this very science is giving mankind the means to destroy itself.... All nations must come to the decision to renounce force as a final resort of policy. If they are not prepared to do this they will cease to exist." This statement, called the Mainau Declaration, was signed by 52 scientists, including Bertrand Russell, Harold Urey, Frédéric and Irène Joliot-Curie, Linus Pauling, and other scientists from Germany, Sweden, France, Switzerland, Finland, England, and Japan.

—John F. Kennedy published in 1955 a book called *Profiles in Courage,* which detailed the actions of a number of political leaders, including John Quincy Adams, Daniel Webster, Sam Houston, and Robert A. Taft, men who had followed courses of action that they believed proper even though public sentiment was against them, and whose careers were endangered or even ruined by their acts. In the first chapter of this book Kennedy says:

> ...our everyday life is becoming so saturated with the tremendous power of mass communications that any unpopular or unorthodox course arouses a storm of protests such as John Quincy Adams—under attack in 1807—could never have envisioned. Our political life is becoming so expensive, so mechanized and so dominated by professional politicians and public relations men that the idealist who dreams of independent statesmanship is rudely awakened by the necessities of election and accomplishment. And our public life is becoming so increasingly centered upon that seemingly unending war to which we have given the curious epithet "cold" that we tend to encourage rigid ideological unity and orthodox patterns of thought.

And thus, in the days ahead, only the very courageous will be able to take the hard and unpopular decisions necessary for our survival. . . .[8]

—Jack Kerouac's book *On the Road,* published in 1955, is an account of the travels and wanderings of several young people across the United States and Mexico by car and bus. They are unemployed or hold temporary, meaningless jobs, and they seem to be interested only in alcohol, jazz, sex, cars, and drugs.

—One of the most widely read and discussed books of 1956 was William H. Whyte's *The Organization Man.* Whyte examined the life-style of a group that, on the surface, appeared to have been one of the most fortunate, successful, and happy ones in postwar America—young businessmen and executives. He says of them:

> For them society has in fact been good—very, very good—for there has been a succession of fairly beneficent environments: college, the paternalistic, if not always pleasant, military life, then, perhaps, graduate work through the G. I. Bill of Rights, a corporation apprenticeship during a period of industrial expansion and high prosperity, and, for some, the camaraderie of communities like Park Forest. The system, they instinctively conclude, is essentially benevolent.[9]

He describes their education, professional training, jobs, family lives, homes, church activities, and relationships with other people. He concludes that in most ways they are very fortunate, that there are many good features to their lives; but he also believes that there is a latent danger in the way things are going for them. Everything about their lives is organized: most of their activities are prescribed by the way of life they have chosen, and there is little opportunity for them to make conscious choices about the way their lives will unfold. He admires the efficient organization of so many phases of life in America, but sees the dangers in this:

> People do have to work with others, yes; the well-functioning team is a whole greater than the sum of its parts, yes—all this is indeed true. But is it the truth that now needs belaboring? Precisely because it *is* an age of organization, it is the other side of the coin that needs emphasis. We do need to know how to co-operate with The Organization but, more than ever, so do we need to know how to resist it. . . .
> The energies Americans have devoted to the co-operative, to the social, are not to be demeaned; we would not, after all, have such a problem to discuss unless we had learned to adapt ourselves to an increasingly collective society as well as we have. . . .
> But in searching for that elusive middle of the road, we have gone very far afield, and in our attention to making organization work we have come close to deifying it.

8 John F. Kennedy, *Profiles in Courage* (New York: Harper & Row, 1956), p. 16. Reprinted by permission.
9 William H. Whyte, Jr., *The Organization Man,* pp. 13, 14, 438. Copyright © 1956 by William H. Whyte, Jr. Reprinted by permission of Simon & Schuster, Inc.

No generation has been so well equipped, psychologically as well as technically, to cope with the intricacies of vast organizations; none has been so well equipped to lead a meaningful community life; and none probably will be so adaptable to the constant shifts in environment that organization life is so increasingly demanding of them.... They are all, as they say, in the same boat.

But where is the boat going? No one seems to have the faintest idea; nor, for that matter, do they see much point in even raising the question. Once people liked to think, at least, that they were in control of their destinies, but few of the younger organization people cherish such notions.

—A new style of popular music, rock and roll, skyrocketed in popularity in 1955. From the beginning it was accepted by young people as "their" music; from the beginning it was opposed and often fought by parents, educators, churchmen, politicians, and other members of the older generations. Derived from the music of several subcultures (black, poor, and rural white), it incorporated from the start an aura of rebellion, of rejection of the patterns and life-styles of white Middle America. Jerry Rubin wrote in *Do It!*:

Elvis Presley ripped off Ike Eisenhower by turning our uptight young awakening bodies around. Hard animal rock energy beat/surged hot through us, the driving rhythm arousing repressed passions.

Music to free the spirit.
Music to bring us *together*.[10]

—The Supreme Court ruled in 1956 that states had no authority to punish persons advocating overthrow of the federal government. Later that year, another ruling declared that the President had violated the law by dismissing as a security risk a federal employee who held a "non-sensitive" post.

—President Eisenhower approved programs for increased exchange of information and persons between the United States and the communist countries of Eastern Europe in the summer of 1956.

—Blacks in Montgomery, Alabama, carried out a boycott against the city's public transportation system in 1956, in protest of segregated seating; on November 13 the Supreme Court ruled that segregation on buses and streetcars was unconstitutional.

—John Hersey's short novel *A Single Pebble* (1956) told the tale of a young American engineer sent to China by a contracting firm to investigate the feasibility of proposing to the Chinese government a vast power project on the Yangtze River. He becomes convinced that dynamiting stretches of rapids and erecting a dam in one of the famous gorges would improve navigation on the river, making it faster and safer. But the Chinese cannot understand this. The river is what it is—its advantages, beauties, even its dangers,

[10] Jerry Rubin, *Do It* (New York: Simon and Schuster, 1970), p. 18. Reprinted by permission.

are fixed points to which humans must adapt. The river should not change; only people should change. The engineer makes his report, passionately urging that the project be undertaken. But nothing comes of it.

—Paul Goodman's *Growing Up Absurd* (1956) is a series of essays relating the "disaffection of the growing generation" to "the disgrace of the Organized System of semimonopolies, government, advertisers, etc." He believes the "organized system" to be characterized by "its role playing, its competitiveness, its canned culture, its public relations, and its avoidance of risk and self-exposure." It is

...very powerful and in its full tide of success, apparently sweeping everything before it in science, education, community planning, labor, the arts, not to speak of business and politics where it is indigenous.[11]

In a series of discussions of patriotism, class structure, community, social life, faith, marriage, and other topics he details patterns and attitudes, prevalent in American culture, that have made some members of his generation "sickened and enraged to see earnest and honest effort and humane culture swamped by this muck." He says that young people in the country are faced with "the lack of bona fides about our liberties, the dishonorable politics in the universities, the irresponsible press, the disillusioning handling of the adventure in space, the inferior and place-seeking high officers of the State, the shameful neglect of our landscape and the disregard of community." He concludes that young people are "growing up absurd" because they "*really* need a more worthwhile world in order to grow up at all." He is encouraged that many of them are resisting the situation they have inherited by turning to eccentric life styles, becoming involved in such intellectual interests as Zen Buddhism, and engaging in radical experimentation in the arts. These "crazy young allies" give him hope that "perhaps the future may make more sense than we dared hope."

—Allen Ginsberg wrote the poem "Howl" in San Francisco in the winter of 1955–56. According to the poet, it was "typed out madly in one afternoon, a tragic custard-pie comedy of wild phrasing, meaningless images for the beauty of abstract poetry." It was a wild, rambling, undisciplined outburst from a young poet who had been dismissed from college for eccentric behavior and who believed that "recent history is the record of a vast conspiracy to impose one level of mechanical consciousness on mankind." The poem begins:

> I saw the best minds of my generation destroyed by
>   madness, starving hysterical naked,
> dragging themselves through the negro streets at dawn
>   looking for an angry fix,

11 Paul Goodman, *Growing Up Absurd* (New York: Random House, 1956), p. 241. Reprinted by permission.

angelheaded hipsters burning for the ancient heavenly
   connection to the starry dynamo in the machinery
   of night,
who poverty and tatters and hollow-eyed and high sat
   up smoking in the supernatural darkness of cold-
   water flats floating across the tops of cities
   contemplating jazz,
who bared their brains to Heaven under the El and saw
   Mohammedan angels staggering on tenement roofs
   illuminated,
who passed through universities with radiant cool
   eyes hallucinating Arkansas and Blake-light
   tragedy among the scholars of war,
who were expelled from the academies for crazy & publishing obscene odes on the windows of the skull,
who cowered in unshaven rooms in underwear, burning
   their money in wastebaskets and listening to the
   Terror through the wall. . . .[12]

First published in 1956, a second printing was restrained in 1957 by a government official who said that "the words and the sense of the writing is obscene.
You wouldn't want your children to come across it." However, a court ruling
later that year found the poem not obscene.

—Vance Packard's *The Hidden Persuaders* (1957), a widely popular
book, claimed that industry's use of advertising, utilizing sophisticated and
unrecognized psychological tricks, often influenced people to purchase items
that they did not need or even want.

—Six Friends (members of the Quaker Church) traveled to Russia on a
friendship mission in 1957. The following year five Americans entered China,
the first to do so since the government banned travel to that country in 1950,
and the American pianist Van Cliburn won first prize in the international
Tschaikowsky piano competition in Moscow, becoming an immediate hero in
both Russia and the United States.

—The Supreme Court reversed the conviction of an American labor
leader, Watkins, an admitted Communist sympathizer who had refused to
answer questions before the House Un-American Activities Committee. It
was held that some of the questions put to him concerned matters not under
the jurisdiction of the committee, and that he had not been properly informed
of either the charges against him or his constitutional rights.

—The governor of Arkansas and the people of Little Rock resisted a court
order for racial integration of Central High School in the fall of 1957. Black

---

[12] Allen Ginsberg, *Howl and other poems* (San Francisco, City Lights Pocket Book-
shop, 1956), p. 9. Copyright © 1956, 1959 by Allen Ginsberg. Reprinted by permission
of City Lights Books.

students assigned to the school were prevented from attending by public demonstrations and the intervention of armed National Guardsmen. President Eisenhower ordered U. S. Army paratroopers there on September 24, and nine blacks entered the school the next day.

—The film *The Bridge on the River Kwai* won Academy Awards for best production, best direction, and best actor (Alec Guinness) in 1957, and was given the New York Film Critics' award as the best picture of that year. The central character, played by Guinness, is a British army officer captured, with many of his men, by the Japanese in Asia during World War II. At first, he refuses to cooperate with his captors in any way, but his pride eventually leads him to supervise the construction of a bridge over a gorge; in the process Guinness drives his own men more mercilessly than the Japanese had. The bridge is an important link in a supply route for the Japanese, and the British send an expedition through the jungle to dynamite it. At the climax of the film, Guinness prepares to demonstrate to his captors how well he has done his job by marching his men across, and having a Japanese train follow. The bridge is blown up just at this moment; Guinness tries to prevent it, even though the saboteurs are British (it has become *his* bridge); the bridge collapses, killing British and Japanese alike, Guinness is shot, and the commander of the British expedition mutters "Madness! Madness!" War is madness, and Guinness's blind passion to complete the job is madness. The only sanity seems to be with the natives who have guided and accompanied the expedition, who have the time and temperament to enjoy the beauties of their country and their relationships with other people.

—Scientist Ralph E. Lapp published a book in 1958 giving an account of a Japanese fishing vessel caught in nuclear fallout when it sailed into a testing area. The book, *The Voyage of the Lucky Dragon,* pointed out the dangers of nuclear testing and attacked the Atomic Energy Commission's policy of secrecy concerning its operations.

—In March, 1958 four people, including three Friends, sailed from San Francisco in the ship *The Golden Rule,* heading for a nuclear weapons testing site in the Pacific. Their plan was to be in the area at the time the United States planned a test blast. They were seized and detained upon reaching Hawaii and were given sixty-day jail sentences in Honolulu.

—The artist Rockwell Kent was denied permission by the government to travel to Helsinki to attend a World Council of Peace; the government had for some time been concerned with some of his associations with "subversive" activities and persons. The Supreme Court ruled in 1958 that the State Department did not have the authority to withhold a passport from a citizen because of his "beliefs and associations."

—Scientist Linus Pauling, in public statements and in his book *No More War!* (1958), called attention to the dangers to health, life, and heredity from radioactive fallout from continued nuclear bomb testing. He claimed that there would be five million defective births and several million cases of cancer in coming generations if nuclear testing continued.

—John Kenneth Galbraith's *The Affluent Society* (1958) argued that American industry was driving itself to maximum production, even overproduction, often without concern for the market or for the genuine needs of American society. The pattern was for industry to decide what to produce, to create a market for these products by advertising, and to persuade people that they needed or wanted these things and were fortunate and affluent once they acquired them. However, millions of American families had difficulty finding enough money for such basic needs as medical and dental care, and the general affluence did not extend to such things as education.

—The Supreme Court ruled in 1958 that the State of New York could not prevent the showing of a motion picture (*Lady Chatterley's Lover*) because it advocates an idea (adultery) contrary to the moral standards or religious codes of the citizens of the state.

—Nightclub comedian Lenny Bruce began attracting widespread attention for his act, which consisted of monologues (liberally sprinkled with "obscenities") on such subjects as sexual freedom, racial and religious prejudices, the drug scene, homosexuality, and the judicial and law enforcement systems of the country. "People should be taught what is, not what should be," he said. "All my humor is based on destruction and despair. If the whole world were tranquil, without disease and violence, I'd be standing in the breadline—right back of J. Edgar Hoover." By 1959 he was commanding fees of $1750 a week. He was arrested for possession of narcotics in Philadelphia and Los Angeles, arrested for obscenity in San Francisco, Hollywood, and Chicago, barred from entering Australia and England, and declared legally bankrupt in 1965; he died in 1966.

—Rachel Carson, author of several poetical books describing the beauties and marvels of the natural world around us (*Under the Sea-Wind, The Sea Around Us, The Edge of the Sea*), became convinced early in 1958 that man, with the aid of science, was destroying his natural environment. Her research lead to the book *Silent Spring* (1962), in which she argued that:

> The most alarming of all man's assaults upon the environment is the contamination of air, earth, rivers, and sea with dangerous and even lethal materials. . . . Chemicals are the sinister and little-recognized partners of radiation in changing the very nature of the world—the very nature of its life. . . . Chemicals sprayed on croplands or forests or gardens lie long in the soil, entering into living organisms, passing from one to another in a chain of poisoning and death. Or they pass mysteriously by underground streams until they emerge and, through the alchemy of air and sunlight, combine into new forms that kill vegetation, sicken cattle, and work unknown harm on those who drink from once pure wells.
>
> Since the mid-1940's over 200 basic chemicals have been created for use in killing insects, weeds, rodents, and other organisms described in the modern vernacular as "pests": and they are sold under several thousand different brand names.
>
> These sprays, dusts, and aerosols are now applied almost universally to farms, gardens, forests, and homes—nonselective chemicals that have the

power to kill every insect, the "good" and the "bad," to still the song of birds and the leaping of fish in the streams, to coat the leaves with a deadly film, and to linger on in soil. . . . The central problem of our age has therefore become the contamination of man's total environment with such substances of incredible potential for harm—substances that accumulate in the tissues of plants and animals and even penetrate the germ cells to shatter or alter the very material of heredity upon which the shape of the future depends.[13]

—Criticism of the American foreign policy, of "brinkmanship," that is, keeping international tensions high by continuing to stress the opposition of the "free world" to the Communist world, reached a crescendo in 1957–59 with the publication of such widely read books as *The Causes of World War Three* (Charles Wright Mills), *The Communist World and Ours* (Walter Lippman), *What's Wrong With U. S. Foreign Policy* (C. L. Sulzberger), and *The Tragedy of American Diplomacy* (William A. Williams).

—As a continuing way of life, national mobilization—military, economic, and political—against "international Communism" was questioned, challenged, and then resisted.

—Support weakened for the idea that American political influence should affect events in nations all around the world.

Though these and other events were at first seemingly isolated from one another and from anything else, they were straws in a wind that grew from random breezes in the early 1950s to a gale by the 1960s, threatening to sweep before it many of the things that had been basic to American life for decades.

National pride in American military and industrial accomplishments, so strong and universal during and after World War II, was gradually replaced by questions, doubts, and eventually hostility and opposition. Many Americans began to question the image of America as a good and righteous country unified against evil. Enforced unity at the sacrifice of certain traditional American freedoms began to appear too high a price to pay, now that there was widespread questioning of the goals that this unity was intended to achieve.

The image of science was tarnished as it continued to develop more powerful and terrible weapons for warfare, to furnish procedures and means for industry to pollute and poison air, earth, and water, and to drink up billions of dollars from the national budget for such things as the space program, an exciting adventure but of little immediate benefit to the millions of people in the country who still needed decent shelter, food, clothing, medical care, and education.

Though the number of Americans in colleges and universities continued to increase, the methods, philosophies, and goals of the educational system were

13 Rachel Carson, *Silent Spring,* pp. 6–8. Copyright © 1962 by Rachel L. Carson. Reprinted by permission of Houghton Mifflin Company.

questioned. American education was not training people to think and reason, claimed many critics, but, rather, was training them to fit blindly into the economy and society of the country.

Governmental policies were openly opposed and resisted. Southern politicians fought integration; speeches led to public demonstrations, and the government eventually found it necessary to use military force against its own citizens. Blacks who felt that the equal rights movement was moving too slowly boycotted, marched, and demonstrated, and were confronted by the armed forces of local and state police and the National Guard. Black urban communities in Detroit, Washington, Watts, and other places—where miserable living conditions seemed unlikely to change, and where the affluence of many Americans was in no way evident—erupted into riots, and again there was the spectacle of American troops confronting and fighting fellow citizens. Protests against U. S. involvement in Southeast Asia grew from small gatherings of college faculty, a few scientists, and some religious groups to mass public marches and rallies; the day came when half a million Americans gathered in the capital of their country to give public testimony of their strong disagreement with policies of their government. Students argued and then acted against certain policies and practices of their universities, in some cases physically taking over buildings and facilities and demanding immediate changes. Here too, the spectacle of law enforcement officers and troops confronting and battling their fellow citizens became common.

The '60s became the age of the underground. Underground films, using techniques and subjects that Hollywood would never have touched, were at first a curiosity and then a strong, vital artistic current. Underground political activity, scorning the two-party system in which the differences between the two parties seemed to grow less and less, ranged from extreme right to extreme left and anarchy. Underground publications used language previously unheard in American journalism as a cutting edge in fiction and non-fiction that dealt in stark, direct ways with sex, radical politics, drugs, and other topics outside the mainstream of American life. This kind of journalism scandalized most people at first but eventually had an effect on American letters. Underground religious movements and underground education ("free universities") likewise explored ideas and methods that in time were more generally accepted.

The '60s was the Age of Aquarius or the age of permissiveness, according to your point of view. It was a time of the Free Speech Movement, of draft card burning, of nudity on stage and screen, of Women's Lib and Gay Lib, of Black Power, of long hair, of the miniskirt and the see-through blouse, of the virtual disappearance of censorship of movies, stage productions, books, and magazines, of topless and bottomless dancers and waitresses, of SDS and Young Americans for Freedom, of Hippies and Yippies, of marijuana and LSD, of wiretapping, mass arrests, Mace, and assassination. The breakdown of faith in American institutions and the suspicion that the state, church, schools, and family were failing to guide people to meaningful lives persuaded more and more persons—not all of them young—to, in the classic phrase of the 1960s, "do their own thing." In a curious parallel to certain earlier periods of religious upheaval, when salvation was sought inside each individual rather than in the canons and traditions of the organized church, Americans tried to find meaning in their lives by turning inwards. In every aspect of behavior—dress, speech, political and religious belief, artistic expression, personal relationships—people tried to discover and follow their own individual desires, tastes, and needs. And if what they found conflicted with traditional American behavior, customs, morals, and even laws, so much the better, because these were the things that seemed to have failed.

Musical activity, like most things at this time, continued much as it had before—on the surface. Symphony orchestras played the same kinds of programs for the same audiences, opera companies staged the same operas, the training of musicians was still done mostly in colleges and universities. Walter Piston and Milton Babbitt wrote more compositions using the techniques discussed above, and many other composers continued to write symphonies, string quartets, operas, and other compositions in the tradition of Western art music. For a composer success was still measured by performances of works by major organizations, publication of these pieces, and the winning of prizes and awards; such success was still rewarded by academic appointments or promotions, or by salary raises. The Musical Establishment remained unchanged.

Other currents were running below the surface, however. Beginning in the late 1950s, traces of new sorts of musical activity occasionally rose to the surface, activity that had no immediate effect on the course of music in America, but which grew steadily more intense and attractive to increasing numbers of younger musicians. This activity seemed purely experimental at first: new ways of shaping a musical composition; new ways of producing sounds; new ideas about structure; different ideas about what was expected of an audience and what role music should play in contemporary society. Eventually, the entire traditional concept of what a piece of music was and what the relationships among composer, performer, and audience should and could be was challenged.

This new activity first took visible form in the way music was notated, or written down. Western music had used a standardized and effective type of notation for many centuries, a system that had remained unchanged except for certain details since the early seventeenth century. But suddenly, in the late '50s and early '60s, performing musicians found themselves asked to play music notated in ways that broke radically with the system they had learned, the system that had been used for all the other music they played. At first, each composer devised his own system, and most scores contained introductory explanations of how the performer should read it. Changes in notation had taken place before in Western music, always signaling some dramatic change in musical style; composers had found that systems devised for one type of music would no longer serve for what they wanted to do. That was the situation in the mid-twentieth century: some composers reached the point of imagining and creating music so different from that of the mainstream of classical music that they could no longer indicate to performers what they should play by using the notational system of that previous time.

Though many musicians were involved in this new activity, the composer John Cage was at the center of it. Born in Los Angeles in 1912, he spent two years at Pomona College, then dropped out of school and spent a year in Paris and other European cities writing poetry, painting, studying architecture and piano, and eventually composing music. Cage returned to California, where he studied piano and composition with Arnold Schoenberg, among others. Later, he spent several months in New York studying contemporary and oriental music at the New School for Social Research.

In 1937 he involved himself with several modern dance groups, at UCLA and then at the Cornish School in Seattle, For many years his main activity— on the West Coast, in Chicago, and in New York City (where he moved in 1942)—was to accompany, compose for, and serve as musical director of dance groups.

Cage's earliest compositions were chromatic, atonal works for traditional instruments, but by the late 1930s he was writing mostly for percussion instruments. Many pieces' were written for "prepared piano"; by inserting various objects among the strings of a grand piano he transformed the usual sonorities of this instrument into a rich variety of percussive sounds. Because much of his music was written for instruments that produced sounds without specific pitch, he experimented with various ways of organizing a composition according to patterns of note durations rather than pitches. Some of his structural techniques resembled those of non-Western music.

Cage's activities were scarcely known to most other musicians; he was writing music that differed in techniques, types of instruments used, and even in intent from the music that most people were involved in. Most of his associates were people from the other arts—the dancer Merce Cunningham, the artists Robert Motherwell, Robert Rauschenberg, Allan Kaprow, and Jaspar Johns, the poet Kenneth Patchen—people who knew his work. Most professional musicians and professors of music had not heard of him, or were unfamiliar with his work. He held no academic positions, won no important prizes, and his music remained unpublished.

In the late '40s Cage began a serious study of Eastern philosophies, Zen Buddhism in particular. He began to use different sources of sound in his music: *Imaginary Landscape No. 1* (1937) used two variable speed phonograph turntables; *Williams Mix* (1952) used various natural and artificial sounds on tape. The composition *4'33"* (1952) required a performer (usually a pianist) to come on stage and sit before his instrument for 4 minutes and 33 seconds without producing a sound. The composition consisted of whatever sounds occurred, within or without the auditorium, during this period of time.

His compositions of the '50s were planned to incorporate variable or chance arrangements of sounds. Each performer in the *Concert for Piano and Orchestra* (1957–58) has for a part a collection of phrases and larger units of music; each decides what he or she will play, and in what sequence. Thus, during the performance no part has a planned relationship to any other part. In other works Cage used the ancient Chinese I Ching tables to generate a random assortment of notes, or he drew a staff on paper and wrote notes on it where he found imperfections in the paper, or he gave the performer a score consisting of several transparent overlays that could be moved around to produce changeable random collections of notes. Cage believed that a person should not force preconceived notions of form and structure onto the notes of a musical composition but should, rather, be able to create his own structure from any combination of sounds. He says in his book *Silence* (1961):

> Our intention is to affirm this life, not to bring order out of a chaos or to suggest improvements in creation, but simply to wake up to the very life we are living, which is so excellent once one gets one's mind and one's desires out of its way and lets it act of its own accord.[14]

This way of thinking leads to the breaking down of all barriers between life and art. Cage has said that if he were successful in getting people to hear any combination of sounds as music—because of structures and coherences imposed on them by the listeners themselves—then people would find it unnecessary to attend a concert in order to hear music; they could hear it in whatever sounds were around them at any time. Each man would be his own creator and his own critic. Standards of taste would not be imposed on an individual by others, would not be established in music schools and universities, would not be systematized and canonized. A musical experience would be a completely private, personal thing, as various as the people in the world.

The late '50s and the '60s saw Cage's position in the musical world change dramatically. At the beginning of this period he was an obscure figure working in a strange musical idiom, writing pieces that were rarely published and almost never played outside of his own circle of dancers and artists; by the end, he was considered by European critics and musicians to be the first truly original figure in American music since Charles Ives. His own countrymen held divided opinions about him. But no one could ignore his music and his ideas about music, no one could deny that what he had done and was

14 John Cage, *Silence* (Middletown, Conn.: Wesleyan University Press, 1961).

doing was having a profound effect on the course of music in America and the world. In 1954 a concert tour, with the pianist David Tudor, through Germany, France, Belgium, Sweden, Sweitzerland, Italy, and England brought Cage's ideas to Europe, and led to lectures at Darmstadt and the Brussels World Fair and a four-month stay at the electronic music studio in Milan. A retrospective concert of Cage's music in New York's Town Hall in May, 1958, gave many persons a first chance to hear samples of works written over a twenty-five-year period, and to more properly evaluate him as a composer; the commercial sale of the recording of this concert made Cage's music even more widely available. He was asked to teach courses in new music and mushroom identification at the New School for Social Research in 1959. Other academic appointments followed: he was appointed a Fellow at the Center for Advanced Studies at Wesleyan University (Middletown, Connecticut) in 1960–61; Composer in Residence at the University of Cincinnati in 1967; an Associate at the Center for Advanced Study at the University of Illinois in Urbana from 1967 to 1969; an Artist in Residence at the University of California at Davis in 1969. There was a concert tour of Japan in 1962, a world tour with the Cunningham Dance Company in 1964, and a heavy schedule of lectures and concerts at colleges and universities throughout the country. He was elected a member of the National Institute of Arts and Letters in 1968. All of this recognition reflected the fact that in the 1960s John Cage was making music that large numbers of people wanted to hear, and that he was saying things about music, art, and life that were interesting, relevant, and provocative.

HPSCHD, composed in collaboration with Lejaren Hiller, is a major piece from this period, when Cage achieved his greatest success and influence. It was commissioned by Antoinette Vischer of Switzerland as a piece for harpsichord, and was performed on the evening of May 16, 1969, in Assembly Hall at the University of Illinois in Urbana.

Assembly Hall is a circular concrete building on the University of Illinois campus that seats some 14,000 persons. It was planned and constructed primarily as a sports arena. The annual state high school basketball tournament is a major event in this basketball-crazy state, and it is said that the state legislature was willing to appropriate money for such an expensive building because the prospect of a spectacular, spacious new site for this tournament was popular among most people in the state, even those who usually objected to expenditures for education. Once constructed, the hall was also used for various musical events—symphony concerts, musicals, operas—despite the fact that it is acoustically unsuited for them. The enclosed area is enormous, the distance from floor to ceiling is staggering and musical sounds, even those produced by a large orchestra, became lost in all of the space, even if they are amplified. Cage was intrigued with the challenge of filling such a huge and unsympathetic space with sound.

The piece turned out to be a vast and incredibly detailed complex of sounds and sights. Seven harpsichordists, playing amplified instruments, sat on raised platforms on the floor of the hall. Three played computer-realized versions of Mozart's "Introduction to the Composition of Waltzes by Means of Dice"; two others played collages of various piano works from the time of Mozart to the present (fragments of Beethoven's *Appassionata* Sonata, Chopin's Prelude in D Minor, Schumann's *Carnaval*, Gottschalk's *The Banjo*, Ives' *Three-Page Sonata*, Schoenberg's Opus 11, No. 1, Cage's *Winter Music*, and an early piano sonata by Hiller) ; another played a part called "Computer Print-out for Twelve-tone Gamut"; and the seventh played any pieces by Mozart he chose. Each harpsichordist was free to play his part any time he wanted to, any number of times, and he was also free to play any other player's part at any time. Fifty-one amplifiers, positioned around the circumference of the hall near its top, were used to play fifty-one different tapes of electronic music that were planned and realized on a computer. Each tape was slightly over twenty minutes long and could be played at any time, any number of times, in the course of the performance—which on this occasion lasted from 8 P.M. until midnight.

For the eye there were slides, movies, and lights. Several screens, including a mammoth continuous 340-foot one, displayed slides of abstract designs done by members of the University of Illinois art school, 5,000 slides loaned by NASA, pages of musical scores by Mozart, computer instructions, and films (most of them concerned with astronomy and space travel). Colored beams of light and spinning mirrorlike balls bathed the hall in continually changing colors.

Nothing was coordinated. Each musician and each operator of a tape recorder, slide projector, or movie camera did what he chose for whatever length of time and in whatever sequence he chose. The eye and ear could pick out any combination of sights and sounds among all there was to choose from. The audience came and went, walked around, chatted with friends and with the performers, sampled the work from the perspectives of various locations. And several thousand people in the audience became part of the piece: they walked, talked, danced, sang, smoked, sat, or stretched out on the floor; some came in bizarre costumes, some painted their faces with Dayglo colors, some wore white shirts imprinted with the likenesses of Beethoven and Cage. Each person made what he wanted of the piece and, thus, it was a different event for everyone who attended; each saw and heard it from the standpoint of when he was there, where he was in the hall, how long he stayed, whom he saw and talked with while there, what mood he was in, and what attitudes he had about such events.

HPSCHD does not have to be performed in this way, or on this scale. It can be performed by from one to seven harpsichords, with any number of tapes (from one to fifty-one), in any kind of hall, for any duration of more than twenty minutes. A recorded version (Nonesuch H-71224) consists of three harpsichordists and a specially condensed version of the tapes.

The jazz world was rocked by similar unorthodoxies. Saxophonist (and occasional violinist) Ornette Coleman arrived in New York in 1959 to play at the Five Spot, after having made two albums for a small company (Contemporary) in Los Angeles. Born in Fort Worth in 1930, he was an almost completely self-taught musician. For a decade he knocked around the jazz world of the South and the West—Fort Worth, New Orleans, Baton Rouge, Natchez, Los Angeles—playing in a style all his own, a style so eccentric and so different from traditional ways of playing jazz that other musicians often refused to play with him, a style that bewildered audiences. It was not until he was in his late twenties, an advanced age for a jazz player, that Coleman found several other players sympathetic to his style who learned to play with him, and it was only then that he achieved some recognition through his two records.

Coleman was still a tremendously controversial figure when he came to New York. The Five Spot was packed for month after month; the crowd including other jazzmen who came to hear—and often to criticize and ridicule. His music was described as anarchistic and nihilistic. Critics spoke of his technical inadequacies and the "incoherence" of his saxophone playing. The famous jazz writer Leonard Feather said that "his rejection of many of the basic rules, not merely of jazz but of all music, did not entail the foundation of specific new rules." Another jazz critic wrote that "there is at least one writer on jazz who not only doesn't understand what Coleman is doing but suggests that it is not worth trying to understand. Not, that is, if you are interested in music." Many jazzmen had similar reactions. "If that's music, I've been doing something else all my life," was the comment of one. Another said, "I listened to him all kinds of ways. I listened to him high and I listened to him cold sober. I even played with him. I think he's jiving, baby. He's putting everybody on. They disregard the chords and they play odd numbers of bars. I can't follow them."

Coleman's playing seemed completely detached from the traditional harmonic foundations of jazz. His melodic lines developed with no apparent reference to the harmonic and metrical patterns that had served jazz for so many decades. He wanted the other players in his groups to do the same; the result was three or four or five independent lines unfolding simultaneously, each unrelated to any other by common beat or harmonic progression.

The album *Free Jazz* (Atlantic SD 1364) is one of the monuments of his art. Coleman collected eight jazz musicians in a New York recording studio in 1964, and grouped them in two quartets: himself, Donald Cherry (trumpet), Scott La Faro (bass), and Billy Higgins (drums) in one; Eric Dolphy (bass clarinet), Freddie Hubbard (trumpet), Charlie Haden (bass), and Ed Blackwell (drums) in the other. With no rehearsal, the eight men performed a free improvisation based on no previously-known tunes, no planned chord progressions, no planned structure. Some times one player or another improvised alone, at other times several of them improvised together. "We were expressing our minds and emotions as much as could be," said Coleman.

"The most important thing was for us to play together, all at the same time, without getting in each other's way." The session lasted fifty-six minutes and twenty-three seconds, enough to fill the two sides of an LP record. In listening, one can notice that although the players listen to one another—an idea played by one may be picked up by others, who play it in their own style— each player, even the drummers and bass players, goes his own way rhythmically, harmonically, and structurally. To ears conditioned to traditional jazz, or traditional music of any kind, this music is chaos. To ears that can listen in other ways, it is a fascinating and exciting collage, rich in detail, that changes with each hearing, depending on which instrument or instruments one listens to most closely.

In summary, America went through a period during and just after World War II in which the emergency of the war, followed by pride in the country's achievements and hopes for a better future unified the country as it had rarely been before. Pride in the victories of the armed forces and American industry, faith in American leadership, a conviction that the country was morally right, the belief that science and education would lead to an even more prosperous, healthy, and happy future—these things created a climate in which Americans saw their role as one of following and trusting their leaders and trying to be good citizens by fitting as smoothly and productively as possible into the economic and social patterns of American life. The mood in the country was one of obedience, trust, conformity, cooperation, discipline, of working with others for the common good—with as little friction and disagreement as possible. Politics was left to politicians, science to scientists, war to soldiers, art to artists.

But the picture began to change. Questions began to grow in the minds of some people. Were political leaders always leading the country in safe, sane, moral directions? Was American industry really concerned about the well-being of American citizens—or were its motives purely selfish? Were the directions science was taking always desirable? Was the military really protecting citizens from some imminent threat to life and property, or was it engaged in its own games—expensive, deadly games? Were educational and religious institutions really training people to lead happy, satisfying lives? Or were they preparing them to fit quietly and unquestioningly into planned patterns in American society? Faith, obedience, and conformity gradually changed to questioning, argumentation, resistance, disobedience, and even conflict.

It is simple enough to relate the musical life of America to these changing patterns. Musical activity that is centered in traditional institutions—music schools, colleges and universities, professional performing groups—and in which new generations of musicians are trained according to methods that will insure the perpetuation of a stable and traditional musical life, is obviously well-suited to a culture dominated by conformity and motivated by a belief that things become even better because of more and better education.

On the other hand, musical activity based on the beliefs that every person must discover for himself what music is, that every individual must find what type of music he best responds to and most wants to create (if he is a composer), that any sounds or combinations of sounds may be music, is just as obviously appropriate in a society in which the basic precepts of government, religion, education, and social behavior are being questioned. Walter Piston, as a composer and teacher, epitomized in music the dominant trends and patterns in America from 1940 to 1955. John Cage, as a composer and philosopher, epitomized some dynamic currents in American society from about 1955 to 1970.

As the times changed, music changed.

But it is not quite that simple. Any culture, at any time in any place, reflects a collection of individuals, each with his own personality, ideas, beliefs, and attitudes. Certain events or the force of a powerful political personality may lead numbers of people—even a majority of them—to agree on enough basic issues to give a particular culture a distinct flavor. When this stage is reached, anything else that seems to fit into the general scheme of things will appear to be part of the culture, regardless of whether there is a cause-and-effect relationship. And even when certain attitudes are predominant, there are always persons who do not share them, who are at odds with the way things are going.

John Cage was writing music from 1940 to 1955—music that was nothing like that of Walter Piston; Piston continued to compose from 1955 to 1970, writing music that had nothing in common with that being written by Cage. There was underground, radical activity in politics and the arts from 1940 to 1955; after 1955, many individuals and organizations were determinedly committed to maintaining the *status quo* in America, to preserving traditional American institutions, morals, and customs. Cage's music and philosophy were representative of one thread in American society and culture during and immediately after World War II, but this thread was not a dominant or even a very important one. Piston's music and his views on art were part of a continuing school of thought that was challenged and at least temporarily overshadowed in the 1960s.

Any period in history can be seen in this way. Historians can identify dominant currents in the culture, musicologists can pick out the most important composers and pieces of music; and, as a result, relationships can be drawn between what was happening in the world and in music. But it must be understood that such a process deals in generalities, that "dominant currents" flow together with less strong and less visible ones, that the "most important composers" coexist with other persons who are also writing music. A rich variety of ideas and attitudes can be found at the same time in the same culture, and events can quickly change the prevailing situation so that something obscure or seemingly unimportant can become significant or dominant.

3

The Role of Music in Culture: Iran, A Recently Developed Nation

BRUNO NETTL

Presumably, we would not have music if it did not do something very important for us. We would not go to all the trouble of composing songs, symphonies, and operas, of learning fiendishly difficult instruments such as the organ and the sitar, of spending a lot of our resources and energies on maintaining concert halls, symphony orchestras, and departments of music in universities, if we did not feel that music is very important in our lives. Music does something for us that is not done by any other activity or any other facet of life. We have great difficulty defining just what this "something" is, but we feel that it is there.

The importance of music in human life can be illustrated in many ways. For example, we know of no culture, no single civilization of the past, no isolated tribal group in a wilderness or jungle, that does not have and has not had, as far back as our knowledge goes, a body of music. Music is one of the few things common to all cultures. Furthermore, throughout the world music has something to do with religion; in most cultures music frequently accompanies or is the vehicle for worship. And everywhere, music appears to be a kind of expression of the most basic values and feelings of people. Thus, whatever it is that music does for people, it somehow involves man's quest for an understanding of the world and of himself. On a larger scale, music (along with the other arts) is a vehicle for the expression of what is happening in the culture of the performer, composer, or listener, an expression of things in that culture that cannot readily be verbalized. At least this seems to be the way it was "in the beginning," and while music obviously does many things, these basic functions are perhaps primary.

The Culture of Iran

Let us try to see how music reflects what is going on in the culture of a typical country of the world, Iran. Why should this rather obscure Asian nation be regarded as a typical modern country? If we examine the roster of the United Nations, we realize that most of the member nations are not highly industrialized and are not part of. the so-called "Communist bloc"; but neither are they simple, isolated cultures resisting or avoiding the change that is being forced upon them by modern economics and technology. Most nations are those whose cultures have been, until recently, relatively little influenced by Western civilization and its most characteristic ingredients, industrialization and technology; nevertheless, these same nations have begun to become industrialized and technologically "developed." Their main task, as they see it, is to absorb those elements of Western civilization that will help them to solve the material problems of life, while retaining those elements of their life style or culture that they regard as integral to their existence as a people. The fact that there is conflict and contradiction between these two goals is a further characteristic of most countries today. The kinds of conflict that occur differ from nation to nation, depending on the particular character of the culture and the kind of contact the country has made with the West.

As a result of the fact that many non-Western countries share the traits discussed above, we can see many of the same kinds of things happening in the cultures of most of these nations—and, for that matter, in the cultures of minority groups in the West. But we also see each culture moving in its own unique way, and at its own speed. An examination of the music of each tends to show that music reflects in a very tangible way what is happening in the life of its people.

Iran is a country in which the above observations are easily illustrated. It is a fascinating conglomeration of old and new, of traditionalism and modernization, of homogeneity and variety. Its economic development has been enormous in the last two decades: its government officially pronounced the country "developed" in 1968; and this development and modernization continues. Therefore, Iran is an appropriate focal point of our examination of music in a contemporary developing culture.

More than twice the size of Texas, Iran has a population of over thirty-two million persons, most of whom speak Persian, a language related most closely to the languages of Northern India and Pakistan, and more distantly to those of Western Europe. There are also many non-Persian-speaking minority groups: Turks in the Western part of the country; other Turkic-speaking tribes, such as the Bakhtiari and the Qashkai, in the center of the country; Kurds in the Northeast and the Northwest; Turkomans near the eastern shore of the Caspian Sea; Armenians and Jews in the cities; and Arabs near the Iraqi border and at the Persian Gulf. There are many racial types, the most typical of which are similar to the inhabitants of Northern India and Kashmir. But there are also Iranians who look very much like Arabs, red-haired people perhaps descended from the neighboring Russians, and black-skinned individuals whose ancestors must have been traders or slaves from Africa. Much of this diversity can be traced in Iranian musical life today.

The history of Iran as a single country goes back about 2500 years. At that time the first Persian empire was established, one of whose capitals was Persepolis, today a tremendous ruined city near the modern city of Shiraz. The existence of Persepolis shows us that at the time of that first empire, a highly sophisticated Persian culture was thriving. At that time—as we can learn from the elaborate relief sculptures of Persepolis—Iran was composed of many ethnic groups, each recognized as distinct by the Imperial government. The Persian empire expanded, fought the Greek city-states (from whom it gained a great deal of knowledge), was conquered by Alexander the Great, and came for a time under strong influence from the Greek-dominated Byzantine empire. In the seventh century Persia reestablished a nationalist dynasty, only to be conquered by the Arabs, under whose influence Islam became the dominant religion. The earlier religious practices, based on the teachings of Zoroaster, have never been completely forgotten: although most Iranians are devout Muslims, they are eager to retain their pre-Islamic heritage, and they do this largely through the arts. After becoming Islamicized, Iran, over the next twelve centuries, conquered large parts of India, which it dominated culturally for a time; it was in turn conquered by the Afghans; lost territory to Russia; and—in the nineteenth century—fell under the strong influence of Germany, France, England, and finally the United States. This history, particularly the multifarious contacts that Iran has had with other cultures—especially in the last hundred years—is very important to us in determining the quality of Iranian musical culture today. Persians consider the history of their country to be essentially tragic, and their explanation of what many of them regard as the essentially sad character of their classical music is that it reflects this tragic quality.

Music Reflects the Broad Issues
in Iranian Culture

As implied above, the way in which a contemporary developing culture like Iran can best be understood is through a series of contradictions. In Iran there is a great deal of difference between rural and urban life; this difference appears to have been important for a long time, for cities have been part and parcel of Iranian culture for many centuries. The nation includes several large cities—Shiraz in the South; Isfahan, one of the world's most beautiful architectural monuments, in the very center; Tabriz (a Turkish-speaking city) in the West; Meshhad (a city that grew largely because of its important shrine, which attracts thousands of pilgrims each year) in the Northeast; and the most distinctive city, the modern capital of Tehran. Life in these cities has always centered on trade, while the villages, which make up the bulk of the Persian population, have been inhabited by peasants who produce the food for the entire nation (in what is largely a desert ecological system), and by artisans, such as the famous rug-makers, who sell their goods in the cities. Evidently, there has always been a great difference in musical culture and musical style between city and country; this difference continues today, for the folk music of the villages seems to be very little influenced by modern life and technology and by Western styles of music, while the musical life of the cities reflects not only the greater sophistication of the city-dweller but also his many contacts with other cultures, especially that of the West.

There is also a sharp difference between life in Tehran and life in the other, smaller cities. Tehran, a city of three million, is by far the most prominent center of commerce, industry, social life, education, and the arts. It is Iran's window to the world, and it is far more modernized and Westernized than the other cities. This difference is again reflected in musical life: the musical culture of Tehran is a tremendous mix of Western and traditional—both local and national—influences, whereas the other cities are much more provincial and parochial in their musical orientation.

One of the most powerful features of Iranian culture is the Islamic religion, particularly the branch of Islam that claims the vast majority of Persians, Shi'ite Islam. Islam is a religion in which the worshipper is relatively free to act as he wishes. There is, strictly speaking, no priest to mediate between the believer and God, but there are teachers who interpret the Koran and the prophets. There is no prescribed liturgy, but the believer does have certain obligations such as prayer, statement of belief in God, alms giving, and pilgrimages. In his daily life he is relatively free to interpret the dictates of religion as he wishes. This is reflected in the attitude toward music. When one goes to Iran, one finds the country full of music. It is heard everywhere, even on the streets, and it is therefore surprising that there is a kind of prohibition of music under Islam. Music, and the arts in general, are frowned upon as ungodly, and one may not perform music at or near shrines or mosques. Instrumental music is particularly to be eschewed. Thus, we see another contradiction in Iranian culture: the importance of Islam, and the tendency to avoid one of its major tenets.

How does this prohibition of music square with the all-pervasive nature of music in Iran? In the first place, there is a kind of music that Muslims do not regard as music proper: the chanting of the Koran, or prayers, and of sermons, which they label as "reciting" or "reading," but which is almost identical in musical sound to the true singing that Persians consider to be music. Thus, while admitting that music cannot be dispensed with, despite the prohibition against it, Iranians tolerate musicians but consign them to a low rung on the socioeconomic ladder. They regard them as unreliable, irreligious, chronic debtors, drug addicts, and guilty of unclean living; in addition, they relegate the profession of musician as much as possible to non-Muslim minorities, which accounts for the fact that in Iran a great many musicians are Jewish. They exalt, at least to a degree, the virtues of being an amateur musician, something that is much less reprehensible than making one's living in music. The amateur class of musicians consists of individuals from wealthy and powerful families who can afford to live in opposition to the dictates of the religious teachers. These amateurs look down upon the professionals because what the professionals perform and when they perform it are dictated to them by their patrons or employers. The amateur can play or sing whatever he wishes, or he can abstain if he wants; this is very important because the ideal of music in Iran is improvisation. Of course, there is in Iran a tremendous quantity of composed songs and pieces.

The importance of the amateur musician's freedom may become more apparent if we consider the three categories of Iranian musical culture (not counting the Western music that has recently been imported). First, there is folk music, which exists largely in villages and small towns, and is performed by the population at large or by several different kinds of semi-professional specialists (to be discussed more fully below). Second, there is the popular music of the cities, which is performed by professional musicians in cavernous music-hall restaurants, on the radio, and most of all, on cheaply produced 45-rpm records. Finally, there is Persian art or classical music, performed by a small group of highly sophisticated musicians, many of them amateurs, who study for years and not only can perform but also can discuss their music in theoretical terms. In the repertory of these musicians of high status we find the main body of Persian improvised music, and within their repertory the improvised material is the most highly regarded. Thus, we are not likely to be mistaken if we conclude that within the context of the Islamic prohibition of music, the high status of amateur as opposed to professional musicians is due to both the freedom of the amateur to play when and as he wishes and the high regard in which improvisation is held. Some forms of western music include improvisation—jazz in particular, but also the performances of organ virtuosos, the accompaniments to dance classes, the experiments of avant-garde musicians—but this is not held in the same high regard as is improvisation in Iran.

The contradiction between the Islamic prohibition of music and the widespread importance of music in Iran is perhaps also explained by the fact that Iranians are very proud of their pre-Islamic heritage, of their ancient empire, of the great age of the Persian language and literature. They are intensely nationalistic, emphasizing that they are not like their Arabic and Turkish neighbors, with whom they are often confused. (For one thing, their language is different from Arabic.) Music has become for them an important symbol of the pre-Islamic past, though this symbolism refers to Islamic elements as well.

Let us look at one example of the mingling of pre-Islamic and Islamic elements in the contemporary scene. Persian men do their daily or weekly exercises in a traditional type of gymnasium, called "zurkhaneh," or "house of strength." Such a gymnasium is really a club, often reserved for the employees of a particular business, or for some other cohesive group. In such a gymnasium some thirty to fifty men will gather at a regular time, and perform feats of strength and skill, in unison and singly. Many of these involve the lifting and manipulation of weights, and some consist of dancing and whirling. These exercises are said to go back to the days of Zoroastrian religion—before Islam. The most interesting thing about these zurkhanehs is that the exercises are always accompanied by singing and drumming. One member of the club, who has the title "Morshed," chants and accompanies himself on a large drum, and also occasionally rings a bell, which signals a change in the prescribed exercise routine. The drum is regarded as ancient, and the words sung by the Morshed are usually taken from the Shan-nameh (Book of Kings), a very long epic poem by the Persian poet Ferdowsi (ca. 935–1020), who gave an account of many of the real and legendary events experienced by the heroic kings, emperors, and nobles of ancient Iran. But as we have pointed out, these pre-Islamic elements are often mixed with Islam, with the result that men in a zurkhaneh feel that they are fulfilling a Muslim obligation, that they are engaged in specifically Muslim activity when performing their exercises. One specific reason for this is that quotations from the Koran are also heard in the zurkhaneh.

There are other examples of the way in which music is used to hold fast the pre-Islamic heritage of Iran. The words of many songs, folk and popular, also refer to pre-Islamic times. The tender story of Leili and Majnun, which dates back to Iran's ancient period, is the basis of many Iranian folksongs; the same story also provides the name for a piece of music that serves as one of the models for improvisation in Persian classical music, and it supplied the words for one of the most popular songs on the Tehran hit parade in 1969. The ancient heritage of Iran is important even in the context of the Western musical tradition that is now a large part of Iranian musical life. The most important Iranian festival of the arts, to which musicians, artists, critics, and dignitaries from the entire world are invited, takes place annually at Persepolis, the capital of the ancient Achimenean Empire. And when the first truly Iranian opera, *The Hero of Sahand* by Ahmad Pezham, was performed in 1968, it characteristically dealt with a subject from the pre-Islamic past (though its music was, of course, in the style of European opera).

Islam affects Iranian musical life in many ways. Although it prohibits music, with the resulting downgrading of musicians, Islam also provides positive influences. One of these relates to the Muslim belief that all men are equal in the sight of God, something that may appear to be negated by the great differences in status and by the hierarchical structure, including the powerful aristocracy, that one finds in Iranian society. But compared with India, a nation with certain cultural similarities, there is in Iran and in other Islamic nations a good deal of social mobility. Today, villagers sometimes go to college, sons of landowners must serve in the army, and members of minority groups can occasionally find government jobs. (Of course, the social difference between landowner and peasant, between scholar and illiterate, is still considerable.) This moderate degree of equality and social mobility extends to musical life and styles.

By contrast, in Western society during the early twentieth century, musical life tended to be rather strictly stratified and classified; a musician or listener was associated with a particular kind of music—classical or "serious" music, popular music, or perhaps another subtype. Violinists in symphony orchestras did not ordinarily play jazz, and, with some notable exceptions, members of dance bands did not play the organ at church services. Of course, in the United States the melting-pot approach to social life and the substantial social mobility of Americans permitted particularly numerous deviations from this system.

India provides an even better example of rigid stratification in a music culture. India is a nation where until recently there was a minimum of social mobility, where the social and economic role of each person was determined by the level, or caste, of his family; its culture includes a tendency to divide musical life very rigorously among the practitioners of classical, popular, and folk music, and in other ways as well. For instance, a musician who performs the ragas of Indian classical music would not demean himself by participating in an ensemble that plays popular film songs. This tendency to divide musics from each other goes further: a practitioner of Northern Indian or Hindustani music would not try to perform South Indian or Carnatic music, despite the fact that both kinds of music enjoy the same amount of prestige. Moreover, an Indian musician who has made a career in Western music—and there are many of these, including the world-famous conductor Zubin Mehta —would not also try to become a performer of Indian classical music.

In Iran there are also many kinds and, in a sense, levels of music; the heterogeneity of the culture guarantees this. There is Western music, both classical and popular, there is Persian classical music, there is a large variety of styles of the kind of popular music that uses elements of traditional and Western music, and there are many regional varieties of folk music. In Iran many musicians participate in a variety of these styles. The most famous singers of Persian classical music can also be heard performing popular songs.

Musicians who specialize in the folk music of a remote region, and who have never visited a large city, do try their hand at classical music, though they frequently cannot perform it with much expertise. The typical Persian violinist is equally at home playing a Vivaldi concerto or improvising on the modes of the classical Persian dastgah system. Iranian musicians do not have all the social mobility they would like in their personal lives; but they can move as they wish among the musical styles existing in their country, and this seems to be related to the general feeling of equality among Muslims, something that is very important in Islamic theology.

Musical Instruments and Iranian Culture

A further characteristic of Iranian life is its broad acceptance of Western ways; this is apparent in the cities, most of all in Tehran, the capital, and especially so among individuals with a Western-style university education. This acceptance is, of course, reflected in the acceptance of Western music, perhaps most clearly in the use of Western instruments. The desire to combine the most desirable elements of modern culture with the most essential components of the older tradition can be seen in the way Western and traditional instruments are used together, and, also, in the ways in which elements of Western music and instrument construction have been incorporated into traditional instruments.

In Iran the most important instruments of the past are stringed instruments. Most of them are lutes, such as the small, delicate four-stringed *setar,* depicted in ancient Persian miniatures; the odd-shaped, somewhat larger *tar,* with six strings and a skin belly; the *'ud,* an Arabian import, which was also brought to Europe in the late Middle Ages, where it eventually became the immediate ancestor of the European lute; the large, simple, two-stringed *dotar;* and others. A few were bowed fiddles, and these were evidently used much less frequently than the plucked lutes. Chief among these bowed instruments are the *kamange,* a three-or four stringed miniature cello with a small, round body and a skin belly, which produced a thin, slightly harsh, and nasal tone; and the *gheichak,* a very curiously shaped instrument once used almost exclusively in tribal music in Eastern Iran, Afghanistan, and Central Asia, and which is closely related to an Indian folk instrument called *sarinda.* Finally, among the stringed instruments of traditional music in Iran we must mention the *santour,* a trapezoid-shaped dulcimer that is played with tiny wooden mallets, and which consists of seventy-two strings. Drums, flutes, and reed instruments are also used in traditional Iranian music, but they are much less prominent. The strings are at the heart of the Iranian musical traditions, classical and folk. These traditional instruments are still in use, but Western instruments have been added to them.

One of the most noticeable characteristics of the musical scene in contemporary Iran is the importance of the Western violin in many types of music—Persian classical, Persian popular, and, of course, strictly Western music. Only in rural folk music has it not become widely used. The violin was introduced to Iran about one hundred years ago; it was soon adopted as a truly Iranian instrument, and began to replace the kamange and the gheichak, both of which would probably have been entirely forgotten had they not been resurrected through the efforts of the cultural branches of the government, which, after World War II, began attempting to restore all sorts of national monuments. Why should the violin have taken on this great importance? For one thing, it is, of course, a technically superb instrument—capable of a great variety of tone color, intensity, dynamics, and sonorities and timbres of sound. Also, it is easily transported. Its success in Iran may be a reflection of its earlier success in Europe, where it drove out and made obsolete most other bowed instruments, such as the viols and other kinds of fiddles. But perhaps more important, it is one instrument that can be used for both Western and Persian music. And it must be remembered that individual Iranian musicians—in contrast with, say, Indian ones—wanted to be able to perform both types of music. Moreover, it was needed because it offered more flexibility and variety of sound than the less successfully built gheichak and kamange; a further advantage of the violin was that it could be played loud enough for large audiences, something the gheichak and kamange were not capable of. The Persian musician holds and plays the violin as in the West, and although he uses different techniques of ornamentation, his style of playing is essentially that of the West. This is in contrast with India, where the violin was adopted some two hundred years ago, and where it is played in two ways. For Western music it is played as in Europe and America. For Indian music the player sits on the floor, barefoot, and holds the violin between his chest and his foot, leaving his arm free to slide up and down the fingerboard; The sounds he produces are quite strange to Western ears. Small wonder that very few Indian violinists play both Western and Indian violin music!

The violin has influenced Persian music in other ways. For example, when the gheichak, the strange-looking fiddle from the Eastern Iranian tribes, was resurrected by the musical nationalists and made a part of urban culture, the number of its strings was reduced from eight to four, and their tuning was changed to match that of the violin; and the instrument was changed in other ways to make it sound more like a violin.

The fact that Western instruments appear in families began to be reflected in Persian music. We have, for example, a string family consisting of violin, viola, cello, and double bass, all more or less the same, but of different sizes, so that a different range of pitch is characteristic of each member of the family; we have a family of flutes consisting of flute and piccolo; we have different ranges of guitars; or saxophones—alto, tenor, and baritone. Traditional Persian music was essentially soloistic. An ensemble would consist at most of two lutes or other stringed instruments, and a drum. But after Western musical ideals were introduced, Iranians began to emulate what appeared to them the most valuable aspect of European and American music—the orchestra, with its families of instruments. Furthermore, they began to speculate about the possibility of developing different sizes and ranges for individual instruments. They didn't develop this idea very much; instead they began to use the most easily accessible Western family of instruments, the violin family. But in order to show the world that their tradition was capable of the same sophisticated development that had occurred in the West, they created alto, tenor, and bass gheichaks and combined them in groups, making an orchestra.

This same development took place in Soviet Central Asia, an area whose traditional musical culture was very much like that of Iran. There, the Russians, who have always dominated the cultural direction of the minority peoples in the USSR, introduced orchestras made of traditional instruments that had previously been used exclusively for solo performance. The Soviets were more successful than the Iranians, partly because government direction was more determined and forceful, and partly because Marxist-Leninist ideology espouses the idea of group and even mass performance.

Orchestras of both native and Western instruments have begun to be very prominent in twentieth-century Iran, even though they only occasionally consist of traditional instruments that have been adapted according to the Western "family" principle of instrument construction. The typical orchestra that performs popular music on the radio consists of some ten violins, two or three cellos, two double basses (played with the bow, not plucked), two santours (Persian hammered dulcimers), and an 'ud, the Arabian lute. In addition, there are two Persian drums, the goblet-shaped zarb, and a tambourine that has about sixty rings instead of a half-dozen bells. The ensemble that ordinarily accompanies belly dancing in the night clubs of Tehran consists of a Western flute, violin, santour, the timpox (an Arabic type of drum made of fired clay, with one skin, which is played with the hands), and the tambourine. The Conservatory of National Music in Tehran has an orchestra consisting of traditional Persian instruments, the most prominent of which are the tar, a long-necked lute with a skin belly (of which there are about twenty), and the santour (four or five); combined with these are a good many violins and cellos. Thus, the role that music occupies in a culture is again shown to reinforce the most important currents of the culture, one of which is, in the case of Iran, to combine traditional modes of behavior with those from the West that are most compatible with their own traditions. Iranian ensembles include both Western and Persian instruments, but the Western ones—the violins and, to a much smaller extent, the flutes and

clarinets—are those that are most compatible with earlier Persian musical culture. Brass instruments, which are so important in twentieth-century Western art and popular music, are rarely used.

The Popular Music Culture of Tehran

The popular music of Iran today reflects both the complexity of modern life in Tehran, and the many currents in Persian culture that are contributing to the generally positive and optimistic flavor of life in the cities, particularly in Tehran. The most obvious characteristics of this popular music culture are its great variety of styles and its relationship to many forces from inside and outside the nation.

Although in many ways the citizens of Tehran consider Iranian and Western popular music to be quite distinct from each other, they enjoy several styles of the latter. Many of them participate rather fully in the popular music trends of the West: they like to listen to rock, soul, jazz, and more old-fashioned European pop music. Western recordings issued by small Iranian record companies are widely sold on 45-rpm discs. Interestingly, these songs are issued four to a disc, and sometimes the four songs exhibit four kinds of Western music so completely different that a typical American buyer would consider only one or two of them to his liking. Perhaps this is done in order to expand the market. More likely, the reason is that Tehran listeners, on the whole, are not sensitive to the differences among Western styles. Just as the classical musician of Iran says, "Persian classical music has a universe of expression, but Western music is very limited and monotonous," the Persian aficionado of Western music seems to be saying, "I like American and European music—but it is really all very much alike." It is interesting that the multitude of stores that sell Western records in Tehran segregate these records from those of the many separate styles of Persian popular music.

This segregation extends also to the places in which one hears live popular music. Western popular music is performed in Western-style nightclubs and restaurants, which are attended by Iranians (and by foreigners who happen to be living in Tehran) whose life style is predominantly Western. They bring their wives, and are dressed in the latest Paris and London fashions. Persian popular music, on the other hand, is performed in large, cavernous music halls patronized mainly by men whose life style is much more traditional. They leave their wives and girlfriends at home, eat Persian food and drink beer, and watch a nonstop and non-repeat stage show that includes, besides music, folk and belly dancing, skits, comedians, and acrobats—something along the lines of the old Ed Sullivan Show on American television. Each music hall has a clientele consisting predominantly of one occupation, such as taxi drivers or small businessmen. Truly Western music is never heard here, though occasionally a Persian popular music act will creep into a show at a Western-style nightclub. The languages used in these two worlds of popular music are also "segregated." The Western-style shows involve both Iranian and Western musicians, but no matter who sings, the songs are rendered in Western languages—English, French, Italian, sometimes Spanish. The Persian-style music halls offer music with almost exclusively Persian words, even when the musical style approaches that of Western music. The musicians themselves—though each involves himself mainly in one type of music, Western or Persian—do not segregate themselves with respect to musical style quite as much as do their audiences.

What we have here called Persian popular music comprises a large number of musical styles. There is a kind of mainstream style consisting of songs in which ensembles accompany the singer in unison and octaves, with each instrument occasionally playing slight variations of the main tune. This use of octaves is interesting because Persian classical and folk music is a predominantly solo tradition. Playing a tune in two or three octaves is foreign to this tradition, but the use of harmony in the accompaniment would be even stranger. The use of octaves in this mainstream style of popular music may be something of a compromise between the old Persian tradition and Western harmonic practice. This mainstream style is shared by Tehran with other large cities of the Middle East—Istanbul, Cairo, Beirut, Baghdad. Its singers are mostly women with full, sensuous voices; most characteristic of these is a type of singer whom we should describe briefly in order to shed another light on the role of music in a culture.

The prototype of this most popular type of singer in Iran is an artist whose stage name is Delkash, a woman who became famous when she was approaching middle age, and who remained perhaps the most prominent singer of both popular and classical Iranian music throughout the rest of her career, which extended to a rather advanced age. Her incredible popularity during the middle decades of the twentieth century is matched by Arabic female singers of similar vocal quality, age, and, to some extent, appearance. The most famous of these was Umm Kalthum, who retired in the 1960s and whose weekly radio concerts were for decades among the great musical and social events in Cairo and other large cities. Such singers were, of course, great artists; but there is no doubt that their appearance symbolized something very important for the predominantly male audiences. The interpretation of this symbolism belongs more properly in the realm of psychology and psychoanalysis; but the fact that the most popular singers in Middle Eastern culture could be regarded as mother-figures, while those of the West much more easily symbolize wives or mistresses, may tell us something significant about the role of these singers in their cultural environment. If we pursue this point one step further, it is interesting to find that the singers and dancers in the traditional music halls of Tehran are usually older or older-appearing, and are more buxom than those in the Westernized nightclubs.

The mainstream style of Iranian popular music is surrounded by other styles. Perhaps next in popularity is one that may be labeled the "Westernized" style, a sort of compromise between the essentially Middle Eastern mainstream style and Western popular music of the '30s and '40s. This style exhibits the Iranian mainstream characteristics of lyrical melodies, usually accompanied by voluptuous strings performing in octaves, but also more frequent use of Western-style harmony.

Other bodies of Iranian popular music symbolize other facets of contemporary Iranian culture. One of these is based essentially on the classical music of Iran; it abstracts from this tradition those elements that involve the greatest amount of technical skill. In the case of vocal music, the borrowed element is the long, drawn-out melisma—a passage of many notes performed with only one syllable of text—delivered with a yodeling or sobbing kind of articulation. In instrumental music, it is the chahār mezrāb, a type of piece that shows how fast the musician can play. The name "chahār mezrāb" means, literally, four plectrums, and represents the idea of speed: "He is playing his lute so fast, it sounds as if he had four plectrums." This type of piece, which is usually based on a short, driving, and endlessly repeated

rhythmic motif (e.g., ♪ ♫♪ ♪ ♫♪), was, in the classical tradition, actu-

ally, a minor part of a performance. In this popular music style derived from the classical tradition, it is an important musical form which may be played alone, without the other parts that would accompany and surround it in a performance in the classical tradition.

Another type of popular music is based on rural folk music, and shows the renewed interest of the urban populace in the minorities and tribal groups of the outlying area. This kind of popular music may consist of folksongs performed more or less as they would be in the villages; indeed, Radio Iran presents a regular program of such authentic folk music for the city-dweller. More frequently, however, songs from the countryside are arranged, played by orchestras consisting in part of Western instruments, and sometimes even harmonized.

Finally, one can hear, among the popular musics of Tehran, types of music that show the influence of (1) folk and popular musics of other Middle Eastern cultures such as the Arabic world, Turkey, and Afghanistan; (2) the music of India and Pakistan; and (3) the Soviet Union, including Central Asia (whose traditional music is closely related to that of Iran anyway), the Caucasus, and Russia itself. Tunes whose musical style could readily be identified as Russian are sung with Persian words in a typically Middle Eastern vocal delivery, accompanied by a mainstream orchestra.

Thus, the popular music culture of Tehran reflects the complex relationships of the modern urban Iranian to his past and to his national and international environment.

Classical Music in Iran and
Other Asian Cultures Today

If the popular music of the cities reflects the contemporary currents of Iranian life, classical music represents an essentially conservative view of Persian culture. It is an ancient tradition that today, however, is practiced by only a very small group of musicians, perhaps not more than one hundred, who live largely in Tehran; a few others live in large provincial cities such as Isfahan and Shiraz (cities that were great cultural and political centers before the rise of Tehran in the nineteenth century). The most important segments of classical music are improvised, performed by solo singers and instrumentalists who are accompanied by individual instrumentalists (usually violin or santour) whose role is to follow, repeat, and paraphrase, phrase by musical phrase, the lines of the soloist; sometimes a drum is also used as accompaniment.

The conservatism that we have mentioned is evident in several ways. First, the body of material upon which a musician may improvise is severely limited. It consists of a number of modes (dastgah), each composed of ten to forty parts (gusheh), which a performer learns in the form of actual tunes. The entire repertory of these tunes takes no longer than ten or twelve hours to perform, and new material that may serve as the basis of improvisation is not admitted (though it does sometimes creep into the repertory in devious ways). Thus, the classical tradition is one that allows little innovation, whereas the popular music tradition permits a great deal of expansion in many directions. This is one respect in which Iran appears to differ from Western culture, for in the West, though the popular traditions are certainly flexible and varied, the classical, or serious, or art music tradition is one in which composers experiment with radically new sounds. If one examines the history of Western art music, he sees that its styles have changed enormously over the last, say, ten centuries; but what little we know about the history of Persian music indicates that the sounds we now hear are not too different from those that were heard a thousand years ago.

Conservatism is also evident in the words that classical Persian singers use for their improvisations; these are poems from the era of classical Persian poetry—the great poets Hafez, Sa'adi, and, best known to Americans, Omar Khayyam—as well as modern poems written in these same classical styles. There are, indeed, avant-garde poets in Iran today, but their works are not used by the singers of classical music. Again, a comparison with Western art music is apt. Composers of the new music in Europe and the Americas make great use of the works of contemporary and experimental poets, beginning with E. E. Cummings and T. S. Eliot, and of newly discovered traditions outside the West, such as Indian and Chinese classics.

Conservatism is also reflected in the attitudes of Persian classical musicians toward their music. They insist that their material is ancient, that much of it originates basically in the pre-Islamic past, that it is peculiarly Persian. They denigrate the obviously close relationship that it has to other classical traditions in South and West Asia, such as the Arabic maqams and the Indian ragas, maintaining that the Persian tradition has not been touched by others. In evaluating their fellow musicians, they praise most highly those whose knowledge of the traditional repertory is most perfect—in contrast with the popular musicians, who stress technical virtuosity in even that part of the popular music that is derived from the classical. Not surprisingly, classical music is something of a whipping boy for that part of the population that is Western-oriented and looks to the West for its inspiration. Western-educated government workers, economists, scientists, and technicians ask themselves what an unchanging musical tradition can contribute to the modernization and development of their country, and some of them would like to see it disappear in favor of a completely Western style of art music.

The traditional place of performing classical music is a small men's gathering, at which the guests eat, drink, sometimes smoke opium, and are entertained by one of their own group. This type of gathering, from which women are rather rigorously excluded, is still found with great frequency, even among families whose style of social life is otherwise quite Western. And though social and educational mobility in Iran has become quite strong (supported as it is by the basic idea of the equality of all men under Islam), classical music remains a vestige of an earlier system in which classes were more rigidly separated, for its audience is almost entirely composed of well-to-do and educated individuals. Thus, the role of classical music in Iran is mainly to reinforce the older values of society.

To be sure, even the classical music has undergone a great deal of change, but much of the change has been made in order to ensure its survival. To a large extent, such change is the result of the almost complete extinction of the tradition in the late nineteenth century, which made necessary a somewhat artificial revival in the twentieth. Among the changes are the following:

Western notation (adapted to the special needs of the Persian musical system) has been introduced, which means that the traditional model for improvisation, once taught by a master to his pupils through performance and listening alone, may now also be learned from a written score. In the past each master developed his own version of this repertory and passed it on to his students, who might again diversify it, so that many different versions could coexist at any one time. Today, the teaching versions of three masters have been published, and while much of the teaching is still done in the traditional way, a certain degree of standardization is coming about. Music is not taught exclusively in the home by great masters to groups of disciples of apprentices; it is also taught in music schools and conservatories that give lessons in the fashion of Western music instruction, and even in the Music Department of the University of Tehran, where students learn the practice of Persian music, as well as its theory (taught in the fashion of Western music schools, with terminology in French) and its history. Classical music has found its way into radio and television and onto the concert stage, and this has obviously had an effect on its performance style. After all, part and parcel of an improvisation at an informal gathering is the fact that the performer may play or sing as briefly or as long as he wishes, or as long as his audience can be kept at attention. On the radio or at a concert, however, he is told in advance that he has a ten- or a fifteen-minute spot and must, accordingly, either plan ahead or break off in the middle of a musical thought. As we have mentioned above, the violin has become prominent in classical music, and other Western instruments—flute, clarinet, even the piano—have begun to establish themselves in this tradition. The tuning of traditional instruments and scales has moved from the uniquely Middle Eastern system to something approaching the Western one, as represented by the piano. All of these changes appear to have taken place as a result of the endangered state of classical music. At the same time Western classical music has become very widely performed by Iranian musicians, and has become a symbol of the forward-looking segments of the educated population.

If we compare the status and role of Persian classical music with that of the ragas of Indian classical music (as performed, for example, by world-famous artists such as Ravi Shankar, Ali Akbar Khan, or Bismillah Khan), we find that this Indian system is not in essence very different from the Persian, except for its rather different cultural role. The Indian system is much larger—there are many, many more ragas than Persian dastgahs, there are tens of thousands of musicians rather than a handful, there are more things that a performer must learn to do, there is a much more elaborate system of musical thought and theory. The Indian tradition is equally conservative, but although it has been less subject to external change than the Persian system, the idea of organic change within the system, is more readily accepted. One may, for example, compose new ragas, while in Iran one cannot compose new dastgahs. In India the classical tradition is even more segregated from other styles than is the case in Iran, but Indian classical musicians are more likely to admit that their music has been influenced by folk and tribal music. The Indian tradition is more alive, probably because it has not been as threatened by extinction from Western influence. Indian culture has not, as a whole, been eager to become Westernized; modernization in a technological sense, yes, but adaptation to Western social, ethical, and aesthetic principles, no. Thus, there has been no need for the conservative intellectual to find a musical symbol for his cultural self-view, no need for him to insist that his classical tradition preserves the heritage of his past and has nothing to do with the present. For the Iranian, classical music is something to be held on to with a certain desperate determination, to be changed by force only in order to assure its survival.

Another view of classical music—one that is comparable to the situation in Iran—is found in Japan, also a nation with a strong classical music tradition. Japanese culture has, over the centuries, developed a special ability to adapt itself to outside influences. It has borrowed elements from many diverse cultures—China, Korea, India, Manchuria, and most obviously, Western Europe and America—and it has fused these into a distinct, characteristically Japanese pattern, but it continues to recognize the sources of the various elements. For example, in the musical repertory of the Japanese imperial court orchestra, one distinguishes "music of the right" (koma-gaku), which is music of Korean origin, from "music of the left" (to-gaku), which is music of Chinese and Indian origin. The Japanese classical tradition is, then, really a group of traditions, each with its own specialist-performers, and each of a different time and place of origin.

Despite the complete modernization of Japan in a technological and economic sense, Japanese individuals have been able to maintain equilibrium between present and past. The Japanese businessman goes to his office in a European suit, but spends the evening in traditional attire. He is also willing to tolerate both Japanese classical music, which he wants unchanged and un-Westernized, and the highest quality of Western music. The Japanese musician specializes, even within his own classical tradition; he does not try to excel in both Western and Japanese music. Nor has he adapted Western instruments to the Japanese classical tradition. He allows his classical music to exist, untouched by modernization, in a corner of his life, much as there are several distinct corners within the classical tradition itself.

If we wish to briefly compare the way in which classical music reflects the contemporary cultures of Iran, India, and Japan, we might do so as follows. India, a nation that wishes to turn to the West only when absolutely necessary in order to raise its material standard of living, maintains its classical music tradition fully, as the ideal of musical sound and practice; the tradition is kept separate from Western music, which, while present, is permitted to occupy only a small slice of Indian musical life. The classical tradition remains alive and is allowed to change internally, as it has in the past—slowly but organically. Japan, a nation accustomed to borrowing from its neighbors, has now borrowed enormously from the West, and this is reflected in the tremendous importance of Western music in Japanese urban life, and in the accomplishments of many Western-oriented Japanese musicians. But the Japanese have for centuries compartmentalized musical styles, adding new ones but leaving the old ones as much as possible unchanged; this continues to be their practice in the face of an unprecedented influx of Western music. In Iran the classical tradition has never been as strong as those of India and Japan, nations in which music played a positive rather than a negative role in religion, and, thus, in a period of both technical and social Westernization it is particularly prone to deterioration; as a result, it has become the focus of a conservative element, but it has also undergone change in its quest for survival.

In this context, it is interesting to briefly note the fate of a group of ancient traditions in the Central Asian republics—the areas of the Soviet Union closest to Iran—traditions whose musical styles are very much like Persian styles.

The notion that music reflects, or should reflect—and even reinforce—the basic values and trends of its culture has been widely accepted by modernized cultures of many political shadings. The sponsorship of music by Western governments is based essentially on this assumption, but Western nations have not made government participation a major ingredient of musical life. Developing nations in the twentieth century have been more interested in this by far, for they—like Iran—have had to grapple with the opposing forces of Westernization and nationalism, of industrialization and tradition, and have seen how the arts can play a major role in underscoring the changing social and economic currents of their peoples. The largest amount of government participation in musical affairs can be found in the Communist countries, particularly the Soviet Union. During the first half of the twentieth century the USSR evolved a rather standardized policy toward music, a policy resulting from a mixture of several forces: Marxist-Leninist theory, nineteenth-century interest in folklore, and Russian domination of minorities, especially the non-Western peoples in Soviet Asia. From Marxist-Leninist philosophy the Soviet managers of music derived the idea that music should be created that would appeal to large masses of people, music that could be performed by the masses—in large choruses and orchestras. This philosophy also promulgated a desire to modernize the music of non-Western peoples in the direction of the styles of music in the industrialized nations—that is, in the direction of Western classical music. During the nineteenth and early twentieth centuries European composers (including such great masters as the Czechs Smetana and Dvořák, the Hungarians Bartók and Kodály, the Norwegian Grieg, the German Brahms, the Rumanian Enesco, and many Russians—Tschaikowsky, Borodin, Rimsky-Korsakov, and others) began to incorporate folksongs and the style of folksongs into their music. This practice, manifested in large works such as operas and symphonies, became something of a standard for Soviet composers. And because the adoption of certain elements of Russian culture, such as a uniform language or at least its alphabet, was urged on the Soviet minorities, it is not surprising that elements of Russian music, including such instruments as the balalaika and Russian folk-music practices, such as choral singing, were also introduced. At the same time, however, Soviet policy has aimed at retaining, on the part of the minorities, a certain degree of cultural independence.

The picture of traditional music in the Caucasus and Soviet Central Asia is, thus, a complex one. The state provides conservatories, music schools, and research programs. It fosters the adaptation of traditional instruments to Western tuning. (For example, the frets of Central Asian lutes such as the tar and the dotar are rearranged to constitute a Western scale.) Instruments are built in families. Orchestras of traditional instruments, which were originally played solo, are established. The state directs musical change by encouraging the development of those elements in traditional music that lend themselves to change.

From this list one can see that some of the aspects of the Westernization of music that is found in Iran are also found in Soviet Central Asia. But there is an important difference in motivation. In Iran traditional music is to a large extent a function of nationalism, and the reconstruction and adaptation of old instruments is done in order to ensure their survival. In Central Asia the old instruments are reconstructed and changed in order that they may serve as vehicles for musical change. For example, the gheichak, the aforementioned folk instrument found in Eastern Iran, Afghanistan, and Central Asia, has been changed in Iran—the number of its strings reduced to four, its tone changed to resemble that of the violin—in order that it may compete with the violin in performing Persian classical music. In Central Asia, the gheichak has been changed in much the same way, but in order for musicians to use it in learning modern, i.e., European music. Indeed, Mark Slobin reports having heard in Tashkent, the capital of the Uzbek Soviet Socialist Republic, sections of the Mendelssohn and Khatchaturian violin concertos played on the gheichak. In short, the role of non-Western traditional musics in the Soviet Union is to serve as a vehicle for bringing about musical change to accompany social and economic change.

Folk Music in Rural Iran

At the base of any complex musical culture is its folk music. It is the music that is most easily intelligible to a large segment of the population, the music that changes least rapidly and is least subject to innovation by individual musicians, and the music that should be the most accurate reflection of the basic values of its culture because it depends for its survival and dissemination upon its acceptance by the entire community. From the folk music of the villages and farms is thought to come the inspiration for the basic content and musical system of the art music that is developed in the cities and at the courts of royalty and nobility. Thus, having commented upon the role of popular and classical music in Iran, it is now appropriate for us to examine the role of folk music in the small towns and villages.

There is obviously a great deal of diversity in it, because Iran includes several isolated regions and several minorities that speak languages other than Persian. The music of the Northwest is close to that of Turkey and the Caucasus, and is in some ways not too different from that of the peoples of the Soviet Caucasus. The music of the Baluchis in the Southeast resembles that of Pakistan. Perhaps most interesting, the Persian Gulf region is inhabited by many peoples who have the physical features of Africans; centuries ago, they were evidently either brought to that area as slaves or came as traders from East Africa by way of Saudi Arabia, and their music has distinctly African characteristics. As an example of Iranian folk music culture, let us look at some of the musical practices of Khorasan, the Northeastern province of Iran, which has been studied in detail by Stephen Blum. I am grateful to Dr. Blum for most of the information in the next two pages. It is difficult to apply the usual definitions of folk music to this region, in which Persian, Turkish, and Kurdish are spoken, and which is characterized by a large number of shrines sacred to the Shi'ite Muslims who dominate all of Iran.

We think of folk music as music that is known and performed by many inhabitants of a village, and we think of a folk culture as a society in which, essentially, the entire community participates in a single repertory. We think of folk music as a type of music that is normally not performed by professional musicians. And we think of it largely as secular music.

This definition of folk music does not apply everywhere; indeed, the kind of distinction made among folk, popular, and art music in the West (and discussed in Chapter 5) is not really satisfactory in many non-Western cultures. In Iran and in many Asian nations, though, there is more or less a stratification of music that makes it possible for us to use the term "folk music" to indicate a particular repertory. In Iran we have designated the largely improvised music of the dastgah system as the art or classical music, and we have labeled as popular music the repertory that is consumed in the cities on 45-rpm records. By the process of elimination, we may label the rest of the non-Western music current in Iran as folk music; indeed, this turns out to be the music performed in villages and small towns, and, to some extent, in the lower socioeconomic classes of some of the cities.

In the province of Khorasan this music differs greatly from the folk music of the West—not only in its sound but also in its cultural context and setting. For one thing, much of it is religious and is not really regarded as music by its practitioners. There are calls to prayer, chants performed on the feast days commemorating the deaths of the most important religious figures of early Islam, chants performed at funerals, musical plays representing the martyrdom of the Iman Hossein (second cousin to Mohammed), calls of a musical nature chanted by beggars asking for alms, and recitations of famous religious stories and of the Shah-Nameh (the eleventh-century account of the historical and mythical past of Iran). Singing and chanting accompanies many kinds of religious events—prayers, sermons, readings of the Koran— and these events may take place in coffeehouses, on the street, in the mosque, and in the home. Musical media (though always vocal, never instrumental) is thus a very large part of the religious tradition of Islam, especially among the unlettered. Thus, a large proportion of the folk music of Khorasan is indeed religious.

Secular folk music is also found. It includes music for weddings and other celebrations of the life cycle such as engagements, birthdays, and circumcision; as such, it also has certain religious connotations, but at these festivals the music may be instrumental as well as vocal. Folk music for entertainment alone is also performed—in coffeehouses, at the bazaar (the commercial and social center of a city), in schools, at picnics (a particularly popular form of family recreation), and in the home. Work songs as such are rarely found, but peasants and laborers are frequently heard singing. Music to accompany dancing is also found, but the dancing is most commonly performed by an entertainer for an audience, not by large groups dancing for their own enjoyment.

All of this music may be heard in villages, in small towns, and in the outskirts of Meshed, the capital of Khorasan. The musicians typically reside in villages, and there are certain villages in which many musicians live, and from which they go out to perform.

A particular distinction of the folk music culture of Khorasan is the way in which its musicians are categorized as specialists. Most of the music is, indeed, performed by specialists who are to some extent professionals and who are paid for their services, though few of them actually make their living from music. The notion of general participation in folk music by the entire community simply does not apply here.

Each specific musical activity has a specialist who is known by a specific label. There is the *naqqal,* a person who recites the Shah-nameh and other poems in coffeehouses; the *morshed,* the man who recites poetry and plays the drum in a zurkhaneh, the traditional gymnasium; the *rozeh-khān,* who recites the story of Hossein's martyrdom; the *vā'ez,* or preacher, whose sermons include passages of chanting; the *khānandeh,* or singer of secular songs; the *bakhshi,* or minstrel, who sings narrative secular songs, accompanying himself on the dotar, and who also acts as a clown; the *motreb,* who is skilled on an instrument, and who sings and dances; the *guyandeh,* who recites poetry to musical accompaniment; the *luti,* who sings popular songs and appears dressed as a woman; the *asheqchi,* who plays the oboe-like zornah, mainly at weddings; and so on. An individual may combine more than one of these roles, but it is nevertheless interesting to find so many different categories of musicians recognized in the folk culture.

Does this kind of categorization reflect something important about Iranian culture? In the first place, the fact that music is officially discriminated against tends to push musicians into these special categories. A man need not exhibit himself as a "musician" at large, something that might make him unacceptable in the eyes of his fellow Muslims. He can say that he confines himself to one or another necessary musical function, but that his career is not musical.

More important, it is interesting to see the generally individualistic character of Persian culture reflected in the musical individualism that results in the thorough classification of musician-types. Persians are individualists. Each man pursues his own goal, throughout his life and in everyday situations. Islam permits individualism; the degree and kind of religious observance is left to the individual. Iranians did not readily take to working in large organizations; even their automobile driving, which, incidentally, results in monumental traffic jams, reflects individualism. The notion that each musician has his own individual type of music is surely related to this phenomenon. And so also is the unwillingness of musicians to represent themselves as a homogeneous class.

In other respects, also, the folk music of Khorasan reflects the individualist tendencies of the Persian. The music (like Persian classical music) is largely soloistic. Choral singing is rarely heard. When musicians do play together, each pursues his own, slightly individual, version of the tune. But side by side with this tendency toward individualism, there is in Persian culture a long-standing hierarchical structure among the people. All are equal in the sight of God, but between any two individuals, one has a (greatly or slightly) exalted position relative to the other, and he tends to speak while the other listens. Similarly, music is not normally an activity in which all join, but one in which an individual—the musician—speaks while the others listen. Thus, it is obviously possible for several of the contradictory patterns in a culture to be simultaneously reflected in musical thought and practice.

The Relationship of Music to Culture Type

We have given a rather detailed account of music in Iranian life, taking into account three segments of musical culture—the popular music of the cities, the classical tradition, and the folk music of the rural areas. This account has given us particulars about the way that music is used in Persian society and some of the ways in which it reflects values and attitudes. Our ultimate aim, however, has not been just to describe, but to see whether a view of music in a culture outside our own can help us to answer the question posed at the beginning of this chapter: What ·is the function of music in human life?

We may therefore ask if there is one main function that music fulfills in Iranian society. There are clearly a number of subsidiary functions: music is entertainment, music accompanies ritual and dancing, it is a vehicle for poetry, it provides outlet for emotional expression. In these respects the musical culture of Iran is very much like that of other cultures, perhaps not in detail (for instance, some cultures have more religious music than others), but in broad outline. If there is a single, basic function of music in Iranian culture, it may also be the same one that exists in all human societies. One suggestion for a basic definition of the function of human music has been made by Alan Lomax: music is the vehicle that man uses to express what is most basic in his relationship with others. Examining both the types of culture found in many societies and the kinds of music that they produce, Lomax found that "a culture's favorite song style reflects and reinforces the kind of behavior essential to its main subsistence efforts and to its central and controlling social institution."[1] Thus, he believes that cultures in which there is considerable freedom of sexual expression have a different kind of music from those in which sexual behavior is severely restricted; that a culture in which people work well together and cooperate with one another has different music from one in which they do not; and that cultures in which there is oppression of a laboring or peasant class by an aristocracy have different music from those in which there is more or less equal treatment of all individuals.

It is difficult to agree with this thesis completely. The type of music a culture develops must be determined by many factors, perhaps including these, but also including types of raw materials available for instrument construction, technological level of the society, amount of contact with other cultures, attitudes towards culture change or continuity, the development of literacy and musical notation, and many others. Nevertheless, it is difficult not to believe that the character of a society and its quality of life do not have a great deal to do with determining the style or styles of its music.

When searching for that aspect of music that most accurately reflects the basic values of a culture, Lomax found that the most frequently studied elements of music—scales, modes, techniques of composition, harmony and polyphony, rhythmic structure—are not the best indicators. Rather, the most useful indicators include the way in which the human voice is used, the kinds of tone color preferred, and the types of relationships among performers in an ensemble.

[1] Alan Lomax et al., *Folk Song Style and Culture* (Washington, D.C.: American Association for the Advancement of Science, 1968), p. 133.

Let us consider how the human voice is used in Iranian musical culture. In Iran there are many types of musical form—from short, repetitive songs to long wide-ranging improvisations. There are many kinds of rhythm— from strict adherence to a beat, or from four beats per measure, to music without any meter or beat at all. There are many ways of combining intervals of many sizes into melodies. In these respects the classical music of Persia, the popular music of its cities today, and the folk music of its countryside differ enormously. But in all of these musics the kind of sound produced by the human voice is essentially the same. It is hard to describe—the field of musicology has not developed a good set of terms to describe singing styles—but the voice is tense, and there is a tendency to produce sobbing or yodeling sounds. There is a great deal of ornamentation of a melody or of a single tone, which means that we hear trills, bending of notes, and short, fast runs of melody on one syllable. The voices, when combined in group singing, do not blend well, and this is a reflection of the fact that singing is primarily a solo activity. This kind of singing is found elsewhere in the Middle East and Central Asia, and also in North Africa and in the folk musics of the Balkan Peninsula and Spain. According to Lomax, it is the kind of singing that accompanies and reflects a culture in which there is exploitation of the broad masses of population by a powerful aristocracy, in which there is restriction of sexual expression, and in which women are either treated badly (e.g., secluded, or made to wear a veil, or left without legal recourse against cruelty) or, on the contrary, placed on a pedestal. It is a culture in which there is a tendency for people to work alone, not in groups, and to establish personal rather than group relationships. In the case of Iranian culture, if we lay aside for the moment the fact that all cultures are complex and that any broad characterization is fraught with exceptions, this description is not too far wrong.

This point of view is based, of course, on the assessment of the relationship between culture and music by an outsider; asking a member of the culture for such an assessment is not expected to yield results. Nevertheless, statements by Iranians about what their music expresses reinforce the above conclusions.

The general view expressed by Iranian experts in the field of their own classical music is that this music has a great variety of emotions inherent in it, that it represents a universe of expression compared to which other musics, such as Western and Indian, are poor, monotonous, and one-sided. The dominant emotion in Persian music, however, is sadness. As we pointed out at the beginning of this chapter, the music is said to express the experiences and feelings of the entire people, experiences that have been overwhelmingly tragic; the Persian people are an old people with many bitter experiences. The entire history of Iran is reflected in Persian music.

The fact that many Persians themselves have a view of their music that fits rather well into Lomax's scheme is certainly significant.

The Role of Music in Other Cultures:
Tribal Groups and Western Civilization

Let us look briefly at the role of music in cultures where industrial development and modernization do not play an important role. In order to find such cultures, we must turn either to the past—which means, almost automatically, the history of European music, for which there is ample information—or to non-Western cultures that have been only slightly touched by the currents of modernization.

The main function of music among the people of Yirkalla, in Northern Australia, is, according to Richard Waterman, enculturation, that is, teaching the people about their own culture. By Western standards this tribe of Australian aborigines has an exceedingly simple way of life, which, when Waterman visited them in 1952, had not been very much touched by Western culture. The arts in this society are largely involved in representing the totem animals and plants and the totemic ancestors of the various clans of the tribe. Waterman writes:

> "Throughout his life, the aboriginal is surrounded by musical events that instruct him about his natural environment and its utilization by man, that teach him his world-view and shape his system of values, and that reinforce his understanding of Aboriginal concepts of status and of his own role. More specifically, songs function as emblems of membership in his moiety and lineage, a validation of his system of religious belief, and as symbols of his status in the age-grading continuum."[2]

A comparison with the high cultures of Asia such as Iran may be pertinent here. The Australian aboriginal sees music as the vehicle whereby he learns his own culture, while the Iranian sees it as a not too necessary way of accompanying social and religious events; the Indian and the Japanese regard music as more essential to life than does the Iranian. In the sense that music is more essential to life in Yirkalla than to life in Iran, its function in these cultures differs; in the sense that music constitutes an essential symbol of identity in each culture, its function is similar. The Iranian regards his music as symbolic of his view of his own culture and of his past—within the wider perspective of the world that he has come to know. The Australian uses it to reinforce his identity within his tribe, and as an indicator of his clan, age, and status; the outside world, of which he is not very much aware, is left aside.

The function of music in the culture of the Blackfoot Indians of the Northern Plains of the United States and Canada is somewhat similar to that in the Yirkalla culture. Although they are now very much (for their

2 Richard Waterman, "Music in Australian Aboriginal Culture—Some Sociological and Psychological Implications," *Music Therapy* (1955), 41.

taste, much too much) aware of the non-Indian world, the Blackfeet have for a long time been in contact with other Indian tribes. For them, music also functions in a number of ways. It is an essential ingredient, perhaps the most essential, in religious observance. But it is also an important symbol of tribal identity. The right way to do something is to sing the right kind of Blackfoot song with it.

Without proceeding to further examples, we may draw some conclusions about music in the non-Western cultures of the world. We find music playing several roles: it is an essential ingredient in religious ceremonies, (even where it is not recognized as relevant to religion as in Iran), it reflects the important values or patterns of the culture, and it is a symbol of individuals and groups in relationship with each other and with their social environment. Of course, it also functions as entertainment, but it is less important in this respect in the simpler cultures and more so in the cultures with complex social stratification and technology.

How do these major functions manifest themselves in Western culture, past and present? We know relatively little about the function of music in medieval Europe. Time was when we believed that all medieval music was religious, that there was very little secular music at all. But this was due to the fact that most of the written information handed down to us by the medieval clerics dealt with church music. There is no doubt that secular music existed in the Middle Ages. But on the whole it was not carried on by learned musicians, and in this respect it was surely closely related to folk music. The area of music that exhibited the greatest complexity, and which was evidently in the vanguard of innovation much of the time, was church music. As far as we know, various kinds of musical practice—types of composition forms, types of polyphony—as well as intellectual theory about music, were the province of the learned monks, and were exhibited most prominently in church music. (Of course, it is likely that some of the innovations first exhibited in written form in the music of the church were actually borrowed from the unwritten secular practice.) We know very little about the secular music of medieval Europe, and it does seem fairly clear that the ideal music of that time, the music where, so to speak, "the action was," was the music of the church. Thus, we see music in Europe, as elsewhere, associated in a fundamental way with religion.

Does medieval music reflect, as does the music of contemporary Iran, the style of life, the kind of relationship that people had with one another? Since this aspect of culture seems to be related most closely to the style of singing and the way the human voice is used, we can only guess at the answer, for we have no tangible evidence of these traits in medieval music— Western musical notation does not provide an indicator for the particular tone color of the human voice. But there is a good deal of evidence that at least some kinds of medieval music (for example, the liturgical chant of the church) sounded not too different from the singing style of Persian art music, or from the chanting of the Koran and the call to prayer. The evidence of which we speak is the chanting in the contemporary Christian churches in the Middle East—the Armenian Christians, the Maronites of Lebanon, the Syrians, Assyrians, and Copts. Further evidence comes from the fact that the structure of a great deal of liturgical music from the Middle Ages, especially the way the words are set to music, appears similar to the structure of the non-metrical improvised classical music or religious chanting of Iran and other Islamic countries. Also, there is a great deal of historical evidence that points to a Middle Eastern origin for some of the musical practices of medieval Europe. And, to be sure, some aspects of medieval society bear resemblances to the contemporary Middle East—for instance, the hierarchical structure of interpersonal relations, and the attitudes toward sex and women. In contrast with Iran, however, group work and the identification of the individual with a group, as illustrated by the practice of congregational worship (versus essentially individual worship under Islam), were part of medieval culture; this is reflected in a practice that became a specialty of the West, complex polyphony, which requires group participation and cooperation at the musical level.

The history of European music is, as one might expect, a rather accurate reflection of the intellectual and social history of Europe. Let us mention only a few examples. Art and folk music, possibly indistinguishable in at least the secular component of medieval music, grew increasingly separate, reflecting the increasing stratification of European society into the learned and unlearned, the elite and the humble. This tendency was slightly reversed in the nineteenth century, when political factors necessitated the recognition of desires and needs of the masses, and when the composers of art music began to recognize folk music as a source of subject matter and inspiration. In the twentieth century we find the homogenization of society in the West again reflected in the creation of an enormous and really dominant body of popular music, which is disseminated largely through the mass media, and which partakes of both folk and art music, providing a middle ground between these two extremes. In this respect the current trends in the West resemble those of contemporary Iran. And in the changing relationships among art, popular, and folk musics, the recent history of Iran is essentially a condensation of the longer history of Europe, just as the economic and industrial development of Iran is accomplishing in a few decades what was accomplished much more gradually in Europe and North America.

Music history in Europe also reflects the growth and eventual dominance of scientific and rationalistic thought. Beginning with a simple and rather approximate system in the Middle Ages, European musicians developed a complex and, eventually, a highly accurate system of notation that today provides possibilities for enormous refinement of the directions given by the composer to the performer. The degree to which a performer was given precise instructions via notation increased constantly, and the distinction between composer (the scientist and the intellectual of music) and performer (the executor or engineer of the composer's ideas) grew throughout the course of Western history. In the middle of the twentieth century, however, the disillusion with and ambivalence toward science and engineering resulted in music in which the composer's directions became less precise and the freedom of the performer, much greater.

Special trends and interests in European intellectual life are also reflected in music. The Renaissance, with its interest in the ancient classical heritage of Europe and its reaction against the church, brought forth a plethora of compositions based in various ways on ancient Greek culture. The subject matter of opera, a form originating at the very end of the Renaissance— around 1600—was at first largely based on Greek mythology; indeed, the musical form of opera was thought to be a reconstruction of the manner in which ancient Greek drama was presented. The tendency toward logical, systematic, rational thought in the late eighteenth century is reflected in the neat, logical forms of Haydn and Mozart. The emotionalism of the nineteenth century had an important musical manifestation in the large orchestral works—especially the tone poems—of Berlioz and Liszt, and in the operas of Wagner. Finally, the enormous complexity of twentieth-century life has its analogue in the many different types of music and the many contrasting schools of composers of twentieth-century art music. Thus, in the history of Europe, as elsewhere, music reinforced the important values and thought patterns of the culture.

We have pointed out the importance of music to religious life and practice in most of the world's cultures. In the tribal cultures music is more closely associated with religion than in the more complex cultures; indeed, there is a sort of continuum in that the more complex a culture becomes, the less and less involved music is with religion. But even in the most complex culture of all, that of the twentieth-century West, music is still strongly tied to religion. We may think of music today as primarily secular entertainment, but churches (and synagogues, mosques, and all of the other places of worship in our religiously very complex society) still depend strongly upon the use of music. Indeed, music has perhaps become more important. The idea of using music as a primary innovating device in churches—for instance, in jazz, rock, and folk services, and in the introduction of English-language music in the Catholic church—underscores the importance of music in the religion of contemporary Western culture.

This strong connection of music with religion draws us to the conclusion that one of the main functions of music for man is communication with the supernatural; indeed, there is, among the many unprovable theories of the origin of music, one that maintains that music was first developed by man for precisely this reason. We will never know how music first came into existence, but we may readily believe that at its beginning it was somehow connected with religion; we can see this tradition carried on in all known cultures, simple and complex, in the world today.

Music in European society also functions—and has in the past functioned —as a symbol of both the identity of individuals and groups and their relative status. The statement that Waterman makes for the people of Yirkalla, whose music is an emblem of clan and a symbol of age, can easily be adapted to Western society. For example, throughout the history of European music the distinction between sacred and secular music, a distinction that Europeans have insisted upon as fundamental, symbolizes the separation of clergy and laity that has always been important in Christianity. Another example, of a sort that could be duplicated in many styles and periods, involves the controversy in the 1750s between the adherents of classical grand opera and a new type of opera that was simpler, more natural, more realistic. This controversy, which took place in Paris, split the opera-loving segment of the population into two camps, divided not only by musical taste, but also by national versus international and conservative versus liberal attitudes. A broader example involves the identification of music with nationality. In the Middle Ages, a time when a person's nationality was evidently not of great importance to him, there was little development in the way of national styles. Empires and kingdoms cut across and exceeded cultural and linguistic boundaries, and the inhabitants of a nation did not regard themselves as single people. But in the nineteenth century, when the development of nations—and particularly the rise of nationalism among the previously dependent peoples of Eastern, Southern, and Northern Europe—became a dominant force in political and social life, we see the creation of national styles and the growing identification of individuals with their national art and folk musics.

A most obvious illustration of music functioning as a symbol of personal and group identity in the West occurs in the popular music culture of the 1960s. Here we find a plethora of musical styles, each serving as the emblem of an age group (teenagers and students regarded rock as their music, while older folks clung to the style of Lawrence Welk) or a racial or cultural minority. (See Chapter 5 for a more elaborate account of this phenomenon.)

What does music do for man? A detailed view of one culture outside our own, and examples from other non-Western cultures and from Western civilization show us that it has three major functions: it is a primary vehicle for man's communication with the supernatural, it symbolizes a person's identity with a group, and it reflects and reinforces the dominant characteristics, values, and directions of a culture.

BIBLIOGRAPHY

The role of music in culture is discussed in a large variety of publications. The best survey is Alan P. Merriam, *The Anthropology of Music* (Evanston, Ill.: Northwestern University Press, 1965). A briefer discussion is found in Bruno Nettl, *Folk and Traditional Music of the Western Continents,* 2nd ed. (Englewood Cliffs, N. J.: Prentice-Hall, 1973), Chapter 1.

Among the general publications on Iranian music, we mention the following: Nettl, "Attitudes towards Persian Music in Tehran, 1969," *Musical Quarterly,* IVI, No. 2 (April, 1970), 183–97; Ella Zonis, "Contemporary Art Music in Persia," *Musical Quarterly,* LI No. 4 (October, 1965), 636–48; Nettl, "Persian Popular Music in 1969," *Ethnomusicology,* XVI, No. 2 (May, 1972); and Nettl, "Examples of Popular and Folk Music from Khorasan," in *Musik als Gestalt und Erlebnis* (Vienna: H. Böhlau, 1970), pp. 138–46. See also Stephen Blum, "The Concept of the 'asheq in Northern Khorasan," *Asian Music,* IV, No. 1 (1972). The material on pages 91–92 is largely based on Stephen Blum's unpublished doctoral thesis, *Musics in Contact, the Cultivation of Oral Repertoires in Meshed, Iran* (Urbana-Champaign: University of Illinois, 1972). The musical culture of contemporary Soviet Central Asia is discussed in Mark Slobin, "Conversations in Tashkent," *Asian Music,* II, No. 2 (1971), 7–13; and in Johanna Spector, "Musical Tradition and Innovation," in *Central Asia, a Century of Russian Rule,* ed. Edward Allworth (New York: Columbia University Press, 1967), pp. 434–84. Comparison of Iran with other Middle Eastern cultures and with India is available in William P. Malm, *Music Cultures of the Pacific, the Near East, and Asia* (Englewood Cliffs, N. J.: Prentice-Hall, 1967), Chapters 3 and 4.

Recordings of Iranian music are *Classical Music of Iran,* ed. Ella Zonis (Folkways FW 8831–32); *Music of Iran, Santour Recital,* 3 discs (Lyrichord LL 165); and *Folk Songs and Dances of Iran* (Folkways FW 8856), which includes examples of popular music as well as folk music. Comparison with other neighboring areas can be made by hearing *Music of the Russian Middle East* (Folkways P 416); *Music for the Classical Oud* (Folkways FW 8761); *Afghanistan* (Anthology AST 4001); and recordings of the UNESCO series, *An Anthology of Asian Music.* Recordings of Umm Kalsum and of Indian virtuosos such as Ali Akbar Khan, Ravi Shankar, and Bismillah Khan are available in large numbers on American LP labels.

The role of music in certain North American Indian cultures is discussed in Alan P. Merriam, *Ethnomusicology of the Flathead* (Chicago: Aldine Press, 1967). Nationalism in European art music, briefly discussed in this chapter, is treated in more detail in Rey M. Longyear, *Nineteenth-Century Romanticism in Music* (Englewood Cliffs, N. J.: Prentice-Hall, 1969), Chapter 8, and in various chapters of Donald Jay Grout, *A History of Western Music* (New York: Norton, 1960). The same trend in the United States is discussed in Gilbert Chase, *America's Music,* 2nd ed. (New York: McGraw-Hill, 1966). Music in aboriginal culture and its role in society is explained by Richard A. Waterman, "Music in Australian Aboriginal Culture—Some Sociological and Psychological Implications," *Music Therapy* (1955), 40–49.

4

The Western Impact on World Music: Africa and the American Indians

BRUNO NETTL

If we view the history of *world* music in the last two or three centuries, there seem to be two events of such magnitude that they must be considered the dominant causes of change. One is the spreading of Western musical styles, musical thought, and musical technology throughout the world, including the isolated parts of the West as well as almost all non-European cultures. The other is the diffusion of musical styles from sub-Saharan Africa to many parts of the world, but especially to Europe and, even more important, to the Americas. These two events have had such an influence on the current state of affairs in world music that they even over-shadow such obviously prominent events as the changing from tonal, eighteenth-century-derived harmony to atonal, largely dissonant sounds in the art music of Europe and the Americas; and the rise of a mass-media-oriented group of popular music styles that have come to dominate the urban-industrial culture of the West.

The interaction of these two major events can be studied in microcosm in the meeting of Western and African musics in Africa and in all parts of the New World. In our musical experience, we have become acquainted with some of the ways in which African and African-derived music has had an impact on various musics in Western society—jazz, blues, gospel, soul;

but it should come as no surprise that Western music and musical culture have also had a great impact on the music of Africa. The role of Western musical styles and thought in contemporary American Indian culture is in some ways similar to but in other ways quite different from the African experience.

Traditional Music in Africa

What was African music like before this Western influence occurred? We can still find a great deal of that music that has been little influenced. Indeed, there are few areas of the world that have managed to preserve their old, pre-modern heritage as well as Africa has. In nations such as Iran, Japan, and the Arabic countries we can still find the old traditions, but they are in a sense hanging on, sometimes only by the thread of a few musicians or as a result of the official action of universities or ministries of culture. In a few places—India and Indonesia, for example—the old tradition remains strong, but it has moved over and made room for a Western tradition to live alongside it. African music has maintained greater integrity, but we should not assume that it has, even south of the Sahara (an area with a predominantly black population), remained completely uninfluenced by outside sources of musical style, thought, and instruments. For example, we are pretty sure that the East Coast of Africa has at times been influenced by South Sea musical cultures, particularly that of Indonesia; this influence resulted from travelers who found their way to that part of Africa, and who perhaps either stayed and merged with the native population, or left the natives something of their own musical culture and departed. We know that there was contact between ancient Egypt and black Africa because certain musical instruments found in Egypt some two or three thousand years ago are now found south of the Sahara. We also know that Arabic traders have for centuries been selling and buying artifacts along the East Coast of Africa, and sometimes even far inland. And we know that the Muslim religion was carried deep into West Africa long ago, giving parts of that area and even its music a decidedly Middle Eastern flavor. Thus, the idea of an untouched, pristine African heritage that existed until the influx of European culture in the nineteenth and twentieth centuries is really a myth.

The music of sub-Saharan Africa does seem to have developed itself into an exceptionally unified and internally integrated unit, though; this accounts for the fact that despite important differences among them, the musics of the East Coast, the West Coast, the Congo area of Central Africa, and South Africa have a great deal in common. It also accounts for the fact that African music is readily identified as such even by the listener who has very little experience with that music.

What are the characteristics that dominate all black African music? (1) Its structure is based essentially on the repetition, with constant and imaginative variation, of a short bit of music; in other words, like European folksong it is strophic: it consists of stanzas. But each stanza is likely to be sung just a bit differently from the previous one, and the changes are improvised, not planned.

(2) Much of it uses, as its basis, alternation between a leader and a chorus, between two groups, between two individuals, or even among several performers; it is thus said to be antiphonal or responsorial.

(3) It makes much use of instruments, of which there are many different types and forms, the predominant ones being percussive instruments. Drums are very important, as are xylophones. Stringed instruments, when used, are more likely to be plucked, which, physically and aurally, is more percussive than is the case when these instruments are bowed. Bowed fiddles are found, but they are not common; they seem to have been imported fairly recently from the Middle East. Even wind instruments are sometimes played with techniques that produce the closest possible equivalent of a percussive sound; sometimes they appear in ensembles, with each flute or horn playing only one note. Melodies are produced by having each instrument play its own note when it is needed.

(4) Considering the prominence of the percussive sound, it is not surprising that rhythm itself should play a great role in African music. We find evidence of this in the almost constant use of music with complex meters, unvarying adherence to an established tempo or speed, and a tremendous emphasis on dancing; of course, great importance—musical and social—is also placed on drumming.

(5) African music is basically dualistic. That is, at various levels its components can readily be divided into two contrasting but complementary portions. For example, melodies are divided between soloist and chorus; when there is polyphony or part-singing, there are usually two voices or parts. In regard to tonality, tunes usually consist of two parts, one centered on the main tone, or tonic, and the other, on a tone of secondary importance.

(6) Polyphony is important in African music. There seems to be a great desire to have more than one sound produced at a time, and, thus, there is a great deal of choral singing. There is a variety of both instrumental ensembles and ensembles consisting of voices and instruments, and drumming is most frequently done in groups. Even when one instrument is played alone, it may have two simultaneous sound sources: some xylophones have rattling beads attached to them, or perhaps the strings of a zither are played by the main player, while a second player raps rhythmically with his knuckles on the back of the instrument.

(7) African singers produce an open-throated, full, and flexible sound, and their melodies abound with leaps and large intervals.

Though these characteristics apply to black African music on the whole, there are some differences among the musics of the various areas of Africa. East and South Africa seem to have a more advanced melody and polyphony, but their rhythmic development is, correspondingly, less sophisticated. The West Coast, the area from which most Afro-Americans are descended, places less emphasis on melody and far more on rhythm; this is the area in which some of the world's most complex rhythmic structures are created. The Congo area tends to combine characteristics of these two areas, while the Pygmies and Bushmen, peoples of very small stature who may have preceded the Negroid peoples into Central and South Africa, have fairly distinctive styles of their own. The areas most prone to Islamic influence—the East Coast and the northern parts of the West Coast (e.g., Northern Nigeria and Northern Ghana) exhibit some traits of Middle Eastern music; these areas combine the long, drawn-out, ornamented melodies reminiscent of the Middle East with the rhythmic complexity typical of West Africa.

Another point to be noted about African culture is the importance of music. Of course, music is important in every culture, and it is hard to find someone who has done field research in a non-Western society who does not maintain that music is particularly important in the culture he is examining. The importance of music in most or possibly even all societies in sub-Saharan Africa can be documented in various ways. The most obvious argument for this is the fact that a tremendous amount of music exists: in each culture there are many different types and styles, and elaborate attempts are made by members of the culture to categorize these and their uses. There is an important association of music with religion—this is, after all, a worldwide trait of musical culture—and with politics. Among the Venda of South Africa, for example, various levels of chiefs control and may sponsor different kinds of music, and one emblem of a chief's prestige is the type of music whose performance he may command, permit, or prohibit. Elsewhere, music is used to praise men of political power: among the Watutsi of Rwanda and Burundi, the king may appear in public only if he is accompanied by his royal drummers. Furthermore, musical instruments are among the most sophisticated creations of the native technologies.

African Music in the New World

When large numbers of Africans were brought to the Americas as slaves, mainly from West Africa, they brought with them their music, but due to the conditions in which they were forced to live then—the breakup of tribal groups, Christian "missionization," a Westernized environment, the disappearance of African political and social systems, and the stimulus of Western music—their music and musical life changed enormously. The amount and kind of change varied from area to area within the New World. Some segments of the Afro-American population, such as Haiti and Bahia (in Eastern Brazil) have music that seems to have changed very little from its African origins. Others, such as Cuba, Puerto Rico, and Jamaica, have music that is essentially African but has been greatly influenced by Spanish and English folk and popular music. In the United States, rural Afro-American populations in the South have music that is essentially Western, but which retains substantial elements of their African heritage. On the other hand, the urban music of Afro-Americans in the United States exhibits only here and there elements that can be traced directly to Africa; it has more in common with music of the Caribbean—Jamaica and Cuba.

The role of music in Afro-American cultures similarly derives much from the African heritage. In Haiti and Bahia one can still find cults that were built around West African deities—cults with their own music and, in particular, their own special rhythms. Remnants of such cults are found in Cuba, Jamaica, and Puerto Rico, and there is evidence that they also existed in the Southern U.S. more than a century ago. The great prestige that drummers enjoy in West Africa is paralleled in various Afro-American cultures and is, no doubt, the basis for the high regard in which jazz drummers are held, even in white society. As in Africa, music in Afro-America is essential to religion, work, and dance. At least some of the tunes that were brought from Africa are still sung—probably in greatly changed form—in various parts of the Americas.

Of course, it is unnecessary to point out the indirect (and sometimes direct) influence of African music, by way of the Afro-American cultures, on various musics of Western white society—mainly the popular musics, but also folk music and, to a significant extent, the art music of many composers, from George Gershwin to Igor Stravinsky.

Highlife Music in Modern West Africa

Recent developments of African music do not involve a sudden break with its tradition but, rather, a fusion of older African elements with European ones. It is interesting that African music, which was brought to the New World by slaves and was transformed by contact with European music into the various styles of Afro-American music, itself became an important influence in the shaping of the new styles of African music. As Africa became a more urbanized continent, these new styles developed largely in the cities, particularly those cities that provided leadership during the 1950's and '60s in bringing about social, economic, and political change in Africa—

Accra (Ghana), Lagos (Nigeria), Nairobi (Kenya), Dar-es-Salaam (Tanzania), Kinshasa, or Leopoldville (Zaire), and the black ghettoes of the cities in the Republic of South Africa. Thus, when we speak of modern African music, we are speaking to a substantial extent of a kind of popular music disseminated largely through the mass media or performed in the bars and coffeehouses of cities. We are speaking largely of a music that is analogous to the popular musics of the West and of Asia. This music ranges from sounds that are almost typically European to others that are very close to the old tradition, and in some ways this spread parallels the kind of continuum from almost African to almost entirely Western that one finds in the various black musics of the New World.

Perhaps the most widely known modern African music is the highlife music of the West African coast. Its recordings are widely known in Europe and the Americas, and its performers are primarily from Ghana and Nigeria. It is a music that fits almost perfectly into the idiom of Western popular music, but it also has obviously African features. Its instrumentation may consist of Western instruments such as saxophones, trumpets, trombones, flutes, and electric guitars, but there is almost always a rhythmic ensemble consisting of several drums (usually Conga drums), bells, and sometimes rattles, which backs up the melody instruments but which also has solo passages. Sometimes native African instruments such as xylophones, mbiras (thumb-pianos), and flutes are used. And some highlife bands consist entirely of percussion ensemble. Singing may be solo, or executed by two or three singers in close, Western-style harmony. The dualism of African music (such as called-and-response patterns and alternating harmonies), the interest in instrumental color, the short and varied forms of melody are all present, but in vestigial form only—perhaps to the same extent that they are present in jazz. What is typically African about highlife is its rhythmic structure, and this is no doubt because the area of Africa that produced highlife specializes in rhythmic technique.

What makes the rhythms peculiarly African is the fact that several of them are produced simultaneously. They fit together in the sense that their beats coincide in length, but their larger units begin at different times. For

example, one rhythm, ♪ ♪ | ♫♫ | , may be combined with another,

♪ |♪ ♪ |♪ , but while in European music they would coincide thus,

♪| ♩ ♪| ♩ ♪| , in highlife the combination is likely to be as follows:

This kind of combination is rather complex though titillating to the Western listener, but it is actually a rather simple form of the rhythmic polyphony that is produced in the more traditional West African music, of which the following is an example:

(After William K. Amoaku, whose help is gratefully acknowledged.)

In order to produce rhythms that fit more easily into a Western musical scheme, many highlife bands have come to use Latin American rhythms—which themselves originated in West Africa.

The words of highlife songs deal with many things, from the mundane to the lofty. In many cases the lyrics reflect the popular love songs of the West. For example, in one popular number a lover pleads with his loved one to accept him as he is; in another, a young man who is trying to sleep cannot keep from thinking about the girl he is courting; in a third, two lovers affirm their confidence in each other. But many songs deal with other matters, and in so doing they reflect a traditional African rather than a Western-popular orientation to composing the words of songs. In one song, for example, a parent cannot bear the thought of dying because he mistrusts the person who would be the guardian of his children. In another, the singer reflects upon the subject of death and concludes that he hopes to die peacefully in his sleep. Some highlife songs deal with religion—Christianity in particular.

One song announces the "good news about Jesus Christ"; another admonishes the listener to stop feeling sorry for himself, for whatever evil has befallen him must surely fit in with God's plans. Other highlife songs voice a -similar sentiment: the singer explains that he does not envy those who are successful and living well; or the singer tries to cheer up his audience, telling them not to despair or cry because sad things happen in this world as a matter of course. Another song praises mothers. In the last one that we shall touch upon, the poet proudly maintains that he expects no favors from anyone; this appears to be a traditional theme.

In summary, the words of highlife may reflect the lyric styles of Western popular music, but there are also texts that seem to come from the older, tribal traditions, and there are still others that reflect the strains and stresses, but also the innovations, of the period of acculturation to the West. Songs in which the audience is encouraged, songs in which the poet philosophically accepts whatever happens, songs dealing with Christianity are examples of this latter trend.

The words of highlife songs are sung in various West African languages—Twi, Fanti, Ewe, Ga, Efik—and also in English. Highlife bands are stable units of ten to twenty musicians; they take their names from Caribbean and North American models (e.g., The Ramblers, E. T. Mensah and his Tempo's Band, The Comets, The Stargazers of Kumasi, The Black Beats, The Modern King Stars, The Ambassador Springboks), and they exhibit the influence of the big-band style of jazz and Western pop that was so prominent in the '40s. Characteristically, the influence of these styles in West Africa lags a decade or two behind their popularity in the West, a point to be noted by the reader interested in historical processes. The elements of Western culture that eventually take root in developing or colonialized societies seem to be imported, widespread, and popular in these societies only after they have passed their peak in the West.

Of course, when an element of culture—be it a style in clothing, a body of theology, a type of tool, a genre of music, a particular song—is taken from one society and adapted to another, its "popularity" in the new cultural environment may frequently peak later than it did in the culture from which it was taken. In the relationship between the Western industrialized nations and their former or present colonies, this pattern is not unlike a typical pattern in the relationship between city and country, and, in earlier times, between the centers of economic and artistic development—the courts and monasteries—on one hand, and the small towns and villages on the other. For example, certain musical instruments that were once widely used in European art music later became popular in European folk culture. Among these were the hurdy-gurdy (a kind of fiddle whose strings are sounded by the cranking of a rosined wheel instead of by using a fingerboard), which was used in the Middle Ages in the church and by learned musicians, and which later became a folk instrument. Violins with sympathetic strings were used in the sixteenth and seventeenth centuries by classical musicians, and later became widely used as folk instruments in Northern Europe. Dulcimers and psalteries—plucked and hammered instruments with several strings—which seem to have been in vogue in art music during the late Middle Ages, came into their own as folk instruments as recently as the nineteenth century. The "lag" is much shorter in Africa and in other developing nations because today communication is easier and quicker, and culture change has generally become more rapid. Our point, then, is that this pattern in the social and economic relationships between an industrial nation and its actual or virtual colonies is somewhat like that which obtains between city and country in the West, and this relationship is reflected in music as well.

Music in East Africa and South Africa

In East Africa the current musical picture is in some ways like that of West Africa, but there are important differences. As in West Africa, we find bands singing in close harmony, the use of Western band instruments mixed with native instruments, and essentially Western styles of music (but with significant elements of native music) performed alongside traditional music. The differences result from the divergence between the musical traditions of West and East Africa, and from a typical difference between the modern population patterns of the two areas; in East Africa there is now a small but significant group of Arabs, Indians, Pakistanis, and other Asians, most of whom live in the cities and exert a great influence on economic and cultural life.

One result of this influx of Asians is that we find in East Africa a style of music that combines African and Asian (particularly Indian) elements. In this kind of music the melodies are drawn out and ornamented, not sung polyphonically, the orchestral accompaniment has very little or no harmony, and the rhythms, though at times as complex as the native African ones, are not flamboyantly displayed but are presented softly and subtly. We have noted that the kind of interaction between African and Western music in Africa is parallel in the Caribbean. The interaction of African and Indian music in East Africa is paralleled in some of the parts of the Caribbean where African and Indian immigrants live in close proximity, particularly the island of Trinidad.

This mixed Asian-African music accounts for a minority of the East African repertory, however. Most of the Westernized music consists of short tunes backed by rhythms not unlike those of Latin America (but not featured as they are in highlife), with an emphasis on harmony. The basic harmonic patterns (tonic-subdominant-dominant-tonic) are simple, however, and in a significant number of pieces they involve little more than an alternation between a tonic chord and its dominant (a chord based on a note a fifth higher than the tonic). Thus, the harmony is much less sophisticated than that of contemporary popular music in the West. This may be due to the culture lag; but more likely, it is an example of a culture clinging tenaciously to some of its musical essentials.

We have mentioned the dualism of African music; the desire to continue using mainly two alternating harmonies may be a manifestation of the importance of this principle to the African musician and listener. But since the tonic-dominant harmony is clearly more prominent in East than in West Africa, we should look further for a reason; in doing so we are immediately confronted by the fact that an indigenous system of harmony, based on the kind of alternation between two chords that we have described, was built, probably long ago. This system characteristically used two chords or chord patterns separated not by the interval of a fifth, but by that of a second. The analogy of the tonic-dominant alternation in Western music with this native system was obviously not lost on the African musician who wished not only to develop a Westernized music, but also to keep the essential elements of his old tradition alive.

The influence of the modern world has also caused old traditions to flourish and prosper, and to live on without absorbing the sound of Western music. This is the case in the music of the xylophone orchestras of the Chopi and their neighbors, peoples of the Eastern part of the Republic of South Africa. Some time ago (we are not sure when, but it was relatively recently), the Chopi developed the use of large xylophone orchestras consisting of thirty to forty players who performed concert music as well as accompaniments to elaborate dances, and who were led by professional composers, conductors (who played and did not wave a baton), and choreographers. A few decades ago, a great many men from the tribes in that area began to make their living by working in the fabled South Africa diamond and gold mines. For entertainment they performed in their xylophone orchestras, and the combination of the contact among men from various tribes and bands and the existence of various mines in one area led to competitions among the orchestras, which developed and perfected the music and dancing. Thus, there can be Western influence on the cultural context of the music without that influence materially affecting the music itself.

Native instruments such as xylophones, drums, rattles, flutes, and thumb-pianos are sometimes used to perform Western or Westernized music, but the instrument that has perhaps played the widest range of musical styles, from completely Western to thoroughly native, is the valiha (tube zither) of Madagascar. The island of Madagascar (now the Malagasy Republic) is geographically very close to Africa, and its cultures are essentially African; however, there are important differences between the two, which are evidently due to the invasion of Madagascar by Indonesian peoples who brought with them their languages—which are still spoken—and probably many cultural traits. These Indonesians probably stayed, but physically they are no longer in evidence, for the people of Madagascar look like Africans. One of their musical contributions seems to have been the tube zither, a large piece of bamboo with several strings stretched along its sides. Today, tube zithers are found in an enormous variety of sizes, shapes, and numbers of strings.

In the middle of the nineteenth century a king of one of the parts of Madagascar imported Western band music, and since then a large variety of music has been performed on valihas. We hear Madagascar-composed pieces that remind us of the simpler forms of seventeenth- and eighteenth-century Western music, pieces that are like the modern popular music of East Africa, and pieces that are not at all Westernized. One recording sounds like the tune and the tone color of a Swiss music box; another, like a typical South African piece accompanied by the one-stringed musical bow or the thumb-piano. The valiha is an example of an instrument that has adapted itself, in one culture, to a large variety of styles, and in that respect it is analogous to the Western piano and guitar. Such instruments are exceptional: most of the instruments in the world are used to play primarily one style of music; if a culture wishes to change its music drastically, it is likely to import (or develop) new instruments and to forget old ones. Only a few instruments in both the Western and non-Western worlds seem to successfully adapt themselves without substantial change to the requirements of musical style change.

South Africa was first settled by Europeans in the middle of the seventeenth century, and its native population has thus been in contact with European-music for a long time. One therefore finds Western-derived sounds in many kinds of South African traditional music; conversely, the modern music of South African blacks has various kinds of African ingredients. Indeed, it may be difficult to separate Western-derived and African-derived music in some of the societies. For example, according to Blacking, the Venda, a people living in the Transvaal, use traditional music (with some Western ingredients) and Western music (with African ingredients) without drawing a sharp line between them; these two musics are part of one complex system in which a large number of musical types accompany a great diversity of activities, social groups, age groups, and political subdivisions. This kind of integration is probably due to the relatively equal complexity of both the old Venda music and the Western music with which the Venda came into contact. True, because of the advanced technology and notation system of the West, much Western music is more complex than native African music; but this was not true of the Western music with which the Venda came (or at least first came) into contact, which was largely folk, popular, and especially church music.

The range of new developments in the African music that in some way uses techniques of traditional music is very great—probably greater than is the case in the black cultures of the New World. Church music is one of the focal points of such developments, for the influence of Christianity in various parts of Africa has been very great indeed. Perhaps the best known example is the *Missa Luba,* a Catholic mass based on tunes of the Baluba of the Congo, which incorporates native choral techniques but retains intact the Latin text of the Catholic mass. Some native black Christian clergymen are known to have composed and notated music that was oriented to Western musical principles in the early nineteenth century in South Africa; this music exhibited a combination of African traits, such as actual tunes from the villages, and Western harmony—but harmony of a sort not completely strange to the African concepts of harmony, with its alternation of tonic and dominant. As African native churches began to separate from those of the white missionaries and take on an independent existence, special styles of music were developed. One source for these was the American Negro spiritual which became an inspiration for Africans early in the twentieth century. The large number of combinations of Western and African elements in South African music (Western hymn tunes sung with African chordal techniques and instruments, native tunes harmonized in the Western hymn style, etc.) makes it clear that the two kinds of music must have been very compatible in many ways. This kind of combination of styles simply did not occur in Asia or among the North American Indians, even though these areas of the world have had to absorb just as many Western musical influences—their technique of absorption had to be different.

New forms of music were created in many other genres as well: freedom songs; music for entertainment in villages, which used Western instruments such as the guitar; folk operas (plays with songs); a special type of jazz called "Congo jazz"; special styles of guitar playing derived from techniques of playing native instruments (such as the style developed by Mwenda Jean Bosco around 1950); military music; and, of course, the songs of Miriam Makeba. Clearly, then, the decades since World War II have seen important developments in Africa, developments that prove the African traditions to be viable and flexible, and by no means in danger of imminent extinction.

This has happened because African cultures were able to maintain—even during the long period of colonization—a high degree of independence. This has been so because African musicians have come into contact with a wide range of Western music but have not talked themselves into believing that all things Western are automatically superior, and because African and Western music are by their nature compatible; that is, important elements of each are structurally capable of being accommodated by the other. This compatibility is probably one of the reasons for the considerable analogy in the developments of African and New World Negro musics. But another reason is the contact–first direct though sporadic, and later constant, through the mass media—that black Africans have maintained with Afro-American societies in North and South America and in the Caribbean.

Music in North American Indian Culture

Let us now look at the situation that developed among some North American Indian cultures, for here we have conditions that are in some ways parallel to those of Africa, but in other ways are clearly different. The North American Indians have been in intensive contact with Western culture as long as Africans have; indeed, there was more pressure on them to either adopt white ways or face cultural and even physical extinction. Like the Africans, the Indians have had to cope with the problem of what to do in their musical lives while the material aspects of their culture were modernized and Westernized. But in contrast with the Africans, the Indians were inundated by whites and rapidly became a minority who could not, as did the Africans, hope for the eventual restoration of their independence. The best that they could expect—after the last vestiges of military resistance were wiped out in the 1880s—was their assimilation into Western culture, with at best the symbolic retention of a few economically unimportant traits. Their tribal groups were much smaller than those of Africa, and white missionaries did not respect their culture as seriously, in attempting to adapt them to Christian ways. The white man in Africa wished to enslave and colonize the natives, and had to use elements of the native tradition to help him. The North American colonists, however, wanted to remove the Indians, either by pushing them into small pockets of land, or by genocide—actual or cultural.

Musically, the difference between Africans and Indians is also considerable. Indian music is less complex in at least most respects, and its styles are much less compatible with Western music and, thus, less easily understood and appreciated by Western musicians. Accordingly, the Indians were hard put to find ways of incorporating Western music into their musical systems.

We know a good deal about the way in which Indian music sounded and functioned before the coming of the white man. In North America it was almost exclusively melodic, and included very little instrumental music other than the accompaniment of drums and rattles. Certain structural principles (for example, the tendency to build songs in two sections, the second of which was in someway a variation of the first) were very widespread, but several styles of music existed, each more or less confined to a geographic area. The music of the sedentary and agricultural Pueblo Indians of the Southwest differed from that of the nomadic, buffalo-hunting Indians of the Plains; from that of the Northwest Coast Indians, who fished for a living and built elaborate totem poles; from that of the California Indians, who had innumerable, tiny tribal groups and lived from small game, berries, and acorns. Despite this variety, it is not difficult to identify an Indian song as Indian by its sound, no matter where it comes from. The music of Mexico and Central and South America was in some ways similar to that of the North American Indians, but in these areas the music of the cultures that were more highly developed, such as the Aztec, Maya, Chibcha, and Inca cultures, was in some ways much more complex.

Although the Indians regarded music as an important element in a great many activities, it was first and foremost associated with religion. There were usually no professional musicians, but the men (and it was almost always men rather than women) who were most active as singers and who knew the most songs were the "specialists" in religion—shamans, priests, medicine men. On the whole, they did not regard songs as something that man could create; however, they had a variety of beliefs regarding the origin of the songs. For example, some songs were believed to have been with a tribe from its very beginnings; some songs could be learned in dreams or visions, from supernatural guardian spirits; and in the case of the Pima of Arizona, songs existed in the cosmos but had to be "unraveled," that is, materially realized by a person in order to become part of human life. The various tribal groups had radically different attitudes toward music, attitudes usually reflecting the different values of the various cultures. The Indians of the Northern Plains, who led a rather informal life that lacked strictly enforced limitations on behavior, took an informal attitude toward music; they did not regard individual ownership of songs very seriously, traded songs with neighboring tribes, and allowed almost anyone to hear any song. The Pueblo Indians had a much stricter view of life and religion, and kept the important rituals of the tribe secret—and continue to do so today. The Indians of the North Pacific Coast stressed the integrity and sanctity of rituals and punished the singer who made mistakes. Music in all Indian cultures was something of great importance, something without which the tribe and the individual could not live.

What did the invasion of North America by whites do to the Indian musical culture? To some extent, it did the same kinds of things that it did to the rest of Indian life. Many tribes have disappeared, their members killed or dispersed without trace, and their songs have gone with them. In other respects, however, Indian music has flourished much more than did other elements of the old Indian culture; this is so because it has been possible for the Indians to keep their songs even where it has not been practical for them to maintain tribal economies and social life. And for the Indian of today music is, perhaps more than anything else, a symbol of his cultural and tribal identity. Of course, the music itself has been influenced by Western culture—its style has changed somewhat, and the attitudes toward it have changed enormously. Musical thought in the Indian world is not at all what it was two centuries ago; but the music is still there, playing an important role in the culture, albeit a different one.

The Impoverishment of Indian Musical Culture

It is not surprising that one major effect of the European invasion on Indian musical culture was destructive. For example, it may have inhibited the development of a kind of native polyphony in Indian music. From the late nineteenth and early twentieth centuries, we have reports by travelers, missionaries, and the like of Indians singing in parts. These reports indicate that the part-singing was sporadic, that it was not really accepted by the tribes, but that individuals who had discovered its principles seemed to be trying to adopt them to use in their own tribes. For example, in one case we hear that visitors to a tribe could join in the performance of songs that they did not know by singing a single, long note, that is, a drone—which they called the "metal tone." In other cases we hear of the singing of rounds. No doubt, in all cultures that have polyphonic singing, the principles of polyphony were first discovered by chance: two people tried to sing the same song, but did so at different pitch levels, or started at different times, or sang two different versions of the same tune; or one of the singers could produce only a monotone. A crucial point occurs when someone regards such a coincidence as a creative act, not just a mistake. A second one is when the polyphonic singing is accepted by the community as real music. Evidently, some North American Indian tribes were on the verge of accepting polyphony, and various individual groups had begun to experiment with it. But then came the white Europeans, and in all probability this inhibited its further development. Thus, contact with Western culture did not obliterate Indian music itself, but as far as we can tell, it obstructed certain internal developments that would have taken place.

Western influence had a much more obviously negative effect in its changing of the native attitudes toward music. Take, for example, the importance of music in Indian religion. Indian ceremonies consisted largely of singing, dancing, ceremonial eating and smoking, and gestures; but music was perhaps the most prominent among these. Gradually, Indians were "missionized" and baptized in Catholic and Protestant faiths, and although they retained their old musical styles, their music changed from being an integral part of religion to serving as a memory of the past and as entertainment for both Indians and whites. As a result, a great deal of the repertory was lost.

Among the Blackfoot Indians of Montana and Southern Alberta, the most important religious ceremonies involved medicine bundles, large pieces of folded cloth that were filled with sacred artifacts such as animal and bird skins, bones, sticks, rattles, rawhide objects, and pipes. One of these types of medicine bundle, the beaver bundle, contained as many as two hundred objects, and its owner, a powerful medicine man, had to "open" it at appropriate times, that is, take out the objects one by one and sing for each its particular song. In the nineteenth century there would be at any one time several beaver medicine men in the tribe, and each would know all of the songs going with his bundle. By 1910 there was probably no one who knew the entire beaver ritual, and today there is hardly anyone who knows even a tiny part of it. Now, when Indians perform the rituals for memorial reasons, they must pool their knowledge and use many performers instead of the one or two originally needed; the bundle rituals are therefore no longer private but public events. Thus, the religious songs, once so important in Indian society, have been to a large extent forgotten. At the same time, Indian music flourishes, but it does so largely through the songs of social dances, which at one time were much less prominent. The point is that in the songs of the medicine bundles there was much more musical variety than in the social dance songs, which are greatly standardized. In this way, among others, the repertories of the Indians have become impoverished.

The same kind of impoverishment is found in the words of Indian songs. Let us again use the Blackfeet of the Northern Plains as an example. Words seem to have been important in the religious songs, for in them man would speak to the supernatural; or on the other hand, the guardian spirits from whom men learned the songs in dreams would speak to him. But evidently, there were also many songs in which words were not important, or which were sung entirely with meaningless syllables; prominent among these were the social dance songs. Some had no words at all, fulfilling a role somewhat like that of instrumental music, others had words that could be changed. Some of them were sung by a war party after it returned from its forays; the men would sing old songs, improvising new words that told of their deeds of bravery. The words were brief, and took up only part of the song, which was otherwise filled with meaningless syllables. These words were gradually forgotten, especially as members of the tribe began less and less to use the Blackfoot language (though most adults still know and speak it along with English). At the same time, as the Blackfeet began to have more contact with other tribes by visiting their reservations, and as they began increasingly to intermarry with other Indians, it became necessary to make songs intelligible on an intertribal basis. As a result, words began to play less of a role in singing, and most songs are now sung with no words and only meaningless syllables as text.

Since the common language of all Plains Indians was (and is) English, English words began occasionally to be used. And because the whites looked upon Indian music as something either barbaric or laughable, Indians also began to have less respect for their music and fitted their songs with funny, undignified words such as these, which are known on many reservations throughout the Plains: "If you wait for me, after the dance is over, I will take you home, in my one-eyed Ford"; or "I don't care if you're married sixteen times, I will get you." These songs, interesting in themselves, bear little resemblance to the dignified and imaginative poetry that is found in older Indian songs and that can be read in collections made at the turn of the twentieth century.

Positive Development in Modern Indian Music

We see, then, that the effect of the white man's ways on Indian music is to a large extent impoverishment of musical style, of words, and of the uses of music.

But there is another side to the picture. Music became, as we have said, a special, cherished symbol to the Indian of his Indian-ness. And the great development of Western music, with its theory, its notation, its emphasis on technical proficiency, has had a positive effect on this particular use of music. Take, for example, the question of musical professionalism. In the old times Indian singers were probably not judged mainly by the excellence of their voices or their ability to sing and drum together, but by the power that their songs had to bend the will of nature and to influence the spirits. Since Indian music today is to a much larger extent entertainment, and since Indians are very much aware of the white man's musical ways, it has become much more customary to judge singers with the same criteria that Westerners use to judge musicians.

On the Blackfoot reservation, as a result, there has sprung up a class of singers—about fifty in a population of about five thousand—who are considered experts at singing social dance songs. They do not make their living from singing, but are accorded respect and are paid for performing. They know many songs and make up new ones, but they are respected primarily because their singing sounds good, because they can learn songs quickly, and because they can keep a steady beat in the drumming. They usually sing in groups, and at a large powwow, when several groups sing alternately, there is considerable competition among them. This contrasts with earlier times, when singing was much more typically solo, and singing in groups was much less formalized. The singers are also the composers, and even though it is difficult to observe clearly the processes they use in making up songs (especially because of the absence of music theory and notation), it is clear that the Blackfeet today accept the notion that people compose, that songs are not brought to man in dreams. (Even so, the Blackfeet song-makers do occasionally resort to the dream explanation.) Furthermore, there has crept into Indian music a certain amount of technical terminology that singers use in talking about their songs.

The songs that are composed have, of course, very little that is new in them. Novelty is not a value in Blackfoot music, and a composer is not praised for bringing about something startling that has never been heard before; his audience and his ideology prefer something that fits into the existing musical system. What apparently happens is that certain stock formulas that appear in songs are reused and recombined, so that old materials are actually used to make up new songs. In this way songs can be made up very quickly, and can also be taught rapidly. A Blackfoot singer says that he can learn a song after one hearing; considering the fact that he is probably already familiar with the materials in the song, from having heard it in other contexts, this seems to be a credible statement. What is perhaps most notable about the modern Blackfoot singer is his relationship with the audience: he is definitely an entertainer who performs *for* his listeners and is applauded by them.

The Blackfoot singers also maintain an interest in Western music. Some of them play in country and western bands, others in military bands, and some sing in church choirs. On the Blackfoot reservations in Montana and Alberta, there is a flourishing musical life in the Western style of music, but it is almost completely segregated from the Indian style. An Indian musician may participate in both kinds of music, but he will keep them separate in his life, and he will not try to present both at the same musical event or performance. And, of course, this segregation continues into the music itself. The Indian has done very little toward creating music that utilizes both Indian and Western elements, even though his approach to music—to perform professionally for an audience, to use music mainly as entertainment—is Westernized.

Actually, some elements of Western music have crept into traditional Indian music. There is some evidence that the intonation of Indian music has moved toward its Western counterpart. It is perhaps necessary to point out here that the systems of pitches used in the various musics of the world, and the intervals between notes, are not alike. No system is any more "natural" than any other, nor are some systems inherently superior to others. But this difference in the scale structure of melodies accounts for the fact that some non-Western music may sound out of tune to the Western listener (and some Western music, no doubt, sounds out of tune to a non-Westerner). Of course, none of these musics is really out of tune; it is simply based on a different system of pitches. The various American Indian systems are different from Western ones, though not extremely so—as are Indonesian or Arabic systems. Indian intervals diverge slightly from Western standards, but, more important, there appears to be somewhat more flexibility in the intonation of individual intervals. For not only are the tone systems of the world different in the sense that they use different intervals; they also vary in the degree to which an interval or a note must be performed accurately in order to be considered "in tune." In the classical music of India, much greater accuracy is expected than in Western music; but most North American Indian tribes appear to have been less insistent in this regard. This does not mean that they do not hear well but, rather, that their conceptualization of music is different. In the most recent recordings of Indian music, however, there appears to be a gradual changing of the Indian intervals toward their closest Western equivalents. The character of the songs is not very much affected, for the kind of interval change noted above fits into the flexible Indian scheme of handling intonation anyway. A result of this Westernization of Indian intervals is that one occasionally hears Indian songs—particularly Peyote songs—accompanied by Western instruments such as guitar and piano; but this is rare.

There are other ways in which Indian music has come to sound like Western music. One is singing style. Chapter 3 included a fairly detailed discussion of this musical phenomenon, which consists mainly of the way the voice is used and the kinds of sound produced by the singer. This is one of the ways in which the musics of the world differ most obviously and consistently. A musical culture may change its songs, scales, and rhythms, but it will tend to keep its singing style unchanged even over many centuries; it appears to be the musical element most resistant to change. Nevertheless, sometimes it does change, and this has happened to Indian music instances. We find that some Indian singers have begun to sing Indian songs in a Western style of singing—a style derived from popular white music of the 1940s and from hymn singing, a style that is perhaps intended to show that the music sung in this manner can be accommodated to Western musical principles. But this does not happen very often. In dancing, Western influence has been very great; Indians have added to their group of social dances several dances performed by couples, rather than by soloists or in lines or circles.

Thus, one positive effect of Western culture on Indian music was to orient Indian musical thought and, to a smaller extent, its musical style toward Western principles. Let us now look at some other developments in Indian musical culture that are positive, that came about as a result of contact with the whites but did not directly incorporate elements from the white culture.

One of these developments was the creation by the Indians of new religions that were intended to cope, somehow, with the problems they faced in the nineteenth century. The first was the Ghost Dance, with which the Indians hoped, by supernatural means, to drive out the whites and restore the decimated buffalo herds. It began in the Great Basin of California and Nevada and spread rapidly, especially in the Plains. It was outlawed in 1890, but it brought with it, wherever it went, songs in the style of the Great Basin Indians, and some of these continued to be sung long after that time. The second of these religions was the Peyote cult, which began in Mexico, was known to Indians in the Southwest by the early eighteenth century, and spread gradually at first and then very rapidly in the late nineteenth and early twentieth centuries. Its role was to effect reconciliation with the whites, and in places it took on elements of Christianity. It also made use of a special song style, probably derived from the music of the Southwestern Apache. It is still very much alive today, its songs constituting perhaps the largest body of songs in Indian society.

The effect of these new religions was to add to the musical repertory and the number of styles in each tribe. The Plains Indians, for example, no longer had music solely in their own, old musical style, but songs in the Ghost Dance and Peyote styles as well; in this way white culture caused, albeit indirectly, a considerable enrichment of the music of at least some of the Indian tribes.

The widespread and rapid diffusion of the Ghost Dance and Peyote religions was possible because of the ways in which Indian tribes were thrown into increased contact with each other. They were repeatedly forced to move, they were split up and recombined in inter-tribal groups, and they were made to live in joint reservations. Communication improved, and Indians began to use trains and trucks instead of horses.

This tendency to break down tribal barriers combined with a growing feeling by Indians that they were not members of a tribe within a larger Indian context; rather, this context had grown so small in comparison with the vast white world that one would have to consider oneself an Indian within an essentially white context. The orientation changed from tribal identity to Indian identity. This also has had musical ramifications, the most important of which is the tendency of the musical style of the Plains Indians, such as the Dakota, Crow, Arapaho, Blackfoot, and Kiowa, to be spread to tribes whose original styles were different. We see, thus, the development of a "pan-Indian" musical style, which is dominated by characteristics of the music of the Plains Indians: sharply descending melodic curves, a strong and stirring singing style, and a harsh, high, and pulsating sound. Of course, not all tribes have participated in this pan-Indian movement; many keep their own repertories while adding pan-Indian songs. Moreover, in the last few years—from the late 1960's on—a return to the ideals of tribal identity can be perceived.

One place for the exchange of musical material among Indians is the large intertribal powwow, an occasion that is at once social event and secular ceremony affirming the Indians' identity. Typical powwows are the festivals at Gallup and Anadarko in the Southwest, and Crow Fair and North American Indian Days in Montana. Powwows take place in the summer, usually around the Fourth of July, and are in some Plains cultures the modern counterpart of the Sun Dance, the most important older religious ceremony of the Plains. On that occasion all bands of the tribe, which had lived apart from one another in the winter, joined together for elaborate social events, dancing, and athletic contests, but primarily for a ceremony several days long, which was important for the welfare of the tribe and also for individuals who were seeking visions of guardian spirits. In some tribes the Sun Dance is still held, but in others its social aspects have been absorbed by the powwow. Powwows are tribal events, but there are, typically, visitors from other tribes on nearby reservations, and there are also white spectators and a number of whites who join in the dancing. (Interestingly, many of the white "hobbyists" are girls, but they usually wear men's costumes and dance in the men's rather than the women's style.) The Plains Indians regard the powwow as a way of affirming their "Indianness," but also as a way of expressing friendship with other tribes and with the white community.

In many large cities in the United States there are sizable American

Indian communities resulting both from the migration of Indians to industrial jobs and from the "termination policy" of the Eisenhower administration, which hoped to end the segregation of Indians by abolishing reservations. In some of these cities American Indian clubs or societies have been formed, whose aim is both political and social. Aside from promoting better housing and jobs and fighting discrimination, these organizations sponsor inter-tribal social events that inevitably include music and dancing. The inter-tribal nature of the powwows of the West is found here in a heightened form.

Musical communication among tribes is also fostered by the growth of record companies that produce material primarily for Indian consumption. Most prominent of these is the American Indian Soundchief label, whose outstanding characteristic—in contrast with the records made primarily for white students and researchers—is that its LP discs are usually filled entirely with one kind of song, for example, Cheyenne Peyote songs, or Blackfoot grass dance songs, rather than merely containing a liberal sampling of short excerpts of a large variety of music in a tribal or area repertory.

Musical Colonization in Other Cultures

The American Indian cultures have thus changed from independent nationhood to minority status in a large industrialized society. And interestingly, the function of music in American Indian culture today resembles in various ways the function of folk music in some of the non-English speaking minorities in American cities. These groups have now been largely assimilated into the mainstream of American society. But early in the twentieth century and, indeed, as late as the '50s, American cities were full of enclaves of Hungarian-Americans, Italian-Americans, Polish-Americans, and other ethnic groups who did not speak English well, and who had difficulty being accepted as Americans and in some respects perhaps did not wish to be. Their difficulties were not unlike those of urban Indians—discrimination in housing and jobs, problems of cultural identity. They, too, formed societies to combat some of their material hardships, and they also used music as a way of keeping their national identity. They published songbooks for their children, established choruses, organized social events such as picnics that included music, and in various ways almost artificially kept alive the folk music culture of their homeland. They seemed to feel that music was an important way of maintaining their national identity, a way of keeping their children from forgetting their heritage and descent. By no means did music achieve this goal completely, however. The second generation usually rebelled and took entirely to American ways, but the third and later generations occasionally produced individuals who took a renewed interest in the culture of their ancestors and who very frequently expressed their interest by hearing, learning, and singing the music of the old country.

We see, then, that one of the functions of music in a minority group is to symbolize the group and its heritage, and when the integrity of the group is endangered by assimilation, music can preserve, at least for a time, the national or tribal identity. In this respect the contemporary musical culture of the American Indians is related to that of other minorities in the United States.

We have seen that the effect of Western music and musical thought on two colonized areas—black Africa and Indian North America—has been quite different, though in both cases the effect was both destructive and constructive. Let us look very briefly at a few other cultures in which a similar social and political process took place.

Latin America presents a much more complex case. In various parts of it—for example, Mexico and Peru—the population is essentially a mixture of Indian and Spanish, and there is no attempt to segregate the Indians; elsewhere, as in Brazil, the Indian element is weaker, though not absent, but there is a large Afro-American ingredient combined with a Portuguese population. In all cases the mixture is racial as well as cultural. What has resulted is a group of mixed styles of folk and popular music, which are, in Peru and Mexico, essentially Spanish but with some American Indian elements. The latter are not prominent, but they do play a role in the mixed styles that represent a situation quite different from the musical and social segregation that exists in the music cultures of the United States and Canada. In Brazil the material is a combination of Portuguese and West African elements, with some Indian ingredients. In general, however, Latin America exhibits many more combinations of musical styles than does North America; this is no doubt due to the fact that political domination of Indians and blacks by Europeans took different forms in the two areas. In neither were the political and military events something that Western civilization should boast about. But in Latin America there has been a much greater willingness to absorb the non-European populations racially and socially, and to develop cultural forms that include ingredients from a variety of sources.

In the history of European art music we also find examples of events that resulted from political domination of one group by another. For example, during the late eighth and early ninth centuries, the Emperor Charlemagne, who conquered and ruled over a large portion of the center of Europe—including most of Germany, France, and Italy—was eager to unify and integrate his empire. The unification of church practices was an important aspect of this process, and Charlemagne imported from Rome the forms and repertory of the Gregorian chants (the liturgical music of the Catholic church) used there. At that time various ritual forms and chant repertories were used in Europe, but Charlemagne adopted for his own court the forms from Rome and then proceeded to establish them in other areas that he conquered and ruled. Thus, the Roman form of the liturgy became dominant in Europe, something that was to affect the history of music in Europe very deeply.

Another Holy Roman Emperor, Charles V, who ruled Central Europe and the Low Countries from 1519 to 1558, inherited the throne of Spain as well. The combination of the Low Countries (which in the early sixteenth century were an enormously important center of musical development) and Spain in one political unit caused musical influence to move from Holland, Belgium, and Northeastern France to Spain. Spanish composers began to compose in a style akin to that of the Franco-Flemish composers. In the late eighteenth and the nineteenth centuries the Austrian influence on lands surrounding it, such as Bohemia (now the Western part of Czechoslovakia) and Hungary, had important musical results. Thus, although the differences in musical style are not as dramatic as those between Western and African or Western and American Indian music, processes not unlike those observed in modern Africa and North America can be observed throughout history.

In the twentieth century there are further examples. The role of Western influence in Iran, a nation that has never been a Western colony but has at times been under strong influence from the West, is discussed in Chapter 3, as is the influence of Soviet ideas about music on the musical culture of Central Asia. An interesting reversal of the usual situation occurred in the relationship between the United States and Western Europe during the twentieth century, particularly after World War II. In this period, the U. S., formerly a colony of Europe, began to dominate Europe economically, and later, politically and militarily. This parallels the constant movement of musical styles from America to Europe, beginning with jazz and ragtime, continuing with rock and soul, and eventually including popular folk music as well. It is interesting, however, that the kinds of music that moved from America to Europe were those associated mainly with the mass media, while a similar current cannot be discerned in the field of art music, in which Europe either maintained hegemony or, at the least, did not succumb to external musical domination.

Further examples could be cited, but perhaps we have done enough to demonstrate the ways in which musical influences follow political ones, and the ways in which colonized or politically dominated peoples react to musical influences, absorb them, ignore them, or use them to create new kinds of musical experience. We have also seen the role that music can play in symbolizing the relationship between two peoples or cultures in conflict, and the ways in which it helps peoples and their cultures to accommodate one another.

BIBLIOGRAPHY

A good introduction to the kinds of change that African culture has undergone is William R. Bascom and Melville J. Herskovits, eds., *Continuity and Change in African Cultures* (Chicago: University of Chicago Press, 1955); this book also contains a lengthy introduction to African music by Alan P. Merriam. Works that deal entirely or partially with modern developments in African music are J. H. Kwabena Nketai, *African Music in Ghana* (Evanston, Ill.: Northwestern University Press, 1963), as well as many other works by the same author; Joseph Kyagambiddwa, *African Music from the Source of the Nile* (New York: Praeger, 1955); and Henry Weman, *African Music and the Church in Africa* (Uppsala: Svenska Institutet för Missionsforskning, 1960); and many articles in the journal, *African Music*. An excellent study of one kind of traditional music is John Blacking's *Venda Children's Songs* (Johannesburg: Witwatersrand University Press, 1967). There is a large number of LP records of traditional and modern African music, of which the best listing—with detailed indexing—is Alan P. Merriam, *African Music on LP* (Evanston: Northwestern University Press, 1970).

The relationship of African and Afro-American musics is discussed in several studies in the book of collected essays edited by Norman E. Whitten, Jr. and John F. Szwed, *Afro-American Anthropology* (New York: Free Press, 1970). An older view, which includes discussion of music as well as other elements of culture, is Melville J. Herskovits, *The Myth of the Negro Past* (New York: Harper, 1941). Among the many surveys of Afro-American music in the U. S., and its relationship to Africa, we mention only Harold Courlander, *Negro Folk Music U.S.A.* (New York: Columbia University Press, 1963); and Eileen Southern, *The Music of Black Americans* (New York: Norton, 1971).

Important records of the music of blacks in Latin America are *The Music of Haiti,* ed. Harold Courlander (Folkways P 403, 407, 432); *Cult Music of Trinidad* (Folkways 4478); *Afro-Bahian Religious Songs of Brazil* (Library of Congress AAFS 61–65); *Cult Music of Cuba* (Folkways 4410); and *From the Grass Roots of Jamaica* (Dynamic 3305). Among the extremely numerous recordings of Afro-American music in the United States, we mention two large sets, *Music from the South,* recorded by Frederic Ramsey, Jr. (Folkways FP 650–58); and *Southern Folk Heritage Series,* ed. Alan Lomax, which contains both black and white folk music (Atlantic 1346–52).

A survey of Blackfoot Indian music and musical culture is found in B. Nettl, "Studies in Blackfoot Indian Musical Culture," *Ethnomusicology,* XI–XII (1967–68). Accompanying ethnology and history is found in John C. Ewers, *The Blackfeet* (Norman, Okla.: University of Oklahoma Press, 1958). David P. McAllester, *Peyote Music* (New York: Viking Fund, 1949); James Mooney, *The Ghost-Dance Religion and the Sioux Outbreak of 1890* (Chicago: Phoenix Books, 1965); William K. Powers, "Contemporary Oglala Music and Dance: Pan-Indianism versus Pan-Tetonism," *Ethnomusicology,* XII (1968), 352–72, deal with recent developments in American Indian music. A survey of North American Indian traditional styles is found in Chapter 8 of B. Nettl, *Folk and Traditional Music of the Western Continents,* 2nd ed. (Englewood Cliffs, N. J.: Prentice-Hall, Inc., 1973.) Recordings of of North American Indian music are numerous. Among the best are the many LP discs issued by the Library of Congress. Modern materials are found in the series, *Songs of the Red Man,* issued by the American Indian Soundchief label.

The question of Western influence in non-European cultures, particularly in Asia, is discussed in many essays in William Kay Archer, ed., *The Preservation of Traditional Forms of the Learned Music of the Orient and the Occident* (Urbana, Ill.: University of Illinois Institute of Communications Research, 1964).

5

The Acculturation of
Musical Styles:
Popular Music, U.S.A.

CHARLES HAMM

Frequently, a body of music that has its own identity, is stylistically homogeneous, and enjoys a well-defined place in a culture, undergoes changes. These may occur as developments within that particular body of music, but they may also result from contact with other types of music. The history of music is filled with examples of different types of music coming into contact with one another, or more accurately, of musicians involved with one sort of music becoming aware of others. This chapter will deal with this common process by examining one body of music, defining it culturally and stylistically, then showing what happened to it when the practitioners of it encountered other, quite different types of music.

"For it's only a paper moon,
Shining over a cardboard sea..."

American popular music was a homogeneous body in the '30s, '40s, and early '50s. By "popular music" we mean music that was most popular in measurable terms: most copies of sheet music and recordings sold, most times played on the radio and jukeboxes. The measurement of popularity has been done for some decades by the music industry, and though the results—

published in weekly charts in such publications as *Billboard*—may not be as scientifically accurate as we have been led to believe, they nevertheless give us a good idea of what music the largest number of Americans listened to during a given week.

This music represents a continuation of nineteenth-century popular music, which was disseminated and consumed in the form of sheet music—single pieces of music (usually for voice and piano, but sometimes for piano, guitar, or organ alone) to be played and sung in the home. In the twentieth century the dissemination of popular music became a more complex matter. Songs were still printed as sheet music, but the invention of the phonograph opened up a new and different means of dissemination; it was most radically different in that while it was necessary to have enough musical ability to play or sing in order to use sheet music (or to at least be in the company of someone with these abilities), a phonograph record could be played by anyone who owned or had access to the proper equipment. In other words, it was possible to consume popular music passively, by merely listening, rather than actively, by performing the music.

Phonograph records were first consumed in the home, and with the introduction and growing popularity of the jukebox they were also played in public. Radio created an even wider audience; as inexpensive radios were marketed and bought by millions of Americans, the potential market for popular music expanded enormously. Sound movies opened up still another audience, as did television several decades later. All of these new twentieth-century media involved people in popular music passively, as listeners.

America was, as it has always been, a conglomeration of peoples with vastly different ethnic backgrounds. In terms of influencing the way of life in America, and controlling the various institutions that shape the country, the most important group was white, middle- and upper-class, and at least moderately educated. Popular music, like so many other commodities, was aimed at this group—at their tastes, likes, and dislikes. Members of ethnic minority groups who wanted to be accepted and to succeed in American society deliberately assimilated the tastes, customs, mores, and life style of this group. Eastern European immigrants, blacks, second-generation Italians, Jews, and others deliberately turned their backs on their own heritage, at least in their public life, and embraced the way of life of white, educated, English-speaking Americans. Popular music was aimed at this latter group, and at any other people who wanted to ally themselves with it. This music was most often heard by pre-high-school, high-school, and college-age Americans—on the jukebox at the local hangout, on radio programs aimed at young people, or on phonograph players at home, alone or with friends. But it was also consumed by people both younger and older. The Lucky Strike Hit Parade, which played the top songs each week, was a family event in millions of American homes, listened to by everyone in the family, from elementary-school children to their grandparents. Many of the movies that launched and popularized so much of this music in the '30s and '40s were family movies. At dinner clubs, night clubs, and country-club dances, parents danced to the same music that their high-school and college children did. A song such as "Going My Way" or "Night and Day" would be listened to, known, and whistled by every member of a family.

Nineteenth-century popular music was an instrument for social and political reform. Abolition, prohibition, women's suffrage, anti-war sentiments, political satire, child labor, destruction of the natural environment, and many other causes were fit and frequent topics for song texts. Many famous performers were aware of their potential role as reformers through song. The Hutchinson Family, popular at mid-century, thought of themselves more as social reformers than entertainers; abolition of slavery and prohibition of alcohol were common topics of their songs. Henry Russell's "Woodman, Spare That Tree" was an eloquent and immensely popular plea against the mindless destruction of our natural environment. "All Quiet Along the Potomac," one of the most poignant anti-war songs ever written, was popular during the Civil War in both the North and the South. Such songs as the touching and enduring "Father, Dear Father, Come Home With Me Now," did more to sway sentiment against consumption of alcohol than any politician's or churchman's oratory.

But by the 1930s popular music had become concerned mostly with personal, private matters. Love—romantic, idealized, sentimental, sincere love—was the subject of an overwhelming majority of these songs. Such events as the Great Depression, the take-over of much of Europe by totalitarian governments, the Second World War, the infringements on basic human rights in so many countries after this war, passed by almost completely unnoticed by the men who furnished lyrics for popular music. This music, aimed squarely at what later was to be called Middle America, was planned by those who marketed it to ruffle no feathers, to raise no questions about the way life was going, to remind no one of unpleasant, painful events across the ocean, in the next block, or across the railroad tracks.

Most songs that became hits during this time were introduced in movies, musicals, or revues. Sheet music copies and recordings would appear on the market at about the same time. If a song began selling well, other singers would record it. There was no feeling at this time that a given song was the property of one singer: even a song closely associated with one singer would be performed and recorded by others. Most songs that became best sellers would rise rather rapidly in *Billboard* charts and appear on the Lucky Strike Hit Parade soon after they were first introduced; many would disappear quickly after this initial popularity, but a significant number remained popular for a long time.

Ira and George Gershwin's "Embraceable You," for example, was first sung by Allan Kearns and Ginger Rogers in the musical *Girl Crazy* in 1930; three film versions of the show were made, in 1932, 1943, and 1965; and the song was interpolated into the films *Rhapsody in Blue* in 1945, *Humoresque* in 1946, *An American in Paris* in 1951, and *With a Song in My Heart* in 1952. The singers in these films ranged from Ginger Rogers, Judy Garland, and Gene Kelly to Jane Froman and Harve Presnell, and during these years the song was sung on radio and recorded by almost every popular singer. The lifetime of this song, then, extended over more than thirty years.

Irving Berlin's "Easter Parade" has a similar history. It was a rewritten version of Berlin's "Smile and Show Your Dimple" (1917), and was introduced in 1933 in the revue *As Thousands Cheer*. It was still being used in movies in 1938 (*Alexander's Ragtime Band,* sung by Don Ameche), 1942 (*Holiday Inn,* sung by Bing Crosby), and 1948 (*Easter Parade,* sung by Fred Astaire and Judy Garland), and was still a best-selling record in 1947, in a version by Guy Lombardo and his Royal Canadians.

Cole Porter's "Night and Day," introduced by Fred Astaire and Claire Luce in the musical *Gay Divorcee,* was sung in a film in 1946 by Cary Grant and Alexis Smith. "That Old Black Magic" by Johnny Mercer and Harold Arlen, first heard in the film *Star Spangled Rhythm* (1942), was sung in later films by Bing Crosby (1944), Frank Sinatra (1952), and Marilyn Monroe (1956). Jerome Kern's "Smoke Gets in Your Eyes" was first sung by Tamara in the 1933 musical *Roberta;* twenty years later it was sung by Kathryn Grayson in the film *Lovely To Look At* (1952), and as late as 1958–59 it was a best-selling record, performed by The Platters.

These several examples illustrate the point that the best popular songs of this period could survive for a long time—ten or twenty years, or even more. This suggests that popular music was static in style. That is, the fact that a song could be just as popular in 1950 as it was in 1930 meant that there had been little change in this music; songs five, ten, or even twenty years old did not sound old-fashioned or out of style because this style had remained very much the same.

This brief sketch has defined the place and function of popular music in American society in the second quarter of the twentieth century, and has suggested that an important characteristic of this music was the limited nature of the types of texts used. The music itself was even more limited in style and scope. To a musician, the term "popular music" defined a particular musical style. A performer, composer, or arranger familiar with various kinds of music would understand exactly what was meant if he were asked to play or write something in the style of popular music. That something would be quite different from "serious" or art music, jazz, rock, or folk music.

To speak first in quite general terms, this popular music style was derived from—and was still more or less close to—a general, "common practice" style of eighteenth- and nineteenth-century European music.

—It is tonal music, music that begins and ends on a certain note or tone. A piece in the key of C begins and ends on the note C, or at least some note in the chord of C. The listener hears this, consciously or subconsciously: he hears the various notes and chords revolve around the note C and its chord, and feels that the piece must inevitably return to C in order to end properly.

—It is polyphonic music, music in which two or more notes sound simultaneously to form vertical clusters of notes, called chords.

—More specifically, it is triadic music. The chords—the vertical clusters of notes—are structures in which the notes are a third apart. A given note, A for example, is combined with the third note above it in the musical scale, C, and the third note above that, E, to form a chord, A C E, called a triad.

—It is metrical music. The durations and accents of the various notes making up a piece fall into regular patterns, or meters, of two, three, four, etc.

—Formally, it is sectional, linear, goal-oriented music. A song consists of several segments, sections, or phrases, each usually corresponding to a formal division in the text. It is "linear" because the music is constructed so that one section, one phrase, leads to the next. The sections or phrases have been put together in some logical order, and rearranging this order—or omitting some of the sections or phrases—would disturb the logic of the piece. The reader can perform a simple experiment by singing a familiar song with the sections in a different order. It will sound wrong partly because the song is already known, but also because the phrases do not make as much musical sense this way, even to the 'ear of a person unfamiliar with the song. The music can be called "goal-oriented" because it is constructed to move with a sense of direction, purpose, or goal; that is, the notes of the melody—and often the chords as well—are put together in such a way that the listener feels the music going somewhere, moving forward, nearing a goal. This goal is often a single note, usually near the end, and it is the climax of the piece, the note that feels like the most important note in the piece because it is the highest one, or the longest, or has some striking chord accompanying it. If the reader will run through familiar songs (mentally or aloud), he will find that almost all of them share this progression toward a climax. Once you think of it, it is quite simple to recognize this note, this climax, when it comes. In "The Star Spangled Banner," it comes on "O'er the land of the *free.*" In America, on "From every mountain side, *let* freedom ring" (an awkward word for a climax, but in the original text, "God save the Queen," the word is "God"). In "White Christmas," on "May your days be merry and *bright.*" And so on.

Most Western music in recent centuries—art music, popular music, religious music, dance music, stage music—has been polyphonic, tonal, triadic, metrical, linear, and goal-oriented. The description of the musical style of popular music has thus far been largely a definition of the basic musical style of Western music. If the reader has access to recordings of music from other cultures of the world—Africa or Bali or Japan, for instance—it would be instructive at this point to listen to some of it, in order to hear that many of the general characteristics of Western music described above are not important elements in other musics. But within the general body of Western music, it is possible to define in a much sharper way the musical character of American popular music in the second quarter of this century.

It is a particular type of polyphonic music. With few exceptions, it is music to be sung by a solo voice with accompanying instruments. When performed professionally (on records, in movies, on radio or television or the stage) the singer is usually accompanied by a combination of instruments forming an orchestra. The makeup of this orchestra may vary, but the usual group is the studio or theater orchestra, a scaled-down version of the symphony orchestra of Western European art music of the eighteenth, nineteenth, and twentieth centuries, the orchestra used to perform symphonies, concertos, and other orchestral works, and to accompany opera and ballet. Stringed instruments—violins, violas, cellos, basses—form the core of the orchestra; they are the largest instrumental group and the one that most often plays the important melodic material. A smaller group of woodwinds includes flutes, oboes, clarinets, bassoons, and sometimes other instruments (in the twentieth century, often saxophones). Brass—trumpets, trombones, French horns, sometimes tubas—and percussion instruments are used more sparingly, and there may be a keyboard instrument supplying a rhythmic and harmonic foundation. The symphony orchestra used for much classical music may number eighty or even one hundred players, but the studio orchestra most often used to accompany popular songs is much smaller—anywhere from a dozen to several dozen players—and does not have the variety of instruments for which the symphonic works of the nineteenth and twentieth centuries are scored.

There are exceptions to the use of an accompanying orchestra. In nightclubs, or for home or other nonprofessional performances of this music, the singer may be accompanied by a single chord-playing instrument, usually a piano but sometimes a guitar, accordion, or organ. And for a few years during World War II, the "big band" jazz sound became so popular that most popular music was performed by a combination of brass (trumpets, trombones) and winds (mostly clarinets and various kinds of saxophones), with a more prominent drummer. This is the sound associated with such famous bands as those of Benny Goodman, Jimmy and Tommy Dorsey, and Glenn Miller. However, this sound never completely replaced that of the theater orchestra, and in a few years such singers as Frank Sinatra, Perry Como, Patti Page, and Doris Day were again performing and recording with string-dominated studio orchestras.

The harmonic vocabulary of popular music was consistent during this period, and bore obvious similarities to that of classical music. As explained above, popular music is triadic and tonal, but the chords and harmonic procedures it derived from late nineteenth- and early twentieth-century "art" music gave it a characteristic sound. The basic three-note triad is often expanded to seventh and ninth chords by adding one or two additional thirds, and notes foreign to the triad, usually the second and/or sixth, are frequently added for additional color. Diminished, augmented, and other chromatically altered chords are common, particularly in the songs of such sophisticated composers as George Gershwin, Cole Porter, and Jerome Kern. Harmonic usage has much in common with the music of Wagner, Puccini, Debussy, Ravel, Grieg, and Rachmaninoff; or at the least, individual chords and isolated progressions of chords resemble those of these men. In a more general sense, though, popular music developed its own harmonic traditions and characteristic chords and progressions, similar in some details to art music, jazz, church music, and other contemporary bodies of music, but distinctly different from any of these in other ways.

And while this music is clearly tonal, the frequent chromaticism and the shifting to notes and chords not in the tonic scale or key make for a tonality quite different from that of a church hymn, a Sousa march, or a Verdi aria. The third section of Jerome Kern's "Smoke Gets in Your Eyes" (1933) and the very beginning of "Temptation" (1933, by Arthur Freed and Nacio Herb Brown) are good and famous examples of characteristic harmonic shifts.

The vast majority of these songs are in one meter, 4/4. The very occasional exceptions are songs in triple meter. This was music to be danced to as well as listened to, and the various sorts of social dancing popular at the time depended on music in duple meter. The most common social dance in triple meter is the waltz, which was not popular during this period. An entire generation of Americans grew up without learning this dance, and if a band at a high school or college dance played a song in triple meter, such as "The Anniversary Waltz" (1941), "Tennessee Waltz" (1948), "The Girl That I Marry" (1948), or "The Touch of Your Hand" (1933), most people would either sit out that dance or somehow try to fit one of their steps to it. Waltzes were music from another generation, music for their parents.

With few exceptions, popular songs of this period consist of 32 bars or measures divided into four symmetrical sections. The most common pattern is AABA—an 8-measure phrase, the same phrase repeated, a somewhat different, contrasting section for 8 measures, and finally a return to the first section, perhaps with some alteration near the end. Jerome Kern's "The Last Time I Saw Paris" is a good example of this formal design, as is Kern's "Smoke Gets in Your Eyes," "If I Loved You" by Rodgers and Hammerstein, Kurt Weill's "September Song," Irving Berlin's "Easter Parade," and almost any other song from this period. Sometimes the B section is shortened, and functions as a transition or bridge back to the repeat of the main tune. Now and then a song is cast in an ABAB pattern; "White Christmas" is an example.

There is often an introductory verse of 8, 12, or 16 bars, the text of which sets the mood or situation for the song proper; such an introduction could be omitted in any given performance. Typically, there is only one chorus. Almost all songs move at a moderate or moderately slow tempo: the chorus (32 bars) took about two minutes to sing. By adding an instrumental introduction, playing part of the song again at the end, or having the singer repeat the last 8 bars, perhaps with some minor changes, the time of performance would become three or four minutes, the proper time for one side of a 78 rpm phonograph record.

Melodies are sectional, linear, and goal-oriented. There is usually a principal melody of 8 bars, a repeat of this, a contrasting section of 8 bars of different melodic material, and then a repeat of the first melody. Within each 8-bar section the notes are put together so as to lead the listener *through* the musical phrase. One note leads to the next, one group of notes leads to the next, with the result that the ear hears the progression of notes as logical and linear. The most common melodic device is the sequence, a group of notes repeated one or more times at a different pitch level. The effect of a sequence is one of continuity and forward movement, of easily comprehended logic and motion.

Sequences and other melodic devices move each 8-bar phrase to a melodic climax, a single note that is the logical and obvious high point or goal of the phrase. This climax usually coincides with some important or significant word in the text, serving to give it unusual emphasis by musical underlining. The usual phrase structure AABA can result in three identical climaxes in a song—one in each of the A sections—but often a composer will change one or more of the A sections in order to make one climax, most likely the one in the last section, more intense.

Now that the musical characteristics of popular music have been more precisely defined, it can be seen that art or classical music bears many similarities to popular music. The usual accompanying group for popular songs is a close relative to the symphonic orchestra. Harmonies have their own character but are often derivative of harmonic practices of art music. The basic forms of popular songs are the same as those of simpler pieces of art music, such as dance movements of symphonies and suites, or brief piano pieces. Linear, goal-oriented tunes moving inevitably to melodic climaxes are common in Western art music. A proof of the kinship between popular and classical music is the fact that from time to time certain nineteenth-century classical compositions, fitted with words and trimmed to the proper length, have become popular songs. Their melodic and harmonic style, only slightly altered, fit so well into the style of popular songs that listeners apparently felt no serious discrepancy. Examples are "If You Are But a Dream," adapted from Anton Rubinstein's *Romance,* "The Story of a Starry Night," from Tchaikovsky's Sixth Symphony, "Tonight We Love," from the same composer's First Piano Concerto, and "Till the End of Time," adapted from Chopin's Polonaise in A Flat. "Sleepy Lagoon," a best-selling record by Harry James and his Orchestra in 1940, was based on a theme from a symphonic work written by the English composer Eric Coates, and Duke Ellington's "Ebony Rhapsody," popular in 1934, was derived from Franz Liszt's Second Hungarian Rhapsody.

We have defined the place and function of popular music in American life and described its musical style described; now we shall briefly discuss several songs to further illustrate these points.

Jerome Kern's "Smoke Gets in Your Eyes," (text by Otto Harbach) was written for the musical *Roberta,* which opened in New York in 1933. It was sung on stage by Tamara, and by Irene Dunne and Fred Astaire in the 1935 movie version; it has been sung and recorded by a wide variety of singers, retaining at least some popularity to the present. The text was designed to allow the composer to use the common AABA form.

Each of the four sections lasts the usual 8 bars. The melody in the A section moves through two sequences to a peak on the word "true," then descends via three shorter sequences. The climax in the second A section comes on the word "blind," and in the final section, on "hide." The B section is likewise built on melodic sequence. Tonally, the song is solidly in the key of E flat, with some chromatic alteration for additional harmonic color. The B section shifts to the key of B Major for tonal contrast. The text, as is the case in most such songs, deals with a very personal emotion, in this case a love affair with an unhappy ending. The music is in 4/4 time—and, thus, can be danced to easily—and it moves at a moderate tempo. It is not a song that in any way touches on any of the social, economic, or political problems of 1933; rather, it is designed to help people forget about such matters, at least for a time. It is very much in the tradition of Western art music. In fact, the musical differences between this song and many of the art songs of the previous century are surprisingly small.

"If I Loved You," by Rodgers and Hammerstein, is a virtually identical song, at least in musical style. This song was written for the musical *Carousel,* which was based on the play *Liliom* by Ferenc Molnar and was produced in New York at the Majestic Theatre in April, 1945. It was sung in the original production by John Raitt and Jan Clayton, and became an immediate hit; it remained popular for many years, being recorded by Frank Sinatra among others. It too is a love song.

The music is tonal, triadic, linear, and goal-oriented. The several verses sung for the stage production are always omitted when the song is done apart from the musical, leaving the refrain, or chorus, which is a full-length song in AABA form. Each of the four phrases moves to a goal and climax. In this case the climax of each phrase becomes progressively more pronounced, with the most important one coming on the words "How I loved you" near the end of the fourth phrase. Thus, there is a single, most important climax to the entire song. As sung on the stage and in most recordings, the singer is backed by the usual studio or theater orchestra. Anything else that might be said about the song would merely repeat both the preceding discussion of the general musical style of popular music, and the remarks about "Smoke Gets in Your Eyes." This is not to say that the song lacks originality. Within the general style used by composers of all popular songs, it is a fine and in its own way original piece of music. But the originality comes from working within a strictly defined and limited set of rules or procedures, not in breaking these. Written in a year when one of the most terrible wars in the history of mankind was coming to an end, the song makes no reference whatsoever to this event or any effects of it, but is designed to take people away from such thoughts.

"Stormy Weather" (music by Harold Arlen and words by Ted Koehler) was written for Cab Calloway in 1933. It was sung by Ethel Waters in *Cotton Club Revue* and further popularized by Lena Horne in the film *Stormy Weather* (1943). Despite the fact that it was written for black performers, the music is in no way different from that of the two songs just discussed. The text, as usual, deals with a purely personal emotion, again unhappy love.

The music exhibits the inevitable AABA pattern. The A phrase moves quickly to a peak and then, for the remainder of the phrase, winds down from this, making use of sequences. The true climax of the song comes in the B section on the word "walk." Harmonic, rhythmic, and melodic details closely resemble those in the two previous songs, and in the thousands of similar songs written during this period. It is a fine song, one which retained its popularity for several decades; but one would look in vain for any deviation from the usual musical style of popular song.

It was very much in the nature of this music that the singer was in the foreground of any performance of any song, that the success of a piece depended to some extent on who sang it. Each of the great singers created a public image, different from that of any of the others. Fred Astaire and Ginger Rogers were enormously sophisticated; Kate Smith was a highly moral, religious, and patriotic American; Doris Day was young and innocent; Frank Sinatra, much more worldly and sexy; Lena Horne was classy, exotic, and always exuded an aura of faint and forbidden sensuality.

But it was Bing Crosby who was the greatest popular star of this era, which he dominated almost from the beginning to the very end. His voice was warm and flexible and he was a good enough musician. But his incredible popularity depended on much more than these things. He projected an easy, affable image, on recordings as well as on the stage and screen. He managed to convey the impression that he was singing directly to whatever person was listening to him, on whatever medium. He came across as a kindly, good, warm, commendable, thoroughly American individual, someone who found life easy and happy and invited everyone else to share in that kind of life. He was a symbol of how a virtuous, simple, gentle, quiet, unpretentious person could succeed in this great country. If only everyone could be a Bing Crosby—at least the Bing Crosby projected in his various screen roles, his radio appearances, and all of his public appearances—if only everyone could believe in what he sang in such songs as "White Christmas" and "Going My Way," there would be no more problems in America, for everyone could live in peace and happiness and prosperity. Life would be just like a movie.

This discussion of popular music in the second quarter of the century has centered on one type of song. There were, at times, songs dealing with topics other than romantic love, songs that sometimes incorporated rather different types of music. Novelty songs turned up now and then, songs with nonsense texts (Saxie Dowell's "Three Little Fishes" of 1939) and even nonsense syllables ("Mairzy Doats" of 1943). An occasional children's song rose high in the Pop charts: Johnny Mark's "Rudolph the Red-Nosed Reindeer" sold over 40,000,000 records after it first appeared in 1949. Sometimes an instrumental piece would become popular, especially if it had been previously heard as theme music in a movie: Anton Karas's "Third Man Theme," taken from the movie *The Third Man,* sold well in 1949. During the height of the big band craze in the late '30s and early '40s, instrumental pieces often made the charts. "Woodchopper's Ball" by the Woody Herman Orchestra (1939) and Glenn Miller's version of "Tuxedo Junction" are examples. An occasional foreign song became popular in this country, sometimes bringing with it slightly different musical sounds. A rash of Cuban and South American songs in the '40s (for example, Consuelo Velazquez's "Besame Mucho" of 1943, Nilo Menendez's "Aquellos Ojos Verdes," which became "Green Eyes" in 1942, and "I'll Never Love Again," from the Mexican song "Tata Nacho") brought some different rhythmic patterns to popular music, and even prompted some Americans to learn new dances. But the core and heart of the popular music repertory remained the sentimental song, as defined and described above. Other musical fads came and went, but the entire period was given continuity by this type of music, which endured and flourished from beginning to end, basically untouched by anything else that happened, musically or otherwise.

There was other popular music in America during this time. Various groups with common ethnic and sociological backgrounds had their own music, often quite distinct in character and musical style. These groups were smaller numerically than the group that consumed the "popular music" just discussed, and their activities were less visible because they were much less involved in the institutions of the country. A certain type of music was popular with the Italian immigrants to this country and their families, with Czechs, Lithuanians, Germans, Poles, and dozens of other groups. None of this music had any effect on popular music. There were, however, three distinct and strong bodies of music that were "popular" with millions of Americans and that ultimately came into contact with one another and with popular music. These were country (or country and western) music, folk music, and black music.

"You load sixteen tons and what do you get?
Another day older and deeper in debt. . . ."

Merle Travis

The base of country music was Anglo-Saxon folk music brought over by settlers, immigrants, and "white slaves" from the British Isles in the seventeenth, eighteenth, and nineteenth centuries. These people settled along the East Coast, mostly from Maryland southwards, retained their most distinctive traits in rural and isolated regions, and gradually worked their way to Tennessee, Kentucky, Arkansas, Missouri, Mississippi, and Texas. Their three most characteristic types of music were:

1. Narrative songs—often tragic, dramatic, and sorrowful—dealing with traditional, historical, and sometimes imaginary people and events. These strophic ballads were originally sung by a single unaccompanied voice and were passed down in oral tradition. Neither words nor music were written down.

2. Dance music, jigs, and other fast dances played on the violin—or, more accurately, the fiddle. These too were passed on as an oral tradition, with each performer trying to retain the tune in a clearly recognizable form, yet also trying to vary it according to his own technique and taste so that his version was distinctive.

3. Religious music—"hymns and psalms and spiritual songs"—brought to the South by Yankee singing-school teachers in the late eighteenth century, and there taking on a distinctive character. Melodies similar to or based on tunes from one of the two above categories were sung in three- or four-part harmony in a crude type of polyphony that frequently incorporated non-triadic clusters of notes. Fourths, seconds, and sevenths—intervals not treated as consonant in western European music—were common components of chords.

This was music for social, family, community, and religious gatherings, and it developed quite independently from other American music. It changed somewhat in character with the introduction of new instruments: both ballads and dance tunes came to be accompanied by guitars or various types of harp-like instruments, and the banjo, an instrument borrowed from the blacks, began to be used as both a melodic instrument in dance music and an accompanying instrument for vocal music.

This music became almost completely Southern—rural Southern. It was the music of people who were isolated, traditional, conservative, slow to accept other kinds of music, though in the nineteenth century some of the sentimental ballads of parlor music and such new religious music as revival hymns became part of this musical tradition. These people also listened to the music that blacks were making.

It was music by and for people on some of the bottom rungs of American society. Whether still on the farm or in the coal mines, working for the railroad, or clustered and crowded in cities looking for a way out, they led lives in which death, illness, hunger, oppression, and exploitation were always present. Songs dealt with these matters in simple, direct fashion. Dying children, ill parents, loved ones torn away by death or violence or the necessity of trying to find money in another way in another place, longing for people and places once known—these are some of the subjects this music concerns itself with. There is no dancing cheek to cheek, no putting on a high hat, no white Christmas, no airline tickets to romantic places. There are pillows soaked with tears, hearses followed to the cemetery, cold cold hearts, company stores, train wrecks, and plenty of religious songs.

Though the number of people who performed and listened to this music was in the millions, it was untapped commercially until the '20s, when radio and the recording industry recognized and exploited the talents of such musicians as the Carter Family and Jimmy Rodgers. The WLS (Chicago) "Barn Dance" and the WSM (Nashville) "Grand Ole Opry" were radio programs with millions of listeners, making country music even more popular and accessible and preparing the way for such stars as the Monroe Brothers, the Blue Sky Boys, Gene Autry, Roy Acuff, and Hank Williams.

In the earliest years of the country-music boom, most of it was still based on traditional Anglo-Saxon folk music, but as the commercial potential of this music became more and more apparent and the demand for it increased, the amount of newly-composed material increased. Some of it was based on traditional music, but much of it was newly composed by musicians who were familiar with other musical styles, such as popular music. Much of the music that such a singer as Gene Autry sang, for example, had more to do with popular music than with traditional country music. But country music as a whole still had musical characteristics that made it as distinct a body of music as popular music.

Even an untrained ear can distinguish country music from popular music. To begin with, the basic sound is quite different. Country singers use a thin, high, nasal vocal sound, descended from the vocal style of traditional Anglo-Saxon ballad singing. One or more guitars form the core of the accompanying group and give it its most characteristic sound. There are various types: 6- and 12-string acoustical ones, steel guitars, and in recent years, bass guitars. Ever since Les Paul and Mary Ford first amplified their guitars in the '30s, electric amplification has been part of the country music scene. Violins—or, more properly, fiddles—mandolins, banjos, and string basses may be used. Some combination of from four to eight of these various stringed instruments is the most common and characteristic accompanying or back-up group for this music. Harmonicas are sometimes used, and it is common for at least several of the instrumentalists to also sing at the ends of verses or in refrains.

Many of the songs are narrative, with the same music repeated for each stanza of the text. There is rarely a sense of a melody moving to a single climactic point. A song unfolds as a succession of identical verses, in schematic form AAAA...A; any intensification, sense of progression, or climax comes in the text, not the music. Melodies usually remain firmly in one key. There is little or no use of melodic sequence; it is more common for a phrase to be repeated exactly one or more times, with a resulting static rather than linear effect. To put it another way, the several phrases making up a musical verse seem to follow one another as successive elements, not as elements leading inevitably to one another and eventually to a single focal point of the entire song.

Harmonies are typically simple, often consisting of only three or four of the most common chords in the key of the song. Chromatically altered chords, shifts to other keys, seventh and ninth chords are foreign to the style. In fact, many of the tunes, both instrumental and vocal, are old tunes constructed as unaccompanied melodies (or new tunes similar in style to these) that were not tied to harmonic progressions. Sometimes, clashes occur (to ears attuned to art music) when chords are fitted to melodic turns that cannot be harmonized with these simple chords. The harmonic style in passages for two or more singers is often derived from that of the religious music found in shape-note collections of the nineteenth century, with such intervals as the fourth and the second used as consonances.

There is a wide range of tempi, from very rapid fiddle tunes and songs based on these to slow ballads. Length is often indeterminant; fiddle tunes can be played any number of times, each repetition varied to show one aspect of the player's virtuosity and imagination. The length of a strophic ballad or song depends on the number of strophes, and this in itself may be variable.

By the third and fourth decades of the twentieth century, country music had a following of millions of Americans, and the commercial potential of this music was being tapped by radio and the recording industry.

> "Hey! Mister Tambourine Man play a song for me,
> I'm not sleepy and there is no place I'm going to...."
>
> Bob Dylan

Anglo-Saxon folk music of the rural South was almost completely unknown outside this region until the first half of the twentieth century, when it was discovered by two groups of people.

Early in the century some scholars of folklore, most of them British, began to recognize that various English folk traditions had been preserved in purer form in isolated regions of the United States (the Appalachian mountains, parts of New England) than anywhere in England. Such scholars as Cecil Sharp visited these regions, wrote down the music, and wrote articles and books about it. Robert Winslow Gordon was the first folklorist to make extensive phonograph recordings of this music; his approximately one thousand cylinder recordings formed the nucleus of the Archive of American Folk Song, which, beginning in 1933, was built into an even larger collection at the Library of Congress in Washington under the direction of John and Alan Lomax. More American scholars began to see this body of music as a rich and unique part of one of America's subcultures, and field recordings and transcriptions of ballads proliferated in the '30s, '40s, and '50s.

As more became known about this music, and as collections of it were printed and became available, a few singers began to see that there was some commercial potential in it. Burl Ives, John Jacob Niles, Richard Dyer Bennett, and others began adapting some of these traditional ballads and songs to their own style and personality, and performing them in ways that retained enough of the character of folk music to be attractive and different to ears accustomed to art, popular, and church music. The music was "prettied up": they sang with a vocal style much closer to that used for art and popular music than the nasal, biting, penetrating quality of the voices of genuine mountain singers; they accompanied themselves with acoustical guitars played in a gentle, non-percussive way; their harmonizations of the tunes used much more sophisticated chords than those of country music. They found a modest but enthusiastic and growing audience for their performances, recordings, and sheet-music arrangements of this music, an audience mostly of educated people of various ages who found popular music of the time too trite and unintellectual, who found country music too common and too closely tied to a people and a way of life with which they had nothing in common, and who wanted an alternative to classical music.

Ives, Niles, Bennett, and others sang traditional songs—discovered and written down by scholars—in their own arrangements. They had not been born into the tradition from which these songs were taken, but, rather, they learned something about it, assuming some of the external aspects of the culture from which this music grew. Their success prompted more and younger people to "learn" to be folk singers, and it also encouraged some musicians such as Jean Ritchie, who had been born into this tradition, to perform for this same new audience. Songs selected by these folk singers were mostly of personal fortune and misfortune—gentle, lyric, sometimes narrative, often humorous. By the '40s and '50s the number of people listening to this music, buying guitars and trying to sing it themselves, and buying recordings of it was considerable. Arrangements of folk melodies for high school, college, and community choruses further popularized it.

At just this same time, Anglo-Saxon folk music was being put to a quite different use by other people. Many traditional songs and ballads were concerned with the hard lot of people forced to lead lives of poverty, repression, and consequent unhappiness, and in the early twentieth century several "folk" composers wrote new songs dealing with mining and railroad disasters, life in prison, harsh reprisals taken against early labor union leaders and members, and the generally miserable conditions of life among the poor in both rural and urban regions. "Protest" songs by such men as Woodie Guthrie and Leadbelly (Huddie Ledbetter) were usually based on traditional melodies, with topical words added and necessary changes made in the melody to accommodate the new words. The new song was then performed with an up-to-date accompaniment.

In the '30s and '40s a curious alliance came about between these men and a group of intellectual political activists who believed that major changes must be made in American society, that the working class must be actively involved in bringing about these changes, and that contact must be made with the "folk" in terms that they could understand, which included using music they could identify with.

Pete Seeger became a central figure in this movement, as a performer, arranger, composer, political theorist, and impresario. He and other performers first sang for small groups, mostly in the East. As the movement gained support, other musicians allied themselves with it. The Almanac Singers, a group of five or more musicians revolving around Seeger and Guthrie, gained a wider following for their programs of various kinds of folk and traditional music, and issued some recordings. After this group disbanded, some of the members formed another group, The Weavers, who at the height of their popularity in 1949–1952, sold millions of recordings of such songs as "Good Night, Irene." Ironically, this activity did not reach many of the "folk" but, rather, became popular among well-to-do Easterners and college students, who were particularly attracted to the "Hootenannies" (evenings of various sorts of folk and traditional music) that further popularized this music. After 1952 political opposition from Washington stifled the movement for a while, but a new generation of musicians—Bob Dylan, Joan Baez, Phil Ochs, and others—attracted such a wide following in the late '50s and throughout the '60s that some of the older people in the movement became suspicious of their success. Nevertheless, the role they and their music played in strengthening opposition to certain policies of the government, particularly the war in Viet Nam, was of a magnitude probably not even dreamed of by those involved early in the folk music movement.

The music itself was similar in many ways to country music. A typical performance—on a college campus, at a coffee house, for some wealthy urban group—was by a single singer accompanying himself on an acoustic guitar. If there were additional performers, they would play guitars, banjos, fiddles, or harmonicas, in any number and any combination. Singers retained, or imitated, the ancient, nasal, coarse singing style of traditional and country music. Songs were almost always strophic, with simple, diatonic, repetitious melodies. Accompanying chords were simple and triadic, with only a few of the most basic chords in a key being used; sometimes repetitious, drone-like patterns imitated such folk instruments as the dulcimer. Some folk singers performed only traditional pieces (often fitted with new words), and some composed new ones—but always in the style of the older ones.

The folk music movement, then, originated in the same music as country and western music, but differed from it in being more sophisticated, with some traces of art music. It was performed for an urban audience, and many of the people involved in the movement used the music to further their political aims and beliefs.

> *"Woke up this morning when the chickens were crowin' for day,*
> *Looked on the right side of my pillow, my man had gone away...."*
>
> Bessie Smith

The first African slaves were brought to the New World in 1501, after the Spanish found that the Indians would not submit to slavery. The slave trade soon became an important and profitable industry practiced by the Portuguese, French, English, Dutch, Swedes, and many others. Almost all slaves came from the West Coast of Africa, the best ones from the region called the Gold Coast, in the vicinity of what is now Ghana. Several thousand were brought over each year at the beginning of the trade; by 1540 the volume had grown to about ten thousand a year. It has been estimated that nearly a million Africans were brought over by 1600. By the end of the seventeenth century the total was probably near three million, and scholars have conjectured that perhaps fifteen million slaves had been transported across the ocean when the trade was finally ended in the late nineteenth century.

Slaves were brought first to the West Indies, then to the mainland of South America. Africans first came to Brazil in 1538. They were brought to the North American continent by the Spaniards in the sixteenth century, probably as early as 1526. The first slaves in the English colonies were the twenty brought to Jamestown in 1619, and the first American slave ship, the *Desire*, sailed from Massachusetts in 1638.

Slavery spread slowly in the English colonies because there were not many large agricultural ventures at first, and white indentured servants from the British Isles proved better for many types of jobs. But there were some 2000 blacks in New York by the end of the seventeenth century and a like number in Boston in 1715; the total number in the British colonies grew to about 300,000 by the middle of the eighteenth century and some 700,000 by the end of the Revolution. The bill to abolish the slave trade was signed by

President Jefferson in 1807, the year of the abolition law in England, but a contraband trade continued for some decades, and the practice of slavery continued to be quite legal until Lincoln's Emancipation Proclamation. By that time most of the slaves were in the South, almost all of them engaged in agricultural work.

African slaves came from cultures in which music played an extremely important role, and of course they brought their native music with them to America. We have no direct evidence of what this music was like; it was not until after the Civil War that attempts were made to write it down. Before this time we have only descriptions of music among the slaves in diaries, journals, letters, and other written documents, mostly by foreigners and Americans visiting the regions of the country populated by blacks. Many of these descriptions could be applied equally well to traditional African music of today, and many scholars assume that this latter music has changed very little in recent centuries and that we can reconstruct the music brought by slaves to America and practiced here for some generations by studying African music.

The slaves proved to be very adaptable, musically. Even though they retained at least some aspects of their own music, they also became involved in and took for their own use some of the music of their masters. There are early accounts of Negroes learning to play Western European instruments and learning to perform white art and dance music. And just as most of them were soon converted to the religion of their masters, so they quickly adopted the hymns, psalms, and spiritual songs of the Christian faith. Though they took over the tunes and perhaps even the harmonies of this type of Western music, their singing style retained obvious elements of African music.

The most characteristic black music of the nineteenth century was the spiritual, which was, musically, more indebted to European than African music, though it was sung with an indescribable but nevertheless real spirit that set it apart from any music made by Europeans. Deeply ingrained racial and cultural traits resulted in several more characteristically black types of music in the late nineteenth and early twentieth centuries. A quite individual way of playing instrumental music, originally the marches and dances of white culture, inevitably developed into a style now known as jazz, which began to emerge in the first years of the present century. Jazz melodies, form, harmonies, and instruments all came from white music, but jazz was different in certain rhythmic elements and, perhaps most important, in the attitude that each player was a creative musician, shaping his part into something that reflected his own skills and personality.

A certain singing style and a certain type of simple, intense, personal expression that might be called folk poetry grew into a form of vocal music eventually called blues. This type of music can be traced back to spontaneous singing among slaves, probably done while they were engaged in one type of work or another. It was a vehicle for the expression of various sorts of private comments and laments, and by the second or third decade of the twentieth century it had become more or less stylized in form: a first line, this line repeated, then a different line. This AAB pattern was repeated as many times as necessary to the same melody and with the same harmonic pattern until the story or situation was completed or resolved.

Incipient jazz and blues were performed by and for blacks for some decades, but eventually some whites began to recognize the originality and excitement of this music. Jim Europe led an all-black orchestra in a performance at Carnegie Hall in 1914, and the same year saw the first publication of music from this tradition, the "St. Louis Blues" by W. C. Handy. 1918 marked the first time that this music was heard in Europe; Jim Europe organized a jazz concert in Paris, which was received with great enthusiasm. The commercial potential of this music was soon tapped. In 1920 a historic record (Okeh 4113) was pressed, featuring blues singer Mamie Smith doing "That Thing Called Love" and "You Can't Keep a Good Man Down." Success was almost instantaneous. The record sold so well that others soon followed, and other companies rushed to tap this market. The first black recording company was established in 1921, the Pace Phonograph Corporation, later renamed the Black Swan Phonograph Company. *Metronome* magazine reported in January, 1922 that one phonograph company had already made over four million dollars on blues recordings. From 1923 to 1927 Okeh Records released 485 new discs, Paramount Records 557, and Columbia 263, a total of 1,305 by these three companies alone. Jazz bands also began recording at this time, the first record of this sort being one by King Oliver's Creole Jazz Band. The term "race record" was soon coined by the recording industry to cover the various types of black music.

Although this music was listened to by both blacks and whites in the beginning, a gradual polarization took place, and by the '30s and '40s most of the market for race records was among blacks. *Billboard* magazine segregated its charts of race records, radio stations playing this music realized that their listening audience would be primarily black, and there were record stores located in black communities dealing mostly with this music. This is not to say that white listeners did not hear black performers; but a sharp distinction was made and maintained between black and white music. Such musicians as Lena Horne, Ella Fitzgerald, the Ink Spots, and even Louis Armstrong were important practitioners of white popular music. When they performed for white audiences, they did mostly popular music, in a style more or less adopted for this market. But for black audiences they performed quite differently. And there were many talented and famous black musicians who were simply not known to whites, whose music was aimed directly at listeners of their own race, whose performing style was much more in the black tradition.

It is difficult to describe black music because of its variety and because of the black musician's ability and willingness to absorb elements of white music into his own style when this is desirable for commercial reasons. A few general comments can be made, however. In both jazz and blues the most popular instruments are the piano, which is the basic supporting instrument, and the saxophone, trumpet, or clarinet, the melodic lead instruments. Performers, both singers and instrumentalists, invariably ornament, embellish, and otherwise change the basic melodic material they are working with, in order to make it something uniquely their own. Performance is a much more creative thing than is the case in most Western music. The blues structure of AAB with its characteristic underlying harmonic movement is an important formal pattern in a great deal of black music. Strophic forms are common, and the lowering or flatting of several notes in the diatonic scale, the 3rd, 6th, and 7th degrees, give black music a quite characteristic sound. These elements may well derive from the African heritage of the musicians who play this music, and sometimes even more obvious elements of African music take over. These include more complex rhythmic patterns than are customary in Western music and melodies consisting of small fragments repeated over and over without development.

These four bodies of music—popular, country, folk, and black or race music—were virtually isolated from one another in the '30s and '40s. People who listened to popular music were not usually interested in country or black music. Composers and performers of country or folk music were rarely involved in popular or black music.

This situation began to change in the early '50s. A primary factor in this was a dramatic change in American living patterns, brought about by World War II. A flood of Southerners, white and black, came to the North seeking lucrative wartime and postwar jobs. Rural Americans moved into large cities in unprecedented numbers during the '40s. The military services were largely segregated, but blacks and whites—both rural and urban, both Southerners and Northerners—were nevertheless thrown together as they had never been before in American history. This same contact occurred in defense plants and large industries during the postwar boom. The GI Bill made it possible for millions of Americans who would otherwise have never considered higher education before to attend colleges and technical schools. All of these factors contributed to a general and unprecedented mix of many ethnic and economic strands.

The changing musical life of the country reflected this same pattern. Radio programs of race music and country-western music became more common and more popular in the large cities of the East, North, and West as the number of both blacks and whites from the South and other rural areas increased. This music was there for anyone to listen to, by choice or by accident. Recordings of this music, and the instruments used to play it, were sold in stores in these cities—stores that also sold recordings and sheet music of popular, classical, and folk music. On a personal level, there was far more potential for the mingling and mixing of Americans from quite different backgrounds—on the job, in the classroom, or elsewhere—and more of a chance to exchange information on any aspect of life, including music. The pattern of a person being born into a socioeconomic-geographic-ethnic group with its own brand of music—which he would accept automatically as *his* music—was still quite possible, but it was also possible for almost anyone to be aware of, involved in, and familiar with other music as well.

The factors in this blending of ethnic and cultural backgrounds were many and complex, but the result, as far as music was concerned, was simple. Bodies of music that had existed in virtual isolation from one another— despite the fact that they were composed and performed in the same country at the same time—now, in the mid-twentieth century, came into contact with one another. Thus, some of the people who listened to, performed, wrote, arranged, bought, and sold popular music came to know some country-western, folk, and black music, and an inevitable process of change began.

A first stage in this process was the assimilation by popular music of some of the musical material of other music; this was done without a change in the basic musical style of popular music. This rather abstract statement can be illustrated by a few specific examples.

—In late 1950 the number one song (for thirteen consecutive weeks), according to *Billboard* charts, was "Goodnight Irene," as done by the Weavers. The song had been written in 1936 by Leadbelly, a black blues singer. The Weavers were a group built around Pete Seeger, long active in the (urban) folk music scene. The original song has many of the characteristics of folk music: strophic structure; a sectionalized, repetitious, linear but not climax-oriented melody; a simple diatonic melodic line, supported by diatonic, triadic harmonies; it was a solo song, accompanied originally by guitar. However, the arrangement of the Weavers' version, by Gordon Jenkins, was for studio orchestra of strings and brass; harmonies were made more sophisticated; the sound was not the nasal sound of mountain folk music or of country-western, but that of more "trained" voices (in the Western European sense). To the casual listener, it was a song in the popular music style. Though the melody and form had much in common with traditional music, the basic sound was such that it would not have been accepted as *his* music by either a folk or a country-western musician.

—The number one song the last week in 1950 and the first eight weeks of 1951 was Patti Page's version of "Tennessee Waltz." This song by Redd Stewart and Pee Wee King had been introduced in 1947 on a radio station in Louisville, Kentucky—a country music station—and had been recorded first by a country group, The Short Brothers. Melodically, it is a country-western song. As recorded by Patti Page, orchestration, harmonization, singing style, and the like were brought in line with popular music style.

—For the last six weeks of 1951, the top song was a version of "Cold, Cold Heart" sung by Tony Bennett, with Percy Faith's orchestra. This was a song by the country musician Hank Williams, who died in 1953. As recorded by him, it had all the characteristics of a country-western song—in sound, vocal style, accompaniment, harmony, etc. As recorded by Tony Bennett, it had all the sound—vocal style, accompanying orchestra, harmonic style—of popular music.

—For seven weeks in late 1955 and early 1956, the number one recording was "Sixteen Tons," sung by Tennessee Ernie Ford. The song was first recorded by its composer, folk-country musician Merle Travis, in 1946; it may have been based on a traditional tune heard by Travis in his childhood in rural Kentucky. His version had all the sound of country music, and would have fallen strangely and harshly on the ears of a popular music audience. Though Tennessee Ernie himself came from the rural South, and in both speaking and singing could retain his native speech mannerisms, he was trained as a classical singer, and the version of "Sixteen Tons" that rose to the top of the popular music charts had the same popular orchestration, arrangement, and reharmonization as the songs above. It has been called a protest song because of its harsh text about the realities of life in a coal mining town. Its strophic, narrative form is in the folk-country style. But just as most ears heard it as a piece of popular music, so most listeners probably understood the text as a quaint bit of regional color.

In the early '50s, then, a number of folk and country songs—and some new songs written in these styles—enjoyed considerable success in the popular music market. They retained some of their stylistic elements and exhibited texts dealing with somewhat more "realistic" matters than was common in popular music. But the originals of these pieces were changed, transformed, rearranged, and prettied up so that the end results sounded to most ears like nothing more than other pieces of popular music.

In July, 1955 "Rock Around the Clock," by Bill Haley and His Comets, hit the top of the *Billboard* charts; it stayed there for eight weeks and became the top song for the entire year. This was not the first record by this group to sell well; "Crazy Man, Crazy" in 1953 and "Dim, Dim The Lights" in 1954 had enjoyed some success, but had not risen as high on the charts and had not had anything like the impact of this song.

The history of rock 'n' roll is discussed in Chapter 6 of this book. The point to be made here is simply that this was a type of music quite different—quite dramatically different—from the popular music before and during this time; the fact that "Rock Around the Clock" became more "popular" this year than any other piece of music was an even more dramatic indication of major changes in popular music than the introduction of popularized elements of folk and country-western music in the preceding several years.

Bill Haley, a white Southerner, was originally a country-western musician. His group, first called the Saddlemen, originally featured a rather routine country-western sound. But like many Southerners at this time he was listening to black music, and the gradual incorporation of elements of this music into his own style led to his playing a leading role in the transformation of the style of popular music.

A few seconds of "Rock Around the Clock" are enough to distinguish it from popular music. Several guitars (one of them electric), a saxophone, and a rhythm section furnish the accompaniment. This group combined instruments used for country-western music—the guitars—and black music—the sax and rhythm section. The singing style is a far cry (no pun intended) from the smooth, crooning, trained vocalization of popular singers. It is harsh—not the nasal sound of country music, but more a shouting style. The harmonic style comes from black music: three basic chords are repeated over and over throughout the piece, and the chord pattern is derived from blues. There are no sophisticated chords, no chromatics, no modulations—just three pounding, persistent, reiterated, basic chords. The vocal phrases are short, and also repeated over and over. There are no extended phrases building to an eventual climax but, rather, the same strophic, melodic patterns over and over, with no real end. The music could go on for an indefinite length of time; the length of the song was obviously dictated by the requirements of the recording industry, not by anything about the music itself. And, perhaps more important, the subject matter was quite different from that of popular music. There is no romantic, sentimentalized love in this music. It is about sex. The verb "to rock" had clear and widely understood sexual connotations in black music. If a white teenager didn't know this, the music itself, with its pounding, pulsing, persistent rhythmic drive, made it clear. Those people who immediately protested against rock 'n' roll, who called it immoral and dirty, who tried to prevent it from being played, who wrote letters and preached about its evils, were of course quite correct: the music did indeed deal openly with a subject that had been taboo in Middle America.

Again, it is not the purpose of this chapter to trace the history of rock 'n' roll. The only purpose here is to point out that beginning in 1955 rock 'n' roll became popular, began to be played and heard more often than any other music, and began to dominate the charts that measured the commercial success of music. Moreover, this music was strikingly different—in basic sound, instrumentation, form, harmony, melody, and intent—from the music that had been most popular until this time.

The infusion of purely black music into popular music was not quite as dramatic and is not as easily traced as the explosion of rock 'n' roll in the mid '50s, but in the end it was an equally important development.

Records by such black artists as The Ink Spots and Lena Horne had often sold well in the '40s and '50s, but they were aimed at the white market; the music was in the style of popular music, and had little in common with the music by black artists that appeared on the rhythm and blues charts.

But in 1953 "Crying in the Chapel" by The Orioles, a black group, sold enough copies to reach the *Billboard* "Hot 100" chart, and was popular enough to be recorded in a new ("cover") version by such popular white singers as J. Valli. "Gee!" by The Crows made the white charts in 1954, and one of the year's top hits—number one for seven weeks in the middle of the year—was the Crew Cuts "Sh-Boom," a cover of a song first done by the black group, The Chords. While these pieces were not yet in the style of rock 'n' roll that was to emerge soon, certain things about them were quite different from white popular music, such as vocal production and melodic and rhythmic patterns more characteristic of black music. The white cover versions were rearranged, reharmonized, and reorchestrated; they had about as much relationship to black music as Tennessee Ernie Ford's "Sixteen Tons" did to country music. But the original music was there, and it was another kind of music.

Black music made the white popular music scene in two different ways; through white artists covering music first done by blacks, and by the increasing popularity in the white market of recordings, by black musicians more oriented to rhythm and blues style. Fats Domino's recording of "Ain't That A Shame" sold well in 1955, but Pat Boone's cover version was the number six song of that year. The Crew Cuts continued to make covers of such black hits as "Earth Angel" and "Story Untold." In 1956 The Platters, a black group, had the number two and number three songs of the year ("The Great Pretender" and "My Prayer"), and Fats Domino's "Blueberry Hill" sold well. "My Prayer" was number one for two weeks, the first record by a black group to reach the top of the weekly charts. Such black rock 'n' rollers as Little Richard and Chuck Berry had hits on both the black and white charts in the '50s, and Harry Belafonte became popular then.

Despite the success of these individuals and groups, the percentage of top-selling records by blacks continued to be low until the early '60s, when a Detroit-based record company, Motown, began issuing a special brand of black music: a combination of gospel music, blues, and some of the milder elements of rock 'n' roll, arranged and performed in a very slick way by such artists as Smoky Robinson and the Miracles, the Marvelettes, and The Four Tops. In 1964 a Motown record ("My Guy," by Mary Wells) was number seven for the year; the following year the Supremes' "Back in My Arms Again" was rated the top seller of the entire year by *Cash Box*. And so it went in succeeding years; such groups as the Supremes and such individuals as James Brown and Aretha Franklin sold equally well among blacks and whites.

These dates and facts serve to document the conclusion already offered, a conclusion obvious to anyone who had any contact with popular music after 1955: the popular music scene had began to change quickly and radically by this time.

These other types of music that became part of the popular music scene came from various American subcultures (blacks, white mountain people, poor white Southerners, the urban poor) in which life was not easy; the attitudes expressed in this music and its texts were foreign to the popular music before this time. The open, joyous sensuality of some black music permeated much early rock 'n' roll. The cynicism toward the institutions and values of Middle America that was found in much black and poor white music carried over into this new popular music. A much wider range of subject matter, including commentary on the injustices perpetrated on the poor, the weak, the outsider, the black, the uneducated, was part of this new music. Some songs still dealt with romantic love. But many of them dealt with sex, loneliness, poverty, religion, prison, old age, drugs, suicide, man's destruction of his environment, and other topics never mentioned in the songs of Cole Porter, Jerome Kern, George Gershwin, and never sung about by Kate Smith, Rudy Vallee, Bing Crosby, and Doris Day.

As young people in the '60s moved into a period of unprecedented involvement in American political and social issues, popular music moved with them. Civil rights, the anti-war movement, a more sane approach to drug enforcement, general resistance to what were thought to be oppressive policies by the government—these all had their songs, their popular songs, their popular musicians who openly allied themselves with these causes. Popular music had, in a very short time, turned away from the voice speaking for the status quo, the voice directing attention away from social and political problems in America. There were Bob Dylans, Janis Joplins, Jim Morrisons, and Joan Baezes, not Bing Crosbys and Fred Astaires and Doris Days. And suddenly, mothers were hoping their children would *not* grow up to be like their popular music idols.

From a body of music created, performed, and consumed by people of various ages, popular music became the music of youth. Performers were in their 20s or even teens. Many wrote their own songs or took over songs written by other young people. Audiences for early rock 'n' roll and other types of popular music became almost one hundred percent young. This music reached a much higher percentage of youth than had earlier popular music, and it cut across economic and social barriers. More young people listened to Elvis Presley and his contemporaries and felt themselves intimately related to this music than had ever felt that way about Bing Crosby, Kate Smith, or even Frank Sinatra.

It was extremely rare for a parent or other adult to listen to this music, least of all in a sympathetic or understanding way. Young people regarded it as "their" music, while older people clung to their own, older music. Not until the mid '60s, with such music as the Beatles' "Sergeant Pepper" album, and that of Bob Dylan, Simon and Garfunkel, and others, did any considerable number of older people listen to this new popular music. Even then, they were mostly either educated people who saw the "artistic" value of this music or musicians and critics who began to treat it seriously—not parents of teenagers and college students.

As for the music itself, the scene changed from one marked by a homogeneous body of songs to one marked by tremendous variety. On any given week, sentimental ballads in the style of the '30s and '40s might share the charts with straight rock 'n' roll songs and others in the traditions of folk, black, and country music. Accompanying groups could range anywhere from the single acoustical guitar of a folk-oriented singer to a full studio orchestra backing a singer like Frank Sinatra or Pat Boone. Texts could range from sentimental love lyrics to quite explicit sexual references or bitter protest statements. Length became quite variable. Although 45-rpm discs were still a mainstay of the record industry, and although jukeboxes and many radio stations used only these (with the resulting limitation on the length of a song), the sale of LP albums equalled and sometimes surpassed that of the 45-rpm singles, and many radio stations—college, underground, and others— were just as willing to play LPs as singles. The range was from thirty-second fragments by the Beatles and others to twenty- or thirty-minute continuous pieces by Steppenwolf and Iron Butterfly; unified song cycles that took up entire sides of albums (Simon and Garfunkel's "Bookends," the second side of the Beatles' "Abbey Road"); and even single unified compositions extending over entire LPs, such as the Beatles' "Sergeant Pepper's Lonely Hearts Club Band."

The year 1966 will serve to demonstrate the great variety of songs that made up this popular music scene. The top songs of this year included "Strangers in the Night" (Frank Sinatra), "Somewhere There's a Someone" (Dean Martin), and "Wish You Were Here, Buddy" (Pat Boone), all very much in the style of popular music of earlier decades. But just as popular were a number of songs by black stars: "You Can't Hurry Love" (The Supremes), "I Got You" (James Brown), "Reach Out, I'll Be There" (The Four Tops), and "Crying Time" (Ray Charles). "Just Like a Woman" (Bob Dylan), "Turn, Turn, Turn" (a Pete Seeger song recorded by the Byrds), and "Sounds of Silence" by Simon and Garfunkel were in the folk tradition; and "The One on the Right Is on the Left" (Johnny Cash) and "I Fought the Law" by the Bobby Fuller Four were by country stars and were very much in the style of true country music.

Each of these songs was so much in the musical tradition of one of the four streams of music mentioned above that it was accepted by listeners who were interested in only one of these types of music. That is, Bob Dylan could have sung "Just Like a Woman" for an activist college audience; "I Got You" was played over stations catering to black audiences; Johnny Cash was perfectly acceptable to country music enthusiasts. It was a remarkable feature of popular music of this time that an audience of many millions of young people was listening to *all* of this music.

But also popular that year were "California Dreamin' " (Mamas and Papas), "Last Train to Clarksville" (Monkees), "Summer in the City" (Lovin' Spoonful), "Yellow Submarine" (Beatles), "Mellow Yellow" (Donovan), and "Good Vibrations" (Beach Boys). These are songs of another sort. They are not clearly in the style of pop music, or black or folk or country music. Some elements of this music are mixed in them, but their overall style was genuinely new.

Thus, the influx of other types of music into the popular music scene—a trend that began in the mid '50s—resulted in a dual situation. On the one hand, many different types of music coexisted; songs of quite different musical styles shared the same popularity charts, were played one after another on the same radio stations and the same jukeboxes, were listened to by the same people. But at the same time, some elements of these different types of music were integrated, which led to a new body of popular music with a homogeneous style of its own.

The songs making up this new body of popular music tend to be somewhat different from one another in style, certainly more so than was the case among songs written in the first half of the century. Yet they share common musical traits, and none of them could be mistaken for a popular song of the pre-World War II period, in either musical style or content. The following brief discussions of several typical and extremely popular songs from this new repertory will attempt to define some of these similarities.

"Mrs. Robinson," written by Paul Simon, was part of the soundtrack of the movie *The Graduate* (1968). Released as a single that same year, it was the number one song for several weeks, and sold over a million copies. Later it was a cut on the album "Bookends," which also sold more than a million. For several years it was a song that almost any young American could sing or whistle—or at least recognize. In other words, it was a very popular song.

The Graduate was a popularization and commercialization of some of the aspects of the "youth rebellion" attracting so much attention at this time. Mrs. Robinson, a central character in the movie, leads the young protagonist into a purely physical, joyless affair, then tries to block his attempts to establish a more healthy, sensible, and permanent relationship and marriage with her daughter. She is the epitome—or caricature—of the frustrated, lonely, alcoholic, desperate Older Generation. The text of the song is a mocking description of the Over Thirty Generation, as seen through the eyes of the young. This is not a song of romantic love, hardly a song to be enjoyed by the entire family, definitely not one designed to support the institutions of American society. It is a song for the young and rebellious.

Musically, it has little in common with earlier popular songs. The accompaniment of acoustical guitars gives it a folk sound, but the rhythm and the character of the bass give it a rock beat. The two voices, often singing in smooth parallel thirds, sound more trained (in a classical sense) and sophisticated than those of country or folk music.

Formally, it is a strophic song. It begins with a chorus; each of the three verses concludes with this chorus, and since the main musical phrase is given twice in each repeat of the chorus, this tune is heard no less than eight times during the song. Thus, the effect is of many repetitions of a musical idea, each exactly the same, rather than a progression through a series of musical phrases, each leading to the next and to a single climactic point in the song. There is no single climax in "Mrs. Robinson," in either the music or the text. Even within the main melody there is no obvious progression to a high point or climax. Thus, the general formal design of the piece is a succession of musical phrases with frequent repetition, rather than a linear, goal-oriented structure with all parts fitted into a single pattern. There are three verses, but there could just as well be four or six.

The key of the song is ambiguous, fluctuating between G Major and E minor. Chords are triadic, but often they occur in successions that do not suggest common tonal progressions. Structurally, the song is clearly more related to folk music than to art music or earlier popular music.

"Eleanor Rigby" (1966), written by John Lennon and Paul McCartney, came just at the midpoint of the Beatles' spectacular popularity. Though it never rose to the top of the charts as a single, it sold over a million copies as part of the album *Revolver,* and it has had a more lasting success than most of the Beatles' songs, being further aided by its inclusion in the movie *Yellow Submarine.* In a reversal of the trend of the early days of rock 'n' roll in which white performers "covered" hits first recorded by blacks, successful recordings of "Eleanor Rigby" were made by Ray Charles (1968) and Aretha Franklin (1969).

It is a strophic song, introduced by a chorus, "Ah look at all the lonely people!" It continues with three musically identical verses that sketch the lives of two of these lonely people: Eleanor Rigby "lives in a dream, waits at the window, wearing the face that she keeps in a jar by the door," while Father McKenzie writes "the words of a sermon that no one will hear." Each stanza ends with a refrain referring back to the opening chorus: "All the lonely people, where do they all come from?"

Except for the chorus, the melody is simple, diatonic, and repetitive, rising to no climaxes, restricted to a narrow range, serving as an almost neutral framework for the recitation of the text. It is not unlike traditional Anglo-Saxon folk tunes; brief melodic ideas are repeated several times within the strophe itself, and the scale used (E minor, but missing the F♯) resembles the "gapped" scales of much traditional music.

There are only two chords in the entire song. The tonic chord of E minor alternates at irregular intervals with a C Major chord. These two chords do not stand in the dominant-tonic relationship so basic to harmonic usage in Western art music and other music related to it. They change and alternate, but there is no sense of tension and release, of one chord having to resolve to the other.

It is sung by a single voice, with all of the Beatles singing only in the opening chorus and in the last refrain. The accompaniment is a string quartet, four solo string instruments playing syncopated chords against the solo voice. The basic sound is not that of earlier popular music. The sound of a string quartet is usually associated with art music, but the form, scale, and melodic design used here resemble the practices of certain types of folk music.

The Doors were a West Coast rock group with a reputation limited mostly to the underground until 1967, when an album and then a hit single, "Light My Fire," brought them spectacular nationwide success. "Light My Fire" was the top song on the *Billboard* charts for three weeks in the summer of that year, and its sales, well over a million, ranked it as the number two song for the entire year.

The Doors were one of the first West Coast groups to become popular in the rest of the country. Their style seemed shocking at the time. Imaginative amplification combined with the sound of an electric organ gave the music a new sound, predominantly electronic. The combination of amplification almost to the threshold of pain and the exaggerated stage deportment of the players made their music almost unbearably exciting, at least to some of their followers. Much was said at the time about the newness of their sound, and with other West Coast groups they brought about a startling change in the rock scene. Amplification, often carried to the point of distorting the natural sounds of instruments beyond recognition, combined with elaborate staging that involved lighting and movement, to became an important feature for many performers and groups in the next several years.

The melody is fragmentary and repetitious. It begins with a brief phrase, "You know that it would be untrue," almost a recitation, using only three notes. Rather than being developed, this phrase is sung three more times, almost exactly the same. With "Come on, baby, light my fire," there is another short melodic fragment, again built on only three notes, in a descending pattern. This phrase is sung twice more, and the first verse is over. The second verse uses exactly the same music. In the third verse the singer suddenly leaps up to a much higher range, singing the same phrases at a different pitch. Thus, the entire song is built on two melodic fragments, each only a bar long, neither one developed or expanded in any way: AAAA BBB AAAA BBB A'A'A'A' B'B'B', and so on. Each of these brief phrases is separated from the others by rests. The melody of the piece, then, is a chain of reiterated, almost monotonous, fragments. There is no hint of the unfolding of a line, no trace of a melodic climax. Coherence comes from the steady, driving pulse of the instruments. And while no one would mistake this piece for black music, the relentless repeat of a short melodic motif is a characteristic of black music, in Africa and elsewhere.

The key of the song is ambiguous. Much of it centers on A, sometimes major and sometimes minor, but it moves also to C and G; there is no strong feeling of dominant-tonic compulsions, and certainly no one would be bothered if it ended on a different chord. Precise pitches are not as important in this music as in traditional Western music, anyway. The guitar, amplified and distorted, often plays notes that the ear does not hear as specific pitches, the organist plays runs and clusters of notes that are often not heard as one chord or another, the singer is hardly concerned with exact pitches. The resulting mix of sound, itself amplified and distorted, is unified much more by the basic beat and repeated rhythmic patterns than by traditional successions of notes and chords.

Kris Kristofferson's career has taken him from a military background (his father was a career officer) to a distinguished academic record at Pomona College and Oxford in England, a four-year stint in Viet Nam, and then to Nashville, where he immersed himself in the country music scene and gradually emerged as a songwriter and performer. Some of his songs have been performed and recorded only by country musicians, others have been successful in the "Top Forty" radio and record market. To date his most successful piece has been "Me and Bobby McGee," written with Fred Foster in 1969. It was recorded by Janis Joplin shortly before her death in the fall of 1970, and was included on her last album, *Pearl,* which reached the top of the *Billboard* LP chart during the week of February 27, 1971, remained the number one album until late April, and continued to sell well for months. As a single, the song was either number one or two for five weeks in March and April.

The song has two rather lengthy strophes, each ending with the chorus "Freedom's just another word for nothin' left to lose. . . ." The melody unfolds as a succession of phrases, each somewhat similar to, but not identical with, the one just before it. It is a simple, diatonic tune, limited in range to an octave, proceeding by the most common and easy intervals, moving rather leisurely from one phrase to the next with little sense of intensification or climax. Janis Joplin's version is backed by guitars, bass, and drums, but Kristofferson often sings it with only a single guitar accompaniment. The song is tonal, squarely in the key of C, using only the three most common chords (C, F, G). Chord changes are infrequent, with some entire phrases sung to a single chord. The melodic and harmonic materials of the song are so simple, so limited, that no discussion of them could possibly explain its success. But successful it has been, among teenagers, college rock fans, and patrons in bars and restaurants catering to country music. Like some of his other songs, like the songs of John Denver and John Prine, it has bridged whatever gap still exists between country and popular music.

Though these four songs are different in many details, they have things in common with each other and with hundreds and thousands of other songs of this time by songwriters such as Carole King, The Band, Melanie, Gordon Lightfoot, Neil Diamond, John Denver, and many others. These are the popular songs of the '60s and early '70s, and they are different in some obvious ways from popular songs of the previous decades:

1. The basic accompaniment is by one or more guitars, often with bass, drums and a keyboard instrument (piano or organ); other instruments may be used, even a small orchestra, but always to support the fundamental guitar sound, not to replace it.
2. Singing styles tend to grow out of or imitate those of country, folk, or black music rather than Western art music.
3. The songs are strophic and narrative.
4. Texts most often deal with matters other than romantic love or other purely personal situations.
5. Melodies tend to repeat simple melodic material, often a number of times, rather than unfolding in a linear, goal-oriented, climax-reaching way.
6. Accompanying harmonies are usually simple, avoiding the complex, chromatic chords of art or other sophisticated music. Chord sequences often do not follow the patterns of traditional Western tonal harmonies.
7. The skills of composition and performance are most often combined; that is, most performers sing songs they have written themselves, and therefore, they identify with them more intensely than if they were singing music written by someone else.

These are simple but profound differences. Teenagers who laugh when they hear the songs that their parents danced to, parents who listen uncomprehendingly and even with disgust to the songs their children play today, are both right. Popular music changed in some fundamental ways in the decade beginning in 1955.

This discussion has shown what happened when a well-defined, homogeneous body of music—American popular music of the second quarter of the twentieth century—came into contact with other types of music—country-western, folk, and black. At first several types of music coexisted, though there were great differences in style among them. Then, various elements of the several different types of music fused into a new type with its own distinct style. Some elements were clearly derived from one or another of the various kinds of music that came together, but in general style and content this new music was distinctly different from any that existed before.

A similar process has taken place time and again in the history of music. For example, American popular music of the early nineteenth century was closely tied to English music. Much of it—songs by such composers as Samuel Arnold, Charles Dibdin, William Shield, and James Hook, for example—was simply imported from England; some of it was written by Englishmen such as Benjamin Carr and Raynor Taylor who came to this country and continued to write the same sort of music here; and some was written by foreign-born musicians such as Alexander Reinagle, whose training and experience had been in England. But around 1815 there began a tremendous influx of music from Italian opera into this scene. Italian opera companies such as the famous Garcia troupe performed with great success in America. Even more popular were performances in English of operas by Rossini, Bellini, and Donizetti. This new, graceful, florid, ravishing music was so pleasing to American ears that it began to invade the popular music scene. Simplified arrangements (of favorite airs and choruses) for voice and piano or piano alone began selling as well as the older English popular songs. For a decade or so these two musical styles, English and Italian, coexisted, equally popular in the American parlor.

Soon, however, some songwriters began combining the simple, strophic style of English music with the characteristic melodic turns of Italian opera. The Englishman Henry Russell, trained as an operatic singer in Italy, became fantastically popular as a singer and songwriter in America. His songs became the most successful commercial items in the history of the publication of sheet music to that point.

Stephen Foster's songs are thought of today as purely American in style, yet he knew Italian opera, English ballads, and the songs of Henry Russell. Certain Foster songs show very clearly, upon analysis or careful listening, the synthesis of English and Italian elements that characterized this period of American popular song.

This process occurred at other times in other places. Sixteenth-century England had a tradition of secular music dating back to the early Renaissance. The carols and part-songs making up this tradition were quite different in style from the polyphonic secular music of Italy, France, and the Germanic countries. The English pieces were largely homorhythmic (all voices singing together in a more or less chordal style), with careful and expressive declamation of the texts. Contrapuntal techniques so prevalent in continental music and to some extent in English church music played a small role in this secular music.

But late in the sixteenth century a few Italian madrigals began to circulate in England. By this time the Italian madrigal was a mature and sophisticated form, having gone through several distinct stages; hundreds and thousands of pieces had been written by the most famous composers of the century, both Italian and foreign. But England had been relatively isolated from many musical developments on the continent, and the madrigal was a new and exciting form for most English musicians. In 1588 a collection of Italian madrigals was published in London under the title *Musica transalpina*, edited by Nicholas Yonge. Though the music was that of the most famous Italian composers of the day, the texts were translated into English. Four similar collections were published in the following years, and for a brief period these "Englished" Italian madrigals coexisted with traditional part-songs. Within a few years a synthesis of Italian and English styles took place. Such composers as Thomas Morley, John Dowland, Thomas Weelkes, and John Wilbye began composing new pieces, English madrigals, in which the melodic sophistication, expressive harmonies, and subtle contrapuntal effects of the Italian secular style were combined with the more robust spirit and masterful declamation of the English. These madrigals have elements of both the Italian madrigal and the English part-song but are distinctly different from both.

No discussion of the music of Johann Sebastian Bach can be complete or totally perceptive without an understanding of the role that different national styles played in his music. Raised and trained in a rich German musical tradition, he recognized the existence of other national styles of music, each quite distinct. Even the titles of some of his compositions indicate this. He came to know music of other national styles by playing it, copying it, and even rearranging it. He became familiar with the Italian style, for example, by copying concertos by such composers as Vivaldi, and in some cases by rewriting Italian violin concertos for the keyboard. It is possible to recognize certain works of his early and middle periods as frankly imitative of one national style or another. But many of his later works represent syntheses of various national styles, drawing some elements from one, some from another.

These are scattered examples of an old but continuing story. There are cultures with an extended, continuous musical style. These are mostly ancient and isolated cultures. But the history of European peoples for many centuries now has been one of exploration, travel, conquest, movement, change, conflict, and integration of people and ideas. All of this has affected music, and every prospect indicates that these patterns will continue and that music, perhaps even more than before, will be a constantly changing and evolving thing.

6

The Formation of a
Musical Style: Early Rock

RONALD BYRNSIDE

The term *style* is often used in discussions of music, as indeed it is used in discussions and assessments of many areas of life. In fact, we often use the term *life-style* to designate a particular mode and manner of existence. To attach the word style to a given phenomenon or set of phenomena is to suggest that it possesses something that is distinctive and individual to such an extent that it may be isolated from other generically similar phenomena. For example, in discussing footwear we can fairly easily separate the sneaker from the boot, the sandal, the thong, and several other types of shoes, on the basis of their distinctive qualities. In doing so we are consciously or unconsciously involved in one of the rudimentary procedures of style analysis.

As used in the arts, the term style refers to various levels, from the very general to the very particular. For instance, on a very general level one can refer to a Western style of music (as opposed to a non-Western style), or to a Renaissance style (as opposed to, say, a baroque style), or to an operatic style (as opposed to, say, a symphonic style). On a more particular level one may speak of a dixieland jazz style, as distinct from jazz style in general. On a still more particular level one can deal with the style of a given composer, or even a specific composition.

On any level the term style usually involves a description of the technical elements of the music. But a more complete assessment of a style takes into account certain things in the music that are not readily illustrated, verbally or graphically—certain aspects of performance, for instance, that are associated with, but not notated in, the music. A full assessment of a style also includes information and sometimes even speculation about the various relationships among the composer, the music, and its audience. A description of technical elements and performance idiosyncracies informs us about *what* is in a style; statements concerning the above-mentioned relationships attempt to inform us *why* the music is the way it is.

An analysis of a piece of music is useful to the extent that it instructs the reader about how the music is made and how it works, and provokes him to more deeply consider the music. But no stylistic analysis, however complete and sophisticated, can substitute for the music being analyzed; the analysis is not the same thing as "having" the piece. In trying to understand the uniqueness of a composition we must keep alive the distinction that exists between analysis and experience, but at the same time, be ready to accept stylistic analysis as something that can feed and broaden a musical experience.

In this chapter we will deal specifically with the formation and development of Rock 'n' Roll style, and also, more generally, with the formation of several other styles that have evolved in the course of Western music. We will be as concerned with the formative process of a style as we will with discovering and isolating its identifying characteristics.

Once formed, some musical styles remain relatively stable; that is, they do not continue to evolve. South Indian classical music, for example, has used the same body of basic melodies and rhythms, the same instruments and approaches to performance for more than two hundred years. Many generations of South Indians have performed this music over the years, and the only aspect of it that has changed has resulted from the differences among performers in improvisational skill and idiosyncracy. Thus, there is an unmistakable and longstanding continuity to this musical style.

Some musics have undergone a change in style as a result of contact with the music of another culture. For example, the music of the Mbuti Pygmies of the Ituri forest in central Africa remained stylistically fixed for many generations, but early in the twentieth century this once completely isolated tribe made contact with other African tribes and with European explorers and settlers. As a result of these contacts the musical style of the Mbuti began to incorporate the sounds of certain instruments that had never previously been part of Mbuti music. There are numerous other examples of this kind of stylistic change.

The history of style in Western music is of a somewhat different pattern. Though some styles of Western music have remained stable for long periods of time, and though some styles have been transformed as a result of assimilating non-Western musical elements, the overriding tendency of Western music has been evolutionary. It seems a basic urge in Western man to change and reshape things, and this is reflected in the history of his music. For many centuries Western music has periodically involved itself in stylistic change. Some styles last longer than others, but whatever their longevity, they generally follow a pattern of formation, crystallization, and decay.

During its formative process a new style somehow detaches itself from its predecessor and, wittingly or unwittingly, emerges as a reaction to the older style. Ordinarily, this reaction to and breaking away from the older style is not clear-cut. In fact the new style usually borrows and/or adapts some element from the older style. After the formative process, the new style becomes crystallized and establishes itself, and its audience begins to recognize the boundaries of it. Finally, having been represented in a substantial body of compositions over a certain amount of time, the style becomes so familiar and certain things about it become so predictable that both composer and audience begin to lose interest. The entire process is then repeated, as another new style forms itself and breaks away from the decaying style.

Why Western man has chosen to create new musical styles for himself and why he has done it so consistently is a complicated and manifold question, to which only part of the answer can be found in the field of music. This is because music is a human activity, and the particular shape that a musical style assumes must be understood not only in the abstract, but in terms of the sociology of the composers of and the audience for that style.

There is a relationship between the human condition in a particular society and the artistic tastes of that society: political events and climates, and economic and sociological conditions shape the basic attitudes of a society, and these attitudes are, in turn, reflected in the arts. As the complexion of a society changes, different attitudes and tastes are formed. It sometimes happens that the basic attitudes of a given generation or age do not (and perhaps cannot) carry over to the next generation or age; many things, including a style of music, that were meaningful to the former, fail to be significant to the latter, which has developed its own attitudes based on its own experiences.

Perhaps unconsciously, or perhaps quite deliberately, new composers and a potentially new audience begin groping for ways to give musical shape and expression to newly emerging attitudes. This groping process is an integral part of, indeed, the first step in, the formation of a musical style.

Probably no one single factor prods a composer or group of composers to create a new style. It is by far more likely that a new style is formed for a combination of reasons and in response to a variety of needs. As a prelude to our investigation of the formation of rock 'n' roll style we will briefly discuss some other examples of musical styles in their formative stages. In each case we will focus on only one aspect, one causal factor in the formation of the style, whether it be the rejection of an inherited style, the adoption of an alternative to an older style, or some other technological, aesthetic, or functional consideration. Eventually, as we examine the formation of rock 'n' roll style, we will take into account all of these factors.

A Style Formed in Response to New Musical-Aesthetic Needs

The formation of opera resulted in part from the desire to create a musical-dramatic kind of composition that simply could not be accommodated within the bounds of the inherited style. The *Camerata,* an early seventeenth-century group of Florentine noblemen, developed their musical style of opera in the shadows of the then prevalent Renaissance style of elaborate choral polyphony. The desire of the *Camerata* composers and dramatists for a clear and affective presentation of drama through song led to the creation of a musical style that emphasized solo singing, virtually eradicated counterpoint, and treated harmony as an accompanimental, supportive force.

This new musical style was also an attempt to recreate the declamatory singing style in ancient Greek drama. Thus, while the *Camerata* style was new, it purported to be based on a very old model. Nevertheless, so many aspects of this style were so new and different from the late sixteenth-century style that composers, critics, and theorists found it appropriate to call the two styles by different names. The older style came to be known as the *prima prattica* ("first practice"), and the new style was called the *seconda prattica* ("second practice"). To some people, one of the implications inherent in this differentiation was that music written in the style of the *prima prattica* was appropriate for sacred purposes, but the *seconda prattica* was suitable only for secular purposes. The general notion that one style of music is acceptable for church use, while another is strictly secular, has persisted for several centuries and, with some exceptions, remains today.

However, jazz and rock, two traditionally secular musical styles, have, since the mid-1960s, been used in sacred contexts—the jazz mass and the rock service. This fact suggests some interesting questions that we will merely pose rather than attempt to answer here: Is there no longer a stylistic difference between sacred and secular music? Was this distinction between the two styles originally based upon something concrete, or was it then, and has it been since, an artificial separation?

The separation of the *Camerata* style of music from other music was not, however, simply a matter of categorizing one as secular and the other as sacred; this new musical style was recognized as something new, above and beyond the question of its presumed secularity or its alledged non-sacredness.

In 1602 Giulio Caccini, a *Camerata* member, published some songs written in this new style, which bore the title *Le Nuove Musiche* ("the new music"). Jacopo Peri, another member of the group, recognizing that his music would strike most listeners as being different, and perhaps even strange, offered an apology for the new style, which begins:

> Before laying before you, gracious readers, these my compositions, I have thought it fitting to let you know what led me to seek out this new manner of music.[1]

The following recorded examples should make obvious some of the major differences between the older style and the new monodic style. In addition to gross differences in texture and harmony, one of the major differences, and indeed one of the dominant concerns of the *Camerata* composers, was in the setting of the text. The aim of the *Camerata* composer was that the text should be understood, and not cluttered up or lost in a web of several contrapuntal lines. It is suggested that the listener follow the texts in translation as he listens to the examples.

Examples in the new monodic style:

Giulio Caccini, "Dovrò dunque morire" from *Le Nuove Musiche. Masterpieces of Music Before 1750,* Vol. 2, No. 30, Haydn Society Records, HS 9039.

Claudio Monteverdi, excerpt from *Orfeo. History of Music in Sound,* Vol. 4, side 4, band 3, FCA Victor, LM 6029.

Giulio Caccini, *Pien D'Amoroso Affete and Amarilli. Masterpieces of the Italian Baroque,* The Bach Guild, BG 565, side 1, bands 1 and 3, respectively.

Examples in the older style:

Palestrina, "Sanctus," from Mass *Aeterna Christi munera.*
De Monte, "Benedictus" and "Agnus Dei," from Mass *Benedictus es.*
Lassus, "Benedictus" and "Hosanna" from Mass *Puisque j'ay perdu.*
(All of the above are found in *History of Music in Sound,* Vol. IV.)

Josquin Des Pres, "Sanctus," from Mass *L'homme armé. History of Music in Sound,* Vol. III, side 3, band 4, FCA Victor, LM 6016.

———, *Ave Maria. Masterpieces of Music Before 1750,* Vol. 1, No. 19.

During its formative stages a new musical style in the Western world almost always has its detractors as well as its practitioners and advocates. We are told by Pietro de Bardi, son of one of the founders of the *Camerata,* that this new singing style was at first "considered almost ridiculous." It is clear that the monodic style of the *Camerata* constituted a distinct reshaping of music. In Western man the strong urge to change and reshape is, ironically,

---

[1] Quoted with permission of W. W. Norton & Company, Inc., from *Source Readings in Music History,* p. 373ff, Compiled and Edited by Oliver Strunk. Copyright 1950 by W. W. Norton & Company, Inc.

balanced by a formidable resistance to change. This accounts for the condescension, skepticism, and derision to which every musical style is subjected during its formative process. Perhaps the audience for an established musical style initially views a new style as inimical not only to traditional musical and aesthetic values, but also to its entire system of values. Part of this attitude was expressed by G. M. Artusi in his essay, *The Imperfection of Modern Music* (1600):

> ...insofar as it [the new music] introduced new rules, new modes, and new turns of phrase, these were harsh and little pleasing to the ear, nor could they be otherwise; for so long as they violate the good rules—in part founded on experience, the mother of all things, in part observed in nature, and in part proved by demonstration—we must believe them deformations of the nature and propriety of true harmony, far removed from the object of music. . . . They [the composers] and their activities die together. By the general judgment of the wise and learned, ignorance, more than anything else, is considered the greatest of the many accidents which makes uncertain for every workman the road of good work. . . . Of ignorance, then, are born compositions of this sort, which, like monstrosities, pass through the hands of this man and that, and these men do not know themselves what the real nature of composition is. For them it is enough to create a tumult of sounds, a confusion of absurdities, an assemblage of imperfections, and all springs from that ignorance with which they are beclouded.[2]

The composers of the *Camerata* circle were interested first and foremost in the drama, and the personality of their musical style was shaped by this overriding interest. The texture, harmony, and form of this style were designed to serve and heighten the effect of the language of the drama. In the end, their reaction to and rejection of the old musical style stemmed from a knowledge that the old style could not accommodate the kind of drama-centered music they wanted to create.

A New Style Created by the Expansion of Elements from the Old Style

No less obvious a break with a stylistic tradition occurred near the beginning of the fourteenth century. In France and Italy some composers began to write a kind of music that was in some respects noticeably different from the general musical style of the thirteenth century—in fact, it was so different that some composers and other spokesmen referred to it as the *Ars Nova* (new art). In the same breath they referred to the thirteenth-century style

[2] Quoted with permission of W. W. Norton & Company, Inc., from *Source Readings in Music History*, pp. 393–404, Compiled and Edited by Oliver Strunk. Copyright 1950 by W. W. Norton & Company, Inc.

as the *Ars Antiqua* (old art). This conscious labeling of styles in terms of old versus new is one of a number of ways in which the formation of the *Ars Nova* style was similar to the formation of the seventeenth-century style just discussed.

The fourteenth century is often, and with good reason, referred to as an essentially secular age. Most of the *Ars Nova* composers of whom we have knowledge invested a considerable share of their energies in the production of secular music. This constituted a major shift, for, in earlier centuries, the church was the principal patron of music, and composers generally spent their time providing the church with music—obviously, sacred music. In a sense, then, beginning with the *Ars Nova* the church relinquished its role as the primary director of musical style.

We have already noted that one of the issues in the formation of the seventeenth-century monodic style was the question of its suitability (or lack thereof) for sacred purposes. That issue was directly anticipated as the music of the *Ars Nova* developed. In contradistinction to the *Camerata* composers, whose need to break with the established style grew out of dramatic rather than strictly musical concerns, the *Ars Nova* composers built from the style they inherited, altering and expanding the rhythmic and harmonic parameters of that style, and at the same time creating musical forms designed to serve secular rather than sacred functions.

We have seen that in their formative years new styles have their detractors; that was the case in the seventeenth century, and it was the case during the formation of the *Ars Nova* style in the early fourteenth century. The composers of this new style incurred the wrath of certain spokesmen for the older style. Notice how Jacob of Liége, the author of the statement below, implies that the new style affects not only musical but ethical values as well:

> Would that it pleased the modern singers that the ancient music and the ancient manner of singing were again brought into use! For, if I may say so, the old art seems more perfect, more rational, more seemly, freer, simpler, and plainer. Music was originally discreet, seemly, simple, masculine, and of good morals; have not the moderns rendered it lascivious beyond measure?[3]

Ultimately, *Ars Nova* style may be viewed as a expansion of certain technical features of the old style, a stretching of these features severe enough to render them unrecognizable in terms of the practices of the old style, and an organization of them consistent enough to justify referring to them as practices of a new style.

[3] Quoted with permission of W. W. Norton & Company, Inc., from *Source Readings in Music History*, p. 189, Compiled and Edited by Oliver Strunk. Copyright 1950 by W. W. Norton & Company, Inc.

A New Style Resulting from a
Rejection of the Inherited Style

Western art music experienced another major stylistic change in the early years of the twentieth century; in fact, it broke from some of the basic musical procedures of art music of the seventeenth, eighteenth, and nineteenth centuries. The most drastic change occurred within the field of harmony: the most unequivocal difference between baroque, classical, and romantic music and a good deal of early twentieth-century music is the absence or distortion of functional harmony in the latter. At this point the reader should listen to as many of the following compositions as he can, so that he may have some idea of the nature and extent of this fundamental difference.

Claude Debussy: "Brouillards," from *Preludes,* Book 1
  "Pagodes," from *Estampes*
  "Et la lune descend sur la temple qui fut," from *Images* (1907)
  "Voiles," from *Preludes,* Book 1
Charles Ives: "Halloween" and "Over the Pavements," from *A Set of Pieces for Theater Orchestra*
Anton Webern: Five Movements for String Quartet, Op. 5
Arnold Schoenberg: Suite for Piano, Op. 25
Igor Stravinsky: *The Rite of Spring* (opening section)
Darius Milhaud: *Bull on the Roof;* Suite Provencale
Paul Mindemith: Piano Sonata No. 3
Edgar Varèse: *Ionisation*

Though baroque, classical, and romantic musics may, on a general level, be easily understood as separate styles, all three, despite their differences, exhibit the principles of functional harmony. In other words, for about three centuries there was continuity to Western art musics—a common central nervous system. Thus, the break from tonality in the early years of the twentieth century represented one of the most radical departures from tradition in the history of Western music.

Many composers continued to write in tonal idioms, and thus extended the long history of functional harmony. In assessing the music of those who did not continue this tradition, one discovers a variety of alternatives to tonality, and a variety of personal styles. But despite different stylistic bents, these composers were united in the belief that the system of functional harmony was exhausted, and that alternatives to this system had to be found.

Debussy's alternative was, at least on the surface, much less radical than some of the others; his approach was not to destroy tonality completely but, rather, to distort it. This he accomplished by organizing his music in such a way that chords became significant more for what they were, in a purely sonorous sense, than for what they did, in a functional sense. (It can be assumed that all composers working within the system of functional harmony were interested to one degree or another in the sonorous qualities of chords. Thus, the suggestion is not that this fascination was invented by or unique to Debussy.)

To remain within the realm of functional harmony, a composer must necessarily select and arrange his chords in such a way that there will emerge from his music that special hierarchy of harmonies described in Chapter 1. If we understand tonality as a musical syntax—a sense-giving, form-giving system—then we can understand that chords in tonal music have a dual nature—functional and sonorous. The composer of tonal music regards his chords primarily as functional elements, restricting himself to using the number, type, and placement of chords that will establish this syntax. The sheer celebration of sonorities is not permitted to damage functionality.

Many of Debussy's compositions are in contrast with this. In such compositions sonorities are used as ends in themselves; they are directionless, and the chordal relationships and progressions that characterize functional harmony are absent. Notice in "Brouillards" how several of the sections—the first section, for example—seem to dwell upon one basic sound; notice, further, that these sounds are devoid of any urgency to progress to some other particular sound. This non-progressive, non-functional harmony might well be described as successive harmony: one sound or section precedes or follows, but does not lead to or result from, another sound or section. This is not true of all of Debussy's music, but it is characteristic of the pieces listed above, and of several of his other works.

The Ives piece, "Halloween," represents a different kind of alternative to functional harmony, for, unlike the Debussy compositions in which tonality is distorted rather than destroyed, this piece abandons tonality altogether. In it, Ives focuses on a body of sounds that are not typical of tonal music; furthermore, the piece consistently avoids arrangements of chords from which traditional functionality would emerge. This kind of music is sometimes referred to as *atonal*—outside the realm of tonality.

We have discovered that on a general level tonality is a musical system organized around a set of basic functional principles, but that on a particular level a great and diverse range of styles has been created within the system. The same is true of atonal music. For example, both the Ives the Webern compositions can be classified as atonal, but as we examine the particularities of these compositions we discover that they sound quite different from each other. Though these composers were united in their desire to avoid tonality, their separate musical personalities suggested different ways of accomplishing this.

Arnold Schoenberg is the inventor of the twelve-tone musical system, within which all pitches are related only to one another, not to a group of hierarchical and functional chords. This system has proved to be a viable and very influential alternative to tonality. Schoenberg's Suite for Piano, listed above, was one of the earliest compositions to. employ systematically the principles of the twelve-tone system.

During the early decades of the twentieth century various other alternatives to tonality emerged, such as bitonality and polytonality—double or multiple tonalities whereby the feel of simultaneously functioning tonal centers was created. Milhaud is one of a group of twentieth-century composers who have from time to time explored these alternatives.

For some composers the loss of interest in tonality led to a de-emphasis on pitches in general, and, concomitantly, to a special and exaggerated interest in other parameters of music, such as rhythm, texture, and timbre. *Ionisation,* by Varèse, is scored for a large battery of percussion instruments, most of which are instruments without definite pitch. The piece is a clear and unequivocal rejection of tonality.

Of course, the above is neither a complete catalogue of early twentieth-century alternatives to tonality, nor a complete list of composers who sought to incorporate these alternatives in their music; it indicates sufficiently, however, that Western art music experienced a dramatic stylistic change early in this century. More than anything else, this change was occasioned by the belief that the old system—tonality—was exhausted, and could not accommodate the aims and intentions of certain composers.

The Role of Economics
in the Formation of a Style

The personalities of some musical styles have been determined to a surprisingly large extent by economic considerations. Since the nineteenth century, some musics have been created, in part, as salable products. To varying degrees, these may be considered commercial musics. The term commercial, as it is herein applied to music, does not necessarily carry with it derogatory overtones, nor is the term restricted to popular musics. The notion of the composer making his living through the sale of his compositions, either to a ticket-buying concert audience, or to purchasers of printed music, is one that developed early in the nineteenth century. (There were, however, numerous, scattered precedents.) With the demise of the patronage system of the eighteenth-century musical world, and with the rise of nineteenth-century industrialization and economics, the role of the art music composer shifted from employee to free agent.

Using industrial terminology in a musical context, we may speak of producer (composer), product (the composer's music), and consumers (the audience). Again, this in no way implies that when a composer attempts to sell his music, he stoops to some kind of crass commercialism, and of necessity forfeits his artistic integrity. We would not, for example, suggest that Renoir, who sold many of his paintings during his lifetime, had less artistic integrity than did Van Gogh, who could sell very few of his. The suggestion here is simply this: beginning in the nineteenth century, many composers adapted themselves to new economic facts of life.

In the early 1800s the piano became a mass-produced instrument, used by professional concert pianists, and purchased in significant numbers by institutions, and by the public for home use. The rising popularity of the piano, as both a solo and an ensemble instrument, called, in turn, for a repertory—one diverse enough to exercise the several functions of the instrument. A number of nineteenth-century composers answered this call with concertos, and chamber and solo music for the piano.

Piano instruction also began to assume the proportions of a business: composers supplied the demand for instructional and exercise books and for piano transcriptions of folksongs, marches, waltzes, and excerpts from popular operas. The financial success and, in fact, the very life of this repertory resulted from the technological development of the piano. At the same time, the commercial success of the piano depended upon an economic scene healthy enough to permit large numbers of people to purchase pianos, piano music, piano instruction, and tickets to concerts of piano music.

The latter point is worthy of further discussion. Perhaps the most obvious area in which economy can affect musical style is the size and scale along which a musical style develops, a process often determined by the relative affluence or depression characteristic of the potential audience. For example, all other things being equal, an audience might welcome, say, a large-scale, theatrical operatic style, featuring a large cast and orchestra, and elaborate stage machinery and costumes. The success of such a production depends upon the price of tickets, as compared with the wages of the potential audience. The price of tickets is determined by production costs. One can readily see that under certain economic conditions an operatic style on this scale could not thrive. In a depressed economy composers and audience of opera would have to content themselves with a much smaller, chamber-like operatic style.

The Role of Technology
in the Formation of a Style

On the surface, the technology of an age may seem far removed from music, but surprisingly often, technology has been a factor in the development of a musical style. Sometimes it directly and obviously affects this process, as, for example, in electronic music, the very sounds of which are produced by instruments from the field of technology. The electronic hardware used in making this music became available to the public only as recently as the early 1950s; thus, electronic music and its several particular styles could not have been created prior to the mid-twentieth century. From one point of view it may be said that electronic music had to wait for the appropriate level of technology to develop; from another, one might hold that the theory of this music developed from the technology, and that composers found out what they wanted to say only after experimenting with the hardware. From any viewpoint it is obvious that electronic music styles have a fundamental relationship with technology.

One of the basic ingredients of the sound of rock music is the electric guitar; here again, a musical style, or a significant aspect of it, was directly affected by a technological development.

The style of American popular music in this century has been effected by technology in another, somewhat more oblique manner. The success of any popular music depends on the mode of its dissemination. Prior to this century the available modes were sheet music or, more frequently, live performances. Today live performances persist, but recordings have replaced them as the mode of dissemination most responsible for the popularity of a piece of music. In fact, today's mechanized modes of dissemination are inseparable components of the popularity of a song. Of course, this is not to imply that every song that is recorded achieves popularity—that is far from being the case. The suggestion, however crass it may have seemed in the past, is that mechanization is as important to the popularity of a given song as are its musical and textual components.

Because the mode of dissemination of much music has shifted from live performance to mechanized reproduction, the idea presents itself that popular music has, in a sense, become dehumanized. Perhaps the loss of live contact between performer and audience should be considered one of the liabilities of mechanization. However, there are other factors that, depending upon one's disposition, could be counted as either assets or liabilities. For example, mechanization in the form of the recording guarantees a performance that is always the same, and, we must assume, the ultimate rendition as a given performer envisions it. Furthermore, mechanization eliminates such human variables as a cracking voice or a momentary loss of memory.

Mechanization has affected the *content,* as well as the form, of some popular music. Over several decades a body of popular songs has been built, which takes as its subject matter certain facets of the mechanical-technological world. Let us direct our attention to a particular category of such songs— those dealing with mechanized modes of travel: trains, cars, airplanes, and so on. A wide range of attitudes towards instruments of travel exists within these songs. Some merely view means of travel as novelties, or they celebrate them as newly found conveniences and luxuries. Other songs tend to romanticize instruments of travel, as, for example, the song in which a man speaks of a locomotive as if it were a friend. Other songs suggest a psychological dependency on modes of travel. Still others mostly of recent vintage, mention instruments of travel, celebrating not the instruments but, rather, travel itself, or the escape or motion therein.

In the first type of travel song mentioned above, the journey usually terminates at home; thus, there is a circular motif to such songs. This is evident in such songs as "Chattanooga Choo-Choo, Won't You Choo-Choo Me Home?" (1941), "In My Merry Oldsmobile" (1905), and "Come Josephine in My Flying Machine" (1910).

In the second kind of travel song the poet often seems to be counting on the instrument of travel to do something for him, to somehow change his situation for the better. This is evident in songs such as "When My Dreamboat Comes Home" (1935).

> When my dreamboat comes home,
> Then my dreams no more will roam
> I will meet you and greet you
> Hold you closely my own.
> Moonlit waters will sing
> Of the tender love you bring
> We'll be sweetheats forever
> When my dreamboat comes home.*

In this kind of song the poet does not do the traveling. He waits. The same is true of "I'm Waitin' for the Train to Come In" (1948), in which the poet not only waits, but also draws a parallel between the instrument of travel and his life.

> I'm waitin' for the train to come in
> Waitin' for my life to begin.
> I've counted every minute of each live long day,
> Been so melancholy since you went away.
> I've shed a million teardrops or more,
> Waitin' for the one I adore.
> I'm waitin' in the depot by the railroad track,
> Waitin' for the choo-choo train that brings you back.
> I'm waitin' for my life to begin,
> Waitin' for the train to come in.

In certain lines of "The Trolley Song" (1944) we sense a connection between the "nervous system" of the trolley and the nervous system of the poet:

> Clang, clang, clang went the trolley,
> Ding, ding, ding went the bell,
> Zing, zing, zing went my heartstrings...
>
> Chug, chug, chug went the motor,
> Bump, bump, bump went the brake,
> Thump, thump, thump went my heartstrings...
>
> Buzz, buzz, buzz went the buzzer,
> Stop, stop, stop went the wheels,
> Stop, stop, stop went my heartstrings....*

* "The Trolley Song." Words & music by: Ralph Blanc, Hugh Martin. Copyright © 1944, Renewed 1971 Metro-Goldwyn-Mayer, Inc. Rights controlled by Leo Feist Inc. Used by permission.

Some recent songs suggest that travel has become a fact, even a way of life. In his book, *Future Shock* (New York: Random House, 1970), Alvin Toffler tells us that "Transcience is the new 'temporariness' in everyday life." "It results in a mood, a feeling of impermanence" (p. 42). Jerry, in Edward Albee's *The Zoo Story,* characterizes himself as a 'permanent transient' (p. 42). Elsewhere in Toffler's book (p. 69) we are told that in 1914 the average American traveled about 340 miles per year by mechanized means. In 1967 the average American travelled 10,000 miles per year by automobile alone. Implicit in statements and statistics of this kind is that mechanization (in this case, only in the form of travel) is with us, around us, and in us; this is a state of affairs that has developed not suddenly, but more like a crescendo. It seems our increasing involvement with technology has changed society in more than merely mechanical ways.

The nature of these changes is reflected in several recent songs dealing ostensibly with mechanized travel, but actually with much more than that. In contrast with earlier types of travel songs, these recent ones view instruments of travel neither as luxuries nor as means to improve life. The impression one gets from these songs is that travel *is* life. In these songs travel is not circular, nor does the poet wait while someone else travels to him. The path is linear; travel doesn't really have a destination; its only direction is out. Consider the lyrics of the song "So Far Away," by Carole King:

> So far away,
> Doesn't anybody stay in one place anymore?
> It would be so fine to see your face at my door.
> Doesn't help to know you're just time away.
>
> Long ago I reached for you and there you stood,
> Holding you again could only do me good.
> How I wish I could,
> But you're so far away.

One more song about moving along the highway,
Can't say much of anything that's new.
If I could only work this life out my way,
I'd rather spend it being close to you.

But you're just time away,
Doesn't anybody stay in one place anymore?
It would be so fine to see your face at my door.
Doesn't help to know that you're so far away.
Yeah, you're so far away

Traveling around sure gets me down and lonely,
Nothing else to do but close my mind.
I sure hope the road don't come to own me,
There's so many dreams I've yet to find.

But you're just time away,
Doesn't anybody stay in one place anymore?
It would be so fine to see your face at my door.
Doesn't help to know that you're so far away.*

Thus, the effects of mechanization are more than merely technical; they are seen in the attitudes and aesthetics of both the composers of travel songs, and the audience, and are clearly reflected in their music and poetry.

All the topics thus far touched upon—the rejection of an inherited style; an alternative to that style; economic, aesthetic, functional, and technological considerations—are factors in the formation of rock 'n' roll style.

The Formation and Development of Rock 'n' Roll Style

Since the late 1950s, rock music of one kind or another has dominated the American popular music scene. It is a music that differs substantially from the predominant popular music of the 1930s and 1940s. Partly for that reason, rock 'n' roll (as rock music was called in the mid to late '50s) was viewed as a very short-lived fad by the practitioners of and the audience for the older style of popular music. During these early years of rock there were numerous predictions that rock 'n' roll was about to die, and that the older style was coming back.

As reported in the April 18, 1957, edition of *DOWN BEAT* magazine, Louis Brecker, owner of New York's Roseland Dance City Ballroom (a kind of temple for the old-style dance music), said: "The people are dancing and *will* turn to enjoy a good danceband. . . . Bands are on the upbeat in popularity. You can almost sense it." Mr. Brecker was so convinced of the truth of this notion that he reportedly spent 2½ million dollars remodeling and refurbishing his Ballroom.

In the same magazine The Rev. Norman O'Connor, a jazz enthusiast, suggested not only that rock 'n' roll was a fad, but also that its popularity was nearly finished, and that it was about to be replaced by a new fad. He said: "Calypso music is gradually edging rock 'n' roll out of the popular music scene . . . rock 'n' roll is a stage in popular music . . . and is now on the way out."

A little earlier (*DOWN BEAT,* May 30, 1956), jazz musician John Lewis said, in reference to rock 'n' roll: "I think it's a transitory thing because you can only take so much of it no matter who you are, because the music is so limited in scope. It's a formula. . . ."

As we have seen, these predictions proved to be erroneous. And rather than remaining the same, rock music has continued to evolve. Indeed, several individual styles of rock have developed. In other words, we may view rock music from the mid '50s to the present as a new style in general (in effect, the new popular music style), but in particular we may say that rock is many styles. The earliest of these, and the subject of our present investigation is rock 'n' roll.

For reasons with which we shall deal presently, it is not possible to assign a specific date of birth to rock 'n' roll, or to single out an "inventor" of the style; we can say that rock 'n' roll became the generally accepted label for a specific musical style sometime in the mid '50s.

The etymology of the term rock 'n' roll leads us back to the earlier blues, where it was often used to describe the sex act. The term "rocking and reeling" was used to describe a particular kind of rural black religious song that called for a very animated and physical performance. Rock 'n' roll seems always to have implied physicalness, excitement, and frenzy. The late '40s and early '50s saw the emergence of several songs that were meant to be danced to, the titles of which use the word rock: "Good Rockin' Tonight" (1948), by Wynonie Harris; "Rock All Night Long" (1950), recorded by the Ravens; and "We're Gonna Rock" (1951), by Gunther Lee Carr. In fact, the closer we approach the time when rock 'n' roll style was formed, the more consistently we find the term rock 'n' roll associated with a dance beat.

One of the earliest to popularize the term among a mass audience was Alan Freed, a Cleveland disc jockey whose radio program, begun in 1952, was called "Moondog's Rock 'n' Roll Party." But it was not until about 1955 that rock 'n' roll style, as it is herein described, fully formed itself and took command of its audience. Also in 1955 the first rock 'n' roll movie premiered —*Rock Around the Clock,* starring Bill Haley and his Comets, and featuring Little Richard.

The influences on and the lineage of rock 'n' roll style can be traced to some earlier musics. Of these, the most closely related to it is the style known as rhythm and blues. Less closely related, but nevertheless very important in the formation of rock 'n' roll, are certain elements from a broad style once known as hillbilly music, but now called country and western music.

Before describing rhythm and blues style, we must first deal with a certain confusion that has grown up around this term. For about two decades prior to 1948 the term "race records" was used by record companies and music trade journals as a label for black popular music. Since several kinds of music were popular among black audiences during these years, "race" did not refer to a single, particular style, but was loosely applied to traditional blues, country blues, some gospel music, some jazz, and some more or less "white-style" ballads as performed by black musicians. Several of the major record companies even had subsidiary labels that recorded songs designed to be popular among and purchased by black audiences. *The Billboard* magazine, one of the principal music trade journals, published lists of the most popular "race records." An examination of these lists reveals the diversity among the musics that were included under the blanket label of "race records."

The Billboard's list of the most popular "race records" for the week ending July 30, 1948, contains the following:[4]

1. "I Can't Go On Without You," Bullmoose Jackson.
2. "Good Rockin' Tonight, Wynonie Harris.
3. "Run, Joe," Louis Jordan.
4. "Long Gone," Sonny Thompson.
5. "My Heart Belongs to You" Arbee Stidham.
6. "Tomorrow Night," Lonnie Johnson.
7. "Messin' Around," Memphis Slim.
8. "Pretty Mama Blues," Ivory Joe Hunter.
9. "Send for Me if You Need Me," The Ravens.
10. "Lollypop Mama," Wynonie Harris.
11. "All My Love Belongs to You," Bullmoose Jackson.
12. "Tell Me Daddy," Julia Lee and Her Boyfriends.
13. "Fine Brown Flame," Nellie Lutcher.
14. "King Size Papa," Julia Lee and Her Boyfriends.
15. "Recess in Heaven," Dan Grissom.

The list includes straight blues (number 8), white-style ballads (1, 11), a jazz group (3), a religious song (15), and some examples of what eventually came to be known as rhythm and blues style (2, 9, 13).

In 1949 *The Billboard* dropped the term "race" and substituted for it the term "rhythm and blues." Thus, rhythm and blues became the general label for the several kinds of music popular with black audiences. Undoubtedly,

[4] Quoted with permission of *Billboard* Magazine.

one of the reasons for dropping the term "race records" at that time was the growing social consciousness of many whites, which suggested that the term was unfair, discriminatory, and certainly racist. Rhythm and blues was, no doubt, a fairer term than "race records," but it was an only slightly more accurate label for this diverse body of music. Lame as it is, this is the term that has been passed on to us. Speaking of it in the most general sense, we can say that there was a slow rhythm and blues music—the blues—and a fast rhythm and blues music—jazz-derived forms.

At about this same time (late '40s), a new and different style of music, which brought together certain elements of both fast and slow rhythm and blues into a dance or "jump" blues, began to develop. This newly emerging musical style added to the existing amalgamation certain elements and accessories of its own, and ultimately resulted in a kind of music that was identifiable and recognizable in its own. Confusing though it is, *this* style should be called rhythm and blues. We must now emphasize that hereinafter, unless otherwise specified, the term rhythm and blues will refer to this particular style, not to the large and diverse body of black popular music, which some of the music trade journals continued to call rhythm and blues.

The Billboard continued to publish a listing of rhythm and blues hits until August 16, 1969. In its next issue (August 23) *The Billboard* carried an editorial that stated, in part:

> Beginning with this issue *Billboard* uses the designation "soul" in place of rhythm and blues. . . . The term soul more properly embraces the broad range of song and instrumental material which derives from the musical genius of the Black American. . . . The term, too, has relevance to a style of performance as well as to musical form.[5]

The first four songs in *The Billboard*'s rhythm and blues chart of August 16, 1969, were:[6]

"Choice of Colors," The Impressions.
"Mother Popcorn," James Brown.
"Share Your Love With Me," Aretha Franklin.
"Nitty Gritty," Gladys Knight and the Pips.

The first four songs in *The Billboard*'s soul chart of August 23, 1969, were:[7]

"Share Your Love With Me," Aretha Franklin.
"Choice of Colors," The Impressions.
"Nitty Gritty," Gladys Knight and the Pips.
"Your Good Thing," Lou Rawls.

[5] Quoted with permission of *Billboard* Magazine.
[6] Quoted with permission of *Billboard* Magazine.
[7] Quoted with permission of *Billboard* Magazine.

This means that on August 16, 1969, "Share Your Love With Me" was a rhythm and blues song, and Aretha Franklin was a rhythm and blues singer. But one week later, "Share Your Love With Me" became a soul song (soul being "relevant" to the form of the song), and Aretha Franklin became a soul singer (soul being "relevant" to her style of performance). This is one of the many ways in which terms that are not based on musical-analytical criteria can be confusing, even misleading. We will, therefore, examine rhythm and blues, this ancestor of rock 'n' roll, as a musical style, not as a marketing label.

The stylistic terms rhythm and blues and rock 'n' roll have on occasion been used interchangeably; in fact, to a considerable extent the former term overlaps the latter both chronologically and stylistically. In the case of some songs from the period around 1953 to 1956, it becomes somewhat academic to argue which of the two terms is more appropriate. To complicate the confusion, we must remember that the term rock 'n' roll is considerably older than the style of music it embraces. And, potentially more confusing, the term rock 'n' roll is older than the term rhythm and blues, though the style of pure or archetypal rhythm and blues is, as has already been suggested, older than rock 'n' roll style. Keeping these semantic and chronological difficulties in mind, but without allowing them to thwart our investigation of the formation of rock 'n' roll style, let us proceed.

The prototypical rhythm·and blues piece is an amalgamation, in that it is music "with a beat," set in the harmonic language and formal structure of the blues, especially the twelve-bar blues. In general, this fascination with beat resulted from the jazz with which the creators of rhythm and blues style were familiar. Rhythm and blues developed a pattern of accents within the 4/4 meter that eventually became a trademark of the style:

$$4/4 \quad 1 \quad 2 \quad 3 \quad 4 \quad / \quad 1 \quad 2 \quad 3 \quad 4$$
$$\text{X} \quad * \quad \circ \quad * \qquad \text{X} \quad * \quad \circ \quad *$$

The X indicates that the metrical downbeat is stressed; the * means that beats 2 and 4 are sharply accented with hard "socks"; and the ° refers to the unaccented or ignored beat in this rhythmic pattern. The following recorded example illustrates this pattern: "Honky Tonk," Part II, by Bill Doggett (*Great Hits of Rhythm and Blues,* Columbia G 30503, side 1, band 1).

Rhythm and blues was dance music, and the accent pattern diagrammed and heard above affords an almost choreographic description of the bodily movements in the dancing: arms extended, hands rigidly slapping the air on beats 2 and 4; a shuffling motion with the feet at beat 3; all accompanied by undulating and snapping movements of shoulders, elbows, and torso.

Many rhythm and blues songs superimpose upon this accent pattern another pattern, which further energizes the music. This pattern is the so-called eight-to-the-bar, or boogie beat, borrowed from the jazz style known as boogie woogie, which enjoyed its greatest popularity in the 1940s. The boogie beat activates all four basic beats in a 4/4 measure by dividing each of them into two, so that there are eight rather than four pulses to the bar:

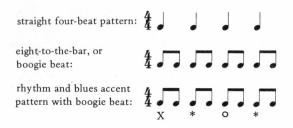

Inasmuch as rhythm and blues was a dance music, it could not borrow or adapt anything from the experimental jazz (such as bop) of the late '40s and early '50s—music that was meant essentially to be listened to, rather than danced to. But boogie woogie provided an eminently inflexible and danceable beat. Pinetop Smith, an early practitioner of boogie, and the man most responsible for the popularization of the term boogie woogie, conceived of it as a dance music. This is made clear in his recording, "Pinetop's Boogie Woogie" (*Encyclopedia of Jazz on Records,* Vol. III—"Jazz of the Forties," Decca DXF 140).

The blues has several forms, of which one of the most frequently encountered is the twelve-bar blues. Its pattern is illustrated below:

A (4 bars) "Oh, I'm feelin' so sad all the live long day."
A(1) (4 bars) "Oh, I'm feelin' so sad all the live long day."
B (4 bars) "Think I'll go down to the river and throw my poor self in."

In terms of text and melody, phrases A and A(1) are identical (they differ in harmony, as you can see below). The first A makes a statement, which the second A repeats and reinforces. The B phrase has a different melodic line, and is usually a lyric that in some way comments upon or draws a conclusion from the statements made in A and A(1). Though there are many possible variations on the harmonic scheme below, it may be taken as a norm for the twelve-bar blues:

		A				A(1)				B		
4/4	1	2	3	4	1	2	3	4	1	2	3	4
	I7				IV7	I7			V7	I7		
		Tonic			Subdominant				Dominant			
					Tonic				Tonic			

The following recorded example illustrates the "X   *   ○   *" beat pattern of prototypical rhythm and blues, the twelve-bar blues format, and (with very minor exceptions) the harmonic scheme outlined above: "Work With Me Annie," by Hank Ballard and the Midnighters (*Great Hits of Rhythm and Blues,* side 1, band 2).

Also present in this example and in many other examples of prototypical rhythm and blues (and also in rock 'n' roll) is an ostinato-like figure that we will hereinafter refer to as an incantation. It is a short, repetitive figure performed by the group supporting the lead singer, and is designed to create a kind of mesmerizing effect. Sometimes, an incantation is the repetition of a few words; just as frequently, it repeats neutral syllables, as in the Ballard song above, where the incantation is "Ah-oom, Ah-oom," etc. The element of incantation is not as crucial to the personality of archetypal rhythm and blues as are the beat pattern and the blues format, but it is used often enough that we might consider it an accessory of the style.

The texts of rhythm and blues songs are usually about love. But by the standard of white radio stations in the '40s and '50s, many of these texts were either (1) downright dirty, (2) heavily and obviously laden with sexual innuendoes, or (3) grammatically unacceptable. By such standards, any or all of these "facts" rendered these lyrics unsuitable for mass public consumption. It is not our purpose here to even attempt to suggest what makes a text dirty or obscene. We can say, however, that many rhythm and blues lyrics speak of love in basic, earthy terms, and that certain words that are consistently used in certain contexts are quite likely sexually connotative. Consider this, and then consider the fundamental differences in approach to the subject of love in the two texts below. The first is the beginning of "Work With Me Annie"; the second is from a roughly contemporaneous song, but one written in the style of popular white ballads.

1.

Work with me Annie,
Work with me Annie,
Work with me Annie,
Work with me Annie,
Work with me Annie,
Let's get it while the gettin' is good
(so good, so good, so good, so good)
Annie please don't cheat,
Give me all my meat.
Ah   oo   oo   oo   oo   oo,
So good to me.
Work with me Annie,
Let's get it while the gettin' is good. . . .

2.

Take my hand, I'm a stranger in paradise.
All lost in a wonderland/ A stranger in paradise.
If I stand starry-eyed/ That's the danger in paradise.
For mortals who stand beside/ An angel like you.
I saw your face and I ascended/ Out of the common place into the rare.
Somewhere in space I hang suspended/ Until I know there's a chance that you care.
Won't you answer the fervent prayer of a stranger in paradise,
Don't send me in dark despair/ From all that I hunger for.
But open your angel's eyes/ to the stranger in paradise,
And tell him that he need be/ A stranger no more.*

In spite of its earthiness and its use of rather obvious innuendoes, the rhythm and blues language does not incorporate words that are commonly recognized as obscene (i.e., four-letter words). Generally speaking, rhythm and blues texts are not violent, nor are they morose (as is often the case in the blues). The lyrics may deal with sex, or perhaps with excessive drinking, or with other topics, but essentially, rhythm and blues texts express a good mood.

The vocal style of rhythm and blues calls for heavy, raspy sounds, but not the moaning quality often associated with blues singing, nor practically any of the crooning of vocalists of white popular music of the late '40s. In addition, rhythm and blues delivery is marked by the occasional use of falsetto, shouts, and growling sounds. Vocal ornamentation and melismas are few in comparison with blues singing, where great melodic and rhythmic freedom and improvisation are expected of the singer.

The typical rhythm and blues instrumentation consists of drums, piano or organ, bass guitar, optional lead guitar, and honking tenor sax. The principal duty of the drums is to keep time and to enunciate the accent pattern. The piano or organ supplies the harmonic background and enunciates the boogie beat, if present; occasionally, it plays solo lines. The bass guitar provides the bass line. If a lead guitar is present, it functions as a solo instrument or as harmonic support, and/or assists the drums in stating the beat pattern. The primary role of the growling. or honking tenor sax is to provide a fairly extended solo between stanzas, while the singer rests. In addition, it may supply simple, unobstrusive countermelodies to the singer or singers. The solos and the countermelodies are, like jazz solos, improvisational in nature, though ordinarily not as intricate and complicated. The sax may also be a lead instrument in introductions and closing formulas. Although there are variations on this basic makeup—for instance, a larger instrumental group—

prototypical rhythm and blues rarely calls for a group smaller than or very different from this one.

Some songs use the standard accent pattern of archetypal rhythm and blues, but have no direct connection with the blues. For these pieces the label rhythm and blues is something of a misnomer; nevertheless, some of their characteristics may persuade us to accept these pieces as members of the family. For example, they may utilize several other elements or accessories of rhythm and blues style, such as its instrumentation, vocal style, kind of text, and incantation. Such songs might be referred to as generic rather than archetypal rhythm and blues. It is with this kind of song that the lines between pure rhythm and blues and rock 'n' roll begin to blur.

Rhythm and blues style crystallized sometime in the early '50s. It was almost exclusively a black American music, made by black musicians, and intended for and listened to by black audiences. In the mid '50s, as it moved from an exclusively black audience to a black and white audience, it was modified, and it acquired some new features, and a new name: rock 'n' roll.

Rock 'n' roll borrowed or adapted a number of technical elements from the rhythm and blues style. In most cases, what was borrowed was modified: it was either exaggerated or simplified. For example, a large body of rock 'n' roll songs (though not all exhibited as many rock 'n' roll elements as others) retained the accent pattern of rhythm and blues. But in these songs there was a tendency to emphasize the downbeat and the hard socks even more than was the case in most rhythm and blues. In rock 'n' roll the downbeat literally became exaggerated.

One way of doing this was to precede the downbeat with some kind of rhythmic confusion or disturbance on the upbeat (or before the theoretically correct place for the upbeat); when this confusion is suddenly resolved on the downbeat, the resulting tendency is to make the downbeat seem much clearer and more emphatic. The drummer in a rock 'n' roll group is usually responsible for accomplishing this. If he begins rhythmic disturbance earlier than the fourth beat, he in effect creates a longer upbeat—he stretches the beginning of the upbeat further back into the measure. Graphically illustrated, this is what happens:

```
1  2  3  4                    1  2  3  4         1
X  *  ///////////////////// X  *  ///////////// X
      fast drum activity, crea-
      ting a rhythmic disturb-
      ance which is resolved HERE!
```

This device can be heard in the following recordings:

"More Than One," by Phil Marks and the Originals. *Roots: the Rock and Roll Sound of Louisiana and Mississippi,* Folkways FJ 2865, side A, band 1. (The device is heard almost every eight bars throughout this song.)

"Lucille," and "The Girl Can't Help It," by Little Richard. *Little Richard Cast a Long Shadow,* Epic EG 30428, side 1, band 1, and side 1, band 2, respectively.

The drummer can elongate the upbeat even further. In doing so, he creates added tension and increases further the anticipation we feel for the downbeat, so that it arrives with even more of a crash. Notice in "Check Up," by Lawrence Bruce (*Roots,* side B, band 4) that the rhythmic confusion, or elongated upbeat, lasts almost an entire measure is some instances.

Rock 'n' roll makes use of other devices that tend to exaggerate the downbeat. One of these is what we might call the ensemble swoop, in which the ensemble pays a small upward slurring motive that, again, begins somewhat ahead of the fourth beat:

One, two, and three are played on the beat, but the pulsation of beat four begins early (after three, but before the theoretically correct time for four).

The eight-to-the-bar approach to ward activating all the beats in the measure was carried over to rock 'n' roll from rhythm and blues. Many rock 'n' roll songs use this device, but perhaps an even more typical rock 'n' roll technique is to divide the beats into triplets, creating a hammer-like effect:

This penchant for triple rather than the duple division of the beat may also be regarded as a borrowed element that is subsequently exaggerated.

A smaller group of rock 'n' roll songs use Latin or quasi-Latin rhythmic patterns, as in "Rome Wasn't Built in a Day," by Al White and his HiLiters (*Roots,* side A, band 3). Here the pattern is:

Notice that beats one, two, and four are played on the beat, while beat three, the ignored beat of rock 'n' roll, is not. The use of such rhythmic patterns may be considered another means of activating the rhythmic life of the music without damaging its danceability.

The instrumentation of early rock 'n' roll was very much like that of rhythm and blues. The biggest exception was that in rock 'n' roll the guitar rose in status; it not only became more important than it had been in arche-typal rhythm and blues, it became louder—to the point of exaggeration, due to the increased use of electronic amplification.

It developed with rock 'n' roll that the more generally public it became, the more exaggerated and theatrical it became in certain respects. The hip-swinging of Elvis ("The Pelvis"), and the stand-up piano thumping and exaggerated pompadour of Little Richard became significant accessories of the style, as did sequined suits and other (at the time) bizarre costumes.

The vocal style of rock 'n' roll resembles that of rhythm and blues, but again, the former modified the latter in some respects. The biggest difference between the two is the introduction of certain white elements into rock 'n' roll vocals. Elvis Presley offered a vocal style that was, in a way, tamer than the sound we associate with rhythm and blues. The shout and falsetto ele-ments of much rhythm and blues were not present in his delivery, and the raspy and growling sounds were watered down. In the pronunciation of many words, Presley compromised between a basic southern black delivery and a basic white vocal style—his was a rural southern voice that partook of both.

Presley and Bill Haley, two of the leading white performers of rock 'n' roll, both came from country music backgrounds. Taken as broad styles, rhythm and blues country and western music of the late '40s–early '50s were more closely related to each other than either was to white popular music of the same era. In the first place, country and western music and rhythm and blues were styles outside the mainstream of popular music. The instrumenta-tion of the two styles was roughly similar, though not exactly so, and both were decidedly different from the instrumentation of mainstream popular music. The vocal style, delivery, and accent of the country and western singer was decidedly different from his counterpart in popular music. In terms of accent the white country singer and the black rhythm and blues singer had something more or less in common: certain pronunciations that were not shared by the white pop singer. Also, the yodelling and hooting of the country and western singer may be considered the counterparts of the falsetto and shouting of the rhythm and blues singer.

In country and western lyrics the treatment of romantic love departed, as it did in rhythm and blues texts, from the idealized, "sophisticated" love lyrics of mainstream popular ballads. In addition, the archetypal rhythm and blues beat is found, though in a slightly softer version, in a large number of country and western songs of the late '40s. Hear, for example, "Walkin' the Floor Over You," by Ernest Tubb (Decca DL 4118), which was popular with "hillbilly" audiences during this time.

Hear also the "X * o *" pattern (with triplets) in a slightly later "hill-billy" song, "A Poor Man's Roses," by Patsy Cline (Starday SLP 291).

During the years in question, these two styles—rhythm and blues and hillbilly (or country and western) music—were, in terms of technical elements and performance practices, surprisingly similar; it must be remembered, though, that the audiences for these two musics were separated by a wide sociological gulf.

In the formation of rock 'n' roll some elements borrowed from rhythm and blues were simplified rather than eraggerated. On the whole, rock 'n' roll lyrics represent a simplification or softening of the texts and sentiments of rhythm and blues. A great many rock 'n' roll songs deal with love, just as rhythm and blues songs before them had done. But in rock 'n' roll, earthiness and blatant sexual references were largely eliminated from the lyrics. In fact, in many rock 'n' roll songs love is spoken of in terms that can be called frivolous.

Herbert Reed of the Platters, a very successful rock 'n' roll group (their "The Great Pretender" sold over two million records, and "Only You" sold over a million and a half), said in an interview in *DOWN BEAT* (May 30, 1956):

> I think that one reason for its popularity is that most rock and roll is really simple thoughts about how people feel.... Criticism concerning objectionable lyrics is no longer valid since, in the majority of new records, the lyrics are clean.

One of the earliest vehicles for rock 'n' roll was the "cover record," in which a performer (usually white) offered a vocally softer and textually less objectionable version of a song previously recorded by a black rhythm and blues performer. A typical "cover" version of a rhythm and blues song removed sexual suggestiveness from the text. For example, Hank Ballard's rhythm and blues song, "Work With Me Annie," with its sexual connotations, was rendered harmless in a "cover" version," Dance With Me Henry," recorded by Georgia Gibbs and others.

Most of the best known performers of rhythm and blues had backgrounds in straight blues and/or jazz of one kind or another. As pure rhythm and blues began to be modified into rock 'n' roll, some of these performers returned to their former backgrounds, some were able to make the stylistic transition from black-based rhythm and blues to black-and-white-based rock 'n' roll. The earliest successful white rock 'n' roll singers—Presley, Haley, Jerry Lee Lewis, and others—broke from their hillbilly music background, but they also brought it with them into rock 'n' roll. It is not surprising that for a short period of time, the music of these people was sometimes called "rockabilly."

Some post-rhythm and blues music moved closer to mainstream white popular balladry while retaining many of the essential ingredients of rock 'n' roll, thereby creating a softer brand of rock 'n' roll. To distinguish between rock 'n' roll and this offshoot, as they existed around 1955–57 or so, we might call the latter by the slightly less colloquial name of rock *and* roll.

Among white performers, the most financially successful of the very early practitioners of this style was Pat Boone, a white crooner, who sang rock 'n' roll lyrics, frequently accompanied by soft strings and a rhythm section mildly enunciating the rock 'n' roll beat pattern. Some black singers also were successful with this softer brand.

Many slow or ballad-type rock and roll songs moved further away from both the lyrics and the formal structure of rhythm and blues, and closer to the sentimental lyrics and formal design of mainstream popular ballads, without, however, becoming mere imitations of such ballads. A case in point is Clyde McPhatter's "Long Lonely Nights" (*History of Rhythm and Blues: Rock and Roll, 1956–1957,* Atlantic SD 8163, Vol. 3, side 2, band 6). Notice the use of eight-bar phrases, and a harmonic language that is more typical of white ballads than of rhythm and blues or rock 'n' roll. Notice also the use of instruments that were foreign to rhythm and blues. Nevertheless, the singer does have the vocal quality and delivery associated with rock 'n' roll; in fact, he makes use of something that we have not yet mentioned, but which is an accessory to rock 'n' roll style. Notice that at the ends of several phrases, he uses a vocal gimmick: a kind of exaggerated whooping falsetto. This is not the raucous shout of rhythm and blues, nor is it the high but masculine yodel of the country and western singer. This seems to be much tamer and simpler, and it has something about it that is almost childlike. Other uses of this device may be heard in two other songs from the above-mentioned album: "Fools Fall in Love," by The Drifters, and "Young Blood," by The Coasters.

The managers and disc jockeys of radio stations that played rock 'n' roll were generally middle-aged men; so were the producers of rock 'n' roll records, and in some cases, the writers of rock 'n' roll songs. But the audience for rock 'n' roll was decidedly, almost exclusively, teen aged. Much has been written about the personality of this audience—its general rebelliousness; its disinterest in the values and habits of its parents; its clannishness, and lack of rapport with its elders. It is possible that this audience, which so enthusiastically adopted rock 'n' roll, took a special delight in the belief that this music belonged only to them. To their elders, rock 'n' roll was either incomprehensible, immoral, or simple-minded.

On April 18, 1956, *DOWN BEAT* carried a feature story under the headline, "Teeners Riot in Massachusetts and Cause Rock and Roll Ban." The disturbance resulted from a misunderstanding between the promoters of a concert at the Massachusetts Institute of Technology and a large group of teenagers who paid their admissions believing they would be permitted to dance. When they were not allowed to do so, a riot erupted. The chairman of the Boston Licensing Board said: "Some of this music is crazy . . . some rock and roll is very acceptable to me, but its exciting tempos could endanger the morals of our youth. The then mayor of Boston said he felt that "Rock and roll concerts incite something that causes a lot of trouble with kids." And a Cambridge police sergeant said, "Modern music apparently has an unwholesome effect on teenagers."

The more the music was ridiculed (in the above instance it was even outlawed), the more firmly welded together the audience became, and the more desperately it attached itself to rock 'n' roll. In fact, several rock 'n' roll songs that became hits were sheer celebrations of rock 'n' roll itself; one of these, "School Days," by Chuck Berry, contains the line, "Hail, hail rock 'n' roll."

The transistor radio became standard equipment for this audience. This inexpensive little box was the source of the rock 'n' roll sound and message, and its portability allowed the audience to take the sound-message anywhere it wished. Even the frowns and complaints of those outside the audience could not silence it, for the transistor was frequently equipped with an earplug amplifier.

In this respect, the audience for a particular musical style had an impact on a certain area of the economy. According to the *Electronic Industries Association Yearbook of 1969,* 1,690,000 portable radios were sold in the United States in 1950. By 1958 sales reached 5,105,000; by 1961 the figure was 14,651,000.

"Nobody likes rock and roll but the public," said Bill Haley (*DOWN BEAT,* May 30, 1956). The public to which he referred was, in fact, the increasingly large teenage audience for rock 'n' roll.

Exactly why this audience was attracted to rock 'n' roll does not admit of a simple answer. In his article, "Popular Music versus the Facts of Life,"[8] S.I. Hayākawa may have touched upon part of the answer when he suggested that the rock 'n' roll audience was reacting negatively to the phony, artificial view of life and love expressed in the white ballads popular among older generations. On the other hand, there is much to be said for the idea that people do not live by facts alone, and that they require a certain amount of fantasy and artificiality.

The lyrics of rhythm and blues songs do deal with the subject of romantic love in a factual, unsophisticated, and unartificial way, especially so in comparison with the lyrics of white popular ballads. But the rock 'n' roll audience was much larger and heterogeneous than the audience for pure rhythm and blues; and as we have seen, the lyrics of rock 'n' roll songs are in general not as hard-nosed, factual, and graphic as are the lyrics of the typical rhythm and blues song. They are a compromise between the sentimental and artificial tone of the lyrics of white ballads, and the gutsy, realistic lyrics of rhythm and blues.

[8] Bernard Rosenberg and David M. White, eds., *Mass Culture* (Glencoe: The Free Press, 1957), p. 400.

This compromise was the result of several factors, probably the most important of which was an economic one: the suggestive lyrics of rhythm and blues could not be put up for sale to the mass public. It may be true that during these years the adult population was losing a certain amount of control over its children; nevertheless, it was by no means a powerless group, and its economic power coupled with its essentially puritanical views had to be reckoned with by the music industry. This puritanical element and the network radio stations which grudgingly (at first), then enthusiastically, "pushed" rock 'n' roll probably precluded the further development of love lyrics in a truly earthy vein.

As we have seen, rock 'n' roll tended to exaggerate a number of things it borrowed from rhythm and blues; it did the same with incantation and nonsense syllables. The same group that was opposed to suggestive lyrics seems not to have opposed lyrics that were grammatically impure, or textual incantations made of nonsense syllables. Partly for this reason, rock 'n' roll seized upon and exaggerated these elements to such an extent that phrases such as "A wop bam a lu ah, A wop bam boom "became an integral part of its style.

Cleaning up the lyrics and making them apparently harmless seemed to assuage the angers and fears of the adult population. For the most part they still, it seems, did not like the music, but in the end they did not prevent it from becoming an enormously successful business.

The rock 'n' roll audience was born at the beginning of the population explosion in this country during World War II. By 1955 there were many more people under the age of 21 than there had ever been in twentieth-century America. If for no other reason than by sheer force of numbers, this segment of the population would have to be catered to. This emerging audience was young, vast, and as a result of the relative affluence of the immediate postwar years, it had some money, and a belief that more money was on call if needed. How different such a belief was from that held by teenagers and young parents during both the depression years of the '30s and the ration-haunted years of the early '40s.

The rock 'n' roll audience also accumulated a kind of independence unknown to earlier generations of teenagers, an independence traceable to a number of things. It was the first generation to grow up with television. Whatever else television may or may not have done to and for this audience, it can safely be assumed that it offered its audience a firsthand, visual acquaintance with many people and things beyond its home towns, and at an earlier age than had previously been typical.

Then, too, for many of this group there was no permanent home town, but rather a series of temporary places to live. This migratory pattern became a fact of life in the '50s for the corporate businessman, or "organization man," and his wife and family. In his book, *The Organization Man*

(1957), William H. Whyte informs us that many of these families moved to different locations as many as seven or eight times in a ten-year span. It is an immensely complicated problem, and one far beyond the province of this book, to try to assess the many possible effects of this pattern upon the rock 'n' roll generation. But one reasonable guess is that it produced in it a feeling or a spirit of rootlessness.

For those not involved in the world of the corporate organization man and the migratory nature of such an existence, many did remain in more or less permanent home towns. However, some of these were exposed to the working mother syndrome that was so much in evidence in the '50s.

From all of this, it is possible to speculate that the new generation may well have been developing a set of attitudes about home, roots, and family that was different in some ways from the attitudes of its elders. In fact, it seems that at about mid-century many new attitudes on many different fronts were being formed, all of which were precipitated by conditions and events peculiar to that time.

But from a musical point of view, why the emergence of rock 'n' roll style at this particular time? A study of popular music in the '40s occupies another chapter of this book. A reading of that discussion reveals that many love songs from the early '40s dealt with the happiness, dreams, longings, and tragedies of young men and women in love, but caught in a wartime situation that necessarily kept them separated, either for the duration of the war (as expressed in songs such as "I'll Be Home for Christmas, if Only in My Dreams"), or—in the most tragic cases—forever (as expressed in, for instance, "I'll Never Smile Again").

The rock 'n' roll generation had no personal experience with such situations; the sentiments and tone of such lyrics were without real meaning to them. Their joys and their tragedies were of a different order: perhaps simpler, thus calling for simpler words; or less dreamy, demanding more realistic, down-to-earth terminology; and more adolescent (they were, of course, younger than the wartime generation mentioned above, but they were also forced to deal with some adult situations at comparatively younger ages), thereby calling for a more direct, less sophisticated expression of sentiments and feelings.

Swing, the jazz style that had been so popular with the parents of the rock 'n' roll audience, was also outside the direct experience of the latter group. By about 1950 or so, big band jazz, and big dance bands in general, were practically out of business. They simply weren't available to the 10- to 13-year-olds who in just a few years would form the core of the rock 'n' roll audience. At this time jazz splintered into smaller groups; the most significant of these dedicated itself to bop and other forms of experimental jazz, which for a variety of reasons appealed neither to the very young teenagers nor to their parents. Thus, a line of continuity, in the form of an interest in jazz, that might have developed between the two generations did not.

The remaining significant body of popular music from the late '40s was either of the topical novelty type (which becomes dated in a hurry), or belonged to a group for which it is difficult to supply a suitable label: the narrative and quasi-folksongs, such as "Mule Train," "The Old Master Painter," "Lucky Old Sun," "Ghost Riders in the Sky," and others. Both types lacked a danceable beat, and it is probably because of this that they failed to capture the imagination of the younger generation.

It is fair to argue that in several ways the late '40s–early '50s was a rather dull time in the United States. The war had ended, and although no reasonable human being was sorry to see it end, the air of electrified tension that accompanies such a holocaust was also brought to an end. The servicemen gladly discarded their military uniforms, but many of them quickly attired themselves in the civilian uniform of the '50s: the grey flannel suit. Equally dull was the kind of newly emerging suburban community like Levittown, Pennsylvania, with its row after weary row of look-alike houses, its supermarkets filled with uniformly packaged frozen foods, and the many chrome-encrusted and tail-finned automobiles that began to crowd the same streets at the same, predictable times of day.

With all of the above factors in mind, it is perhaps not too difficult to see why rock 'n' roll became such a quick and smashing success with its new, young audience. It did everything that the old style of popular music did not do for it. It used the right kinds of texts, expressed the right sentiments in an easily approachable manner, was not cluttered up with virtuosity, and had an utterly consistent, danceable beat.

Moreover, it belonged to this audience—the whole audience. It was not rooted in one section of the country or a particular kind of background or even in one ethnic group. This fact was eventually one of considerable pride to the audience—this was one kind of ownership this somewhat rootless group understood. Furthermore, this style of music belonged to them because no one else wanted it. In fact, as we have seen, some people didn't even want them to have it, which probably made it all the more appealing. Finally, at a time when many things, musical and otherwise, seemed rather dull, the audience found that rock 'n' roll music was exciting.

DISCOGRAPHY

Many recordings of rhythm and blues and rock 'n' roll songs are still available; however, as time goes by, they become more difficult to locate and, in many cases, much more expensive than they were several years ago. The recent revival of interest in this music has prompted record companies to reissue many of the biggest hits in albums. However, such albums usually include non-hits and sometimes, irrelevant material. But in the long run, the albums provide the best, most practical, and least expensive introduction to this music. Below is a very selective list of albums devoted to this music, as performed by several of the most significant practitioners of the styles. In the interest of economy, no attempt has been made to include every important performer and song. Instead, the list aims to be representative. The albums are divided into three groups: indispensable, important, and very useful. Following this is a supplementary list of recordings that are useful in the study of rhythm and blues, rock 'n' roll, and rock and roll.

Indispensable

Great Hits of R&B, Columbia G 30503. In addition to the selections already mentioned in this chapter, this album also contains other crucial performers and songs, such as "Fever," Little Willie John (Peggy Lee made a successful "cover" version of this song); "Sixty Minute Man," Billy Ward and the Dominoes; "Only You," The Platters; "Trying," LaVerne Baker.

ELVIS PRESLEY, *Elvis' Golden Records* (March, 1958), Volume I, RCA Victor. There is also a Volume II to this set, but it is this first volume that is crucial. The album includes, among others, "Hound Dog," "All Shook Up," "Heartbreak Hotel," "Teddy Bear," "Jailhouse Rock."

History of Rhythm and Blues, 4 volumes, Atlantic SD 8161, SD 8164. Volumes 2 and 3 are crucial; Volumes 1 and 4 are useful. In addition to the selections already mentioned in this chapter, Volume 3 has several important rock 'n' roll songs. "Corrina, Corrina," Joe Turner; "Ruby Baby," The Drifters; "Jim Dandy," LaVerne Baker; "C.C. Rider," Chuck Willis. Especially important in Volume 2 are: "Money Honey," The Drifters; "Shake, Rattle, and Roll," Joe Turner; "Tweedle Dee," LaVerne Baker.

Bill Haley's Greatest Hits (June, 1968), Decca DL 5027. Particularly important are: "Rock Around the Clock"; "See You Later Alligator"; "Shake, Rattle and Roll."

Little Richard: Cast A Long Shadow 4 sides, Epic EG 30428. The album contains a number of Little Richard's most important early rock 'n' roll hits, plus some later material. Hear especially: "Lucille"; "Tutti Frutti"; "Long Tall Sally"; "Good Golly Miss Molly"; "Whole Lotta' Shakin' Goin' On."

Important

Chuck Berry's Greatest Hits (April, 1964). The album contains many important rock 'n' roll songs, such as "School Days"; "Roll Over Beethoven"; "Maybelline"; "Johnny B. Goode."

PAT BOONE, *Pat's Greatest Hits,* Dot 3071, S 25071. The album contains several of the singer's rock and roll best-sellers from the mid '50s.

FATS DOMINO, *Rock & Rollin'* Imperial 9004, 9009. The album contains several of the best songs of one of the central figures in rock 'n' roll, including 'Aint It a Shame" (Pat Boone made a very successful cover version of this song); "You Said You Love Me"; "Fat Man."

Very Useful

PAUL ANKA, *21 Golden Hits* (1963). Most typical of this rock and roll performer are "Diana," and "Puppy Love."

FRANKIE AVALON, *15 Greatest Hits* (1964). Avalon and Anka are very much in the same (soft) vein. Hear especially: "Bobby Sox to Stockings."

BIG BOPPER, *Chantilly Lace* (1958). The title song from this album was a big rock 'n' roll hit in 1958.

Bo Diddley's 16 Alltime Greatest Hits (1964). The album contains several songs typical of the style of this important early rock 'n' roll singer.

THE DRIFTERS, *Rockin' and Driftin'* (1958). "Ruby Baby" and "Fools Fall in Love" are included in Vol. 3 of *History of Rhythm and Blues*, but this album also includes several of their other hits, such as "Drip Drop."

BUDDY HOLLY (1958). Another important early rock 'n' roll performer; this album includes his two biggest hits: "Ready Teddy," and "Peggy Sue."

Golden Hits of Jerry Lee Lewis. The album includes "Whole Lotta' Shakin'," and "Great Balls of Fire."

RICKY NELSON (1958). Very typical of the lyrics and singing style of the soft rock and roll style of the late '50s.

CARL PERKINS. Another rock 'n' roll performer with a country music background. This album contains his biggest hit, "Blue Suede Shoes," also made famous by Elvis Presley.

JOE TURNER. This well known and highly respected blues singer had some success as a rock 'n' roll performer. "Chains of Love" and "Corrina, Corrina" are included in *History of Rhythm and Blues*. In addition to these, this album contains "Shake, Rattle, and Roll," "Flip Flop," and "Honey Hush."

Richie Valens Memorial Album. Hear especially "Donna" and "Come on, Let's Go Rockin' All Night."

BIBLIOGRAPHY

In the past four or five years a great many books on various aspects of rock have been published. The quality of these sources is very uneven. Moreover, the majority of them either discuss the history of rock, giving general attention to each style, or concentrate on rock from the Beatles to the present. Below is a very selective list of sources that deal in useful ways with early rock and/or its ancestors.

BELZ, CARL, *The Story of Rock.* New York: Oxford University Press, 1969.

COURLANDER, HAROLD, *Negro Folk Music, U.S.A.* New York: Columbia University Press, 1963.

GILLETT, CHARLIE, *The Sound of the City.* New York: Outerbridge & Dienstfrey, 1970.

KEIL, CHARLES, *Urban Blues.* Chicago: University of Chicago Press, 1966.

ROXON, LILLIAN, *Rock Encyclopedia.* New York: Grossett & Dunlap, 1969.

SHAW, ARNOLD, *The Rock Revolution*. London: Crowell-Collier Press, 1969.

SHELTON, ROBERT, *The Country Music Story*. New York: Bobbs-Merrill, 1965.

The following items provide many useful insights into the sociology of the rock 'n' roll era:

JACOBS, NORMAN, *Culture for the Masses?* Princeton, N. J.: Van Nostrand, 1959.

McLUHAN, MARSHALL, *Understanding Media*. New York: McGraw-Hill, 1964.

ROSENBERG, BERNARD, and DAVID M. WHITE, eds., *Mass Culture*. Glencoe: The Free Press, 1957.

WHYTE, WILLIAM H., *The Organization Man*. Garden City, N. Y.: Doubleday, Anchor Books, 1956.

7

Words and Music:
English Folksong
in the United States

BRUNO NETTL

Throughout the world one of the functions of music is to provide a vehicle for the presentation of words—stories, religious incantations, emotional outpourings. Just as we know of no culture without music, we can find no culture, past or present, that does not have song. The relationship of the words to the melody that carries them varies greatly from people to people, and the relative significance of words and tune differs. There are songs without meaningful words and cultures in which the words of songs are relatively unimportant, but the use of melody to accompany words that are put together in some sort of artistic framework is a cultural universal. Indeed, the tie between these two elements, language and music, is so great that we may even be justified in believing that at one time, at the dawn of humanity, they were one and the same, and that from this form of communication that had elements of both music and speech, these two separate, audible forms of human expression eventually evolved.

Today, man everywhere is at a level far beyond this kind of generalized communication pattern, but he clings to the close relationship of language and music, in the form of song. The composer who sets words to music, or music to words, is engaged in a very complex but nevertheless very basic artistic activity. And this is true whether he composes the most esoteric, experimental music or the simplest sort of folksong. An understanding of the process of setting words to music may best be begun with an examination of folk music, for this is the music that is intelligible to large masses of people, the music that the largest segments of population regard as their own, and the music that probably expresses most clearly the personality of its culture.

Folk Music and the Mass Media

Many students have attempted to define precisely the concept of folk music, and they have had difficulty doing so, probably because its exact nature, cultural function, and relationship with other kinds of music differ from culture to culture and from period to historical period. Before the advent of industrialization and the development of mass media, European and American culture had a kind of music that was the property of peasants and farmers, of villages and homesteads, that was taught only by word of mouth, that had a relatively simple style of tune and poetry, and that was performed by more or less anyone in the community—the musically talented and the villager with the tin ear. Of course, people everywhere have always recognized the fact that some individuals sing better than others, learn songs more quickly, and know more songs; and in some folk cultures people sing in groups, while in others the singer performs solo, for others. But despite these differences, folk music was the music of all the people. The kind of folk music practice described above still exists in relatively isolated pockets of European and American culture. But as literacy became more wide-spread, and as printing and then radio and records and finally television and film became accessible to all, the nature of folk music changed.

The first of these developments, the invention of printing in the fifteenth century, began to become a force in the dissemination of folk music around 1600. Instead of continuing in the rural tradition of keeping its old songs, and to occasionally create variants of them, song writers of the towns and cities, among which London was prominent, began to compose new songs, which were printed on large sheets of paper called broadsides and were then sold very cheaply. These broadsides were usually poems—the tunes were only occasionally printed along with the words—which were, according to directions given on the broadside, to be sung to well-known folk, hymn, or popular tunes. Although the words at first dealt with lyrical themes such as love or nature, they soon came to be concerned more frequently with current events of local interest such as crimes, accidents, or inexplicable happenings that seemed to be supernatural. Thus, there developed a kind of narrative song, the broadside ballad, which shared the musical and textual style of folk song—many of the texts were sung to tunes taken from true folksong—and, in many ways, really became folksong. Many of these ballads passed into the rural folk tradition and, though originating in print, continued to exist in an oral tradition. In the United States the printing of broadsides began in the eighteenth century, and many of the most widely known folksongs of the nineteenth century, such as the songs of famous murders, outlaws (Jesse James), folk heroes (John Henry), and railroad wrecks ("The Wreck of the old 97"), began as broadsides. Even in the twentieth century, broadside ballads, largely by anonymous writers, continue to appear, commemorating events such as the death of Franklin Roosevelt and the assassination of John Kennedy.

Printing was thus the first of the mass media to have a great influence on the history of folksong. The broadside ballad is only one example of this; there are many other instances of the complementary influence of the printed and oral traditions.

The invention of recording near the end of the nineteenth century also played an important role in the development of folk music. Folk singers began to make records for public consumption in the second decade of the twentieth century, but even before this, scholars who wished to hold on to the rapidly disappearing rural folk traditions began to collect songs on wax cylinders and later on discs (and they continue to do so, with unabated interest, on tape). Then came radio and television.

What has happened to folk music in the West, particularly in the United States, is the gradual amalgamation of folk music, once a more or less isolated musical phenomenon, and musical styles of the cities; this has resulted from the development of visual and sound technology. One result of this amalgamation has been the evolution of a large number of distinct folk music styles used by a segment of the population that at one time was almost totally ignorant of folk music—the city dweller, the intellectual, the academic. The folk music tradition in the United States is carried on today by a few older individuals in small towns who still maintain a purely oral tradition, perhaps centered on the family or on a small clique of friends. But at the same time, this tradition has also been maintained by professional country and western musicians; by folk singers who appeal largely to college students, such as Joan Baez, Judy Collins, Joni Mitchell; by widely popular groups such as the Byrds and Simon and Garfunkel; by singers who try to maintain the oldest ways of singing the oldest songs they can find, such as Mike Seeger; singers who sing traditional songs in their own styles, such as Burl Ives and Pete Seeger; singers who use traditional styles to create new songs of contemporary relevance, such as Bob Dylan; singers who use elements of mainstream in a primarily folk context, such as Peter, Paul, and Mary; groups who use elements of folk music in what is essentially the mainstream itself, such as the Mamas and the Papas and other folk-rock musicians.

Many music lovers and scholars would argue that much of the music of the singers just mentioned is not folk music. And we might agree, depending on where we would set the outer limits of folk music, or depending on whether the distance between the old, rural, orally-transmitted amateur style and the new styles have become so great that we must admit that we are dealing with two phenomena. But at the very least, all of these musical styles contain ingredients of folk music among their essential elements. And probably one of the most prominent of these ingredients is the particular relationship that exists between words and tune.

Structure of Words and Music

The relationship between the words and the music of a folksong is probably closest and most obvious in their structure. The problem of meaning in music is enormously complex, and we will not be able to make very many concrete statements about the way in which the melody of a song, especially a folksong, reflects the meaning of its words. But we can rather easily observe the way in which musical and textual forms work together and the ways in which they contrast. And we can examine a single song in detail, as well as making generalizations about this kind of relationship in an entire repertory or in the total musical output of a culture. Our major concern in this chapter is the body of American folk music that originated in England and Scotland, or was created in America in the British tradition.

In this American folk music the most obvious and most widely used kind of structure is the strophic form, whereby a song consists of several stanzas of words, all different in word content but alike in number of lines, rhyme scheme, and rhythmic arrangements of the syllables; all of the stanzas of words are sung to the same tune.

There are several types of stanzas that are widely used in folksong. The most common is called "ballad meter" because of its great importance in many of the oldest English ballads. It consists of four lines and uses iambic feet, which means that a line consists of alternations of unstressed and stressed syllables, beginning with unstressed. The typical arrangement is for the first and third lines to have four iambic feet, and the second and fourth, two feet, as in the following stanza (with the stressed syllables underlined):

> She <u>mount</u>ed <u>on</u> her <u>milk</u>-white <u>steed</u>
> And <u>led</u> the <u>dap</u>ple <u>grey</u>,
> And <u>when</u> she <u>got</u> to her <u>fa</u>ther's <u>house</u>
> 'Twas <u>one</u> long <u>hour</u> till <u>day</u>.

It is difficult in the folk tradition (in contrast with the English and American learned poetic tradition) to find stanzas that do not at some point or other depart from the scheme. Even in our quoted example the third line has an extra unstressed syllable ("her"). Some stanzas in ballad meter have four feet to each line:

> Lord Bateman was a noble lord,
> A noble lord of high degree
> And he was restless, discontent
> Some foreign lands he wished to see.

The departure from set patterns is actually a special characteristic of folk music. Songs may well be composed with strict adherence to ballad meter or to some other scheme, but because songs are learned by word of mouth, and because each singer who learns a song feels free to make certain changes or tends to forget the precise way in which he learned the song, irregularities creep in. Of course, these irregularities are strictly circumscribed; certain kinds are acceptable to the culture, while others would render a song unpalatable. Thus, while folksongs permit departures from set patterns, these departures themselves become strictly patterned. For instance, in the example just cited, the third line is also sung as "he was restless, discontented," or "and he put his foot on a little boaten," or "he put his foot into some little boat," or "he became uneasy, discontented"—all slightly different in meaning and also irregular in regard to the four-foot iambic line. Thus, in some songs that appear to have been created in the ballad meter we have described, there are sections that have only vestiges of the ballad meter:

> There was a youth and a jolly, jolly youth
> And he was the squire's son.

Of course, other kinds of meter are also found in American folksong. The second most widespread has four lines to the stanza and four feet per line, but the feet are anapest (two unstressed syllables plus a stressed one); the first unstressed syllable in each line is lacking:

> Come all you young huntsmen that handles the gun
> And ever go hunting at the down setting sun
> I will tell you a story that happened of late
> Concerning pretty Molly whose beauty was great.

(From the booklet accompanying the record *Ohio Valley Ballads,* sung by Bruce Buckley, Folkways Records FA2025.)

The number of lines in a stanza is most commonly four; but five (this is found mostly in cases in which the fourth line is simply repeated), six, and eight are also found. The point to be remembered is that these kinds of poetic form were dominant in the oldest known English folksongs, and have been so ever since, even in those songs composed in recent times.

One reason for the integrity of the poetic forms of English and American folksong may be the fact that they are accompanied by tunes that fit the stylistic scheme exceedingly well. Most of the songs fit into a few types of musical meter. The songs with iambic feet are usually set to music in either duple meter, with all notes of equal length, or triple meter, with the fourth and eighth syllables elongated. Sometimes the elongated note is longer or shorter, creating measures in duple or even 5/4 meter. The songs that use anapest meter, on the other hand, are either in duple meter, with the stressed note longer than the others, or 6/8 meter, with the notes of equal length. Lines of song in these various meters are illustrated in Ex. 1.

Ex. 1. Examples of Meter in Anglo-American Folksong.

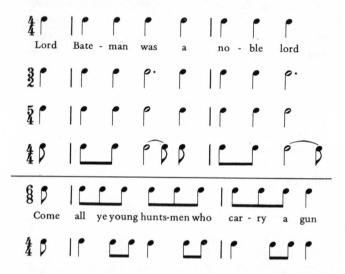

Many folksongs, old and new, differ in certain details from the given schemes, but most of them are somehow based on one of these types of arrangement. We may conclude, therefore, that in that part of American folk music based on the British tradition, there is close structural correspondence between words and music. At various levels—stanza, line, verse foot, and musical measure—units of words and music correspond closely. Stressed syllables are set to musically stressed notes.

One area of word structure of which the composers of English and American folksongs evidently took no cognizance is the rhyme scheme. In most four-line stanzas it is ABCB; that is, the second and fourth lines rhyme. But there is nothing in the music to suggest this. There is another aspect of the structure of the text that seems not to be reflected: the overall structure of the stanza. In most English songs each line of words appears only once; we may describe this structure as ABCD. However, the music of the four-line stanzas may include a good deal of repetition, and we find forms such as AABA, ABBA, ABCB, along with the very commonly found ABCD.

Of course, each folk music tradition in Europe (and its counterpart in America) has its own group of patterns and relationships; this is also true of Afro-American folk music. As an interesting contrast to the English forms used in the United States, let us briefly look at the blues form, which is so important in Afro-American folk and popular music. The most typical form for the words of blues consists of three lines. The second is a repetition or a paraphrase of the first; the third is a conclusion based on the premise of the first line. All three lines rhyme; that is, they end in syllables that rhyme with each other, but there is usually no scheme of metric poetry:

> My house is full of bedbugs, and chinches just crawl around: ‖
> But they bite me so hard at night, I can't hardly stay on the ground.

(From Harold Courlander, *Negro Folk Music U.S.A.* [New York: Columbia University Press, 1963], p. 135.)

> Well I'm sittin' down in jail, down on my knees;
> Well I'm down in jail, down here on my knees.
> And I ain't got nobody to come here and help me please.

(*Ibid.*, p. 132.)

The musical form of blues is similar to that of these words. The first two lines of music may be identical, or slight variations of each other, while the third line is usually in contrast, though its conclusion is often like that of the other lines, perhaps reflecting the fact that while the word content of the third line contrasts with that of the others, its last syllable nevertheless rhymes. In view of the fact that the rhyme scheme of Anglo-American songs is not usually reflected in any way in the music, we may say that the relationship between words and music in the blues is in certain respects closer. That is, in the blues the relationship among the lines of words, so far as their meaning is concerned, is reflected to some extent in the relationship among the musical lines; we must conclude from this that the structure of the words directly influences the music.

In some cultures the structure of words can have a profound influence on the structure of the accompanying tunes. The most dramatic examples are found in cultures that speak tone languages, that is, languages in which the relative pitch level of individual syllables helps to determine the meaning of a word. Such languages are spoken throughout Africa south of the Sahara, in China and Southeast Asia, and in some American Indian groups. Jabo, spoken by a tribal group in Liberia, has four tones—high, upper medium, lower medium, and low. According to Herzog, one word, "ba," can have a different meaning when spoken at each of these four pitch levels:

> "Spoken on a high pitch, *ba* means "namesake"; on a somewhat lower pitch, it means "to be broad"; in the middle register, it means "tail"; and spoken quite low, it is a particle expressing command.... The pitch is as much a part of each word in this language as its consonants and vowels."[1]

[1] George Herzog, "Speech-melody and Primitive Music," *Musical Quarterly*, XX, No. 4 (October, 1934), 453.

When Jabo words are set to music, there is no doubt that the melody made by the sentences of text has a good deal of influence on the melody that is composed as accompaniment. Composers do not appear to slavishly follow the melody of the words, however; they take it into account but depend on the context of the words and on certain poetical conventions to do the rest. A good deal of music is nevertheless derived from the tone-patterns of words. In the first place, the system of spoken tones is the basis for drum and horn signalling; indeed, it is the basis for most of the "talking drum" systems of Africa. Also, sentences—often making fun of a member of the tribe—are used as the basis of melodies, and people must guess what the melodies say.

Another culture in which words and music are closely related is that of the Tepehua of Mexico; here, specific bits of melody are thought to represent certain thoughts, ideas, and objects, much as European composers from J. S. Bach to Wagner used musical motifs to identify ideas that they wished to comment on musically. Here, then, are examples of cultures in which the structure of music and the structure of words are much more closely related and much more interdependent—in the sense that both have an impact on the meaning of the music—than is the case with English and American folksong.

Does Music Reflect the Meaning of Words?

Let us now see how the meaning of words can actually be reflected in the music. There are many levels at which this could take place. The kind of structural relationship that involves the meaning of the words, as well as the structure of the words and music—as just shown in the case of the blues—is certainly a possibility. The general mood of the text can be reflected in the overall character of the music; or changes in mood can be reflected by analogous changes in the tune. In order to provide that sort of change in folk music, we would need to provide different music for the various stanzas of a song, since changes in mood are most typically exhibited over longer stretches of a song, not within a single stanza. This kind of changing musical accompaniment is, thus, hardly found in folksongs, which are almost always strophic; but it is found in many songs in the realm of art music, a few examples of which are discussed in a subsequent section of this chapter.

A composer can, of course, go much further. For example, in opera each personage may have his own musical style, which then reflects not only what he says, but his entire character. In the late music dramas of Richard Wagner—especially *The Ring of the Nibelung,* in which the entire assembly of singers and orchestra work along the same lines in order to underscore what a character is saying—the accompanying music as well as the singer's melody may simultaneously reflect (through the association of individual musical motifs with specific characters, events, ideas, and even the attitudes of the individuals in the drama), various levels of drama, such as the specific content of the words being sung, what a character is actually thinking, and past and possibly even future events in the story. In folk music there is nothing that even comes close to such a complex structure.

Even so, the relationship between words and music in folk music is important, and even where we fail to find it, its absence may be significant. In English and American folk culture—and in others as well—singers have difficulty separating words and music. If a singer (and we are now speaking of unlettered, rural folk singers) is asked to recite the words of a song, he frequently cannot do this without singing them. In fact, in many cultures there is but a single word for "song," not separate words for "music" or for "words that are sung."

Generally speaking, although folksongs change in the process of oral transmission, a tune remains associated with a particular set of words. If we take a sample of the versions or variants of a popular folksong such as "Barbara Allen" or "Lord Randall"—versions that differ considerably from one another because they have been circulating orally for so long—we find that most of them are sung to tunes that are related to one another, that is, tunes that can be assumed to be variants of one original tune. Thus, we can say that many of the tunes that are sung to the words of "Lord Randall" (and B. H. Bronson, in *The Traditional Tunes of the Child Ballads,* presents over a hundred of these) belong to one tune family, just as all of the versions of the "Lord Randall" poem, different though they may be in detail, belong to one text family. A folksong and its tune tend to grow together.

There are important and significant exceptions to this kind or parallel development, however. If we examine the folk music of all of Europe (and of that part of American culture that is derived from Europe), we find that each nation has its own musical style, its own typical forms of song, its own scales, rhythms, kinds of harmony, and so forth. But we also find that some tunes in, say, England are very similar to some tunes in France, Czechoslovakia, even faraway Hungary and Rumania. The similarities are not great, but they are significant. It is possible that in the remote past a tune would be composed in one country and carried to others by wandering minstrels (who we know were very important in the dissemination of music in the early Middle Ages), or taught by people near a border to their neighbors on the other side. In any event, members of a tune family seem to coexist in various countries; but they are almost never accompanied by the same set of words, even in translation. A tune will be sung with the words of a narrative ballad in one country, and elsewhere its musical relative will be a love song, a ritual song, or a children's game ditty. The practice of taking a song and substituting new words for the original ones is widely used within countries as well. In American culture broadside ballads made use of hymn tunes, and hymn writers borrowed from the folk tradition. But whereas on a national level there is a tendency for a tune and its words to stay together, on an international level this is hardly ever the case.

Not that a set of words may not also have an international existence. On the contrary, the stories of most of the famous English ballads that are so important in American folk music are found also in the balladry and sometimes in the folk-tale repertory of other countries. For example, let us take the story of "Lady Isabel and the Elf Knight." The Finnish scholar Iivar Kemppinen searched folksong collections throughout the world and found that almost 2000 variants of this song had been collected, mainly in Europe, but including 162 in North America. This story—rather typical of the old, complicated balled stories—concerns a young lady whose home is visited by a man with whom she falls in love. He prevails upon her to elope with him, and to take much of her parents' riches. They leave, and when they arrive at a river (or at the sea), he tells her that he will now drown her for her gold. She remonstrates and finally finds a way both to escape from him and to do away with him (usually by drowning), and she then returns home. This story is obviously very old, and it must certainly have spread from country to country, for it is too complex to have been created independently, on different occasions, with the main elements of the story intact in each version. Different forms of this one story, varying in detail, are found, particularly in the nations of Northern Europe. Kemppinen found about 800 versions in the Germanic-speaking countries (England and North America, Germany, Holland, Scandinavia), a great many in Finland, some in Hungary, many again in the Slavic countries, and a few in Italy, France, and Spain. From this geographical distribution we may assume, incidentally, that the story arose in England or Scandinavia and thence spread to other nations. The point to be noted here, however, is that while the English versions of "Lady Isabel" are sung to tunes that are related to each other, and the Finnish ones to another group of related tunes, etc., the story, as it spread, does not appear to have taken its tunes along with it, despite the fact that we know from our previous example that tunes can and do cross national boundaries.

All of this tells us something about the ways in which words and music in folksong are and are not related. In general, it must be admitted that the relationship between a text and its tune in English and Anglo-American folk music, and perhaps in European folk music generally, is not really organic. Structural relationships are considerable, but they apply to a whole class of materials, and there are few cases in which the peculiarity of structure of a *single* song are reflected in the music. Again, the *way* in which words and tunes travel (through space and time) is similar, though the traveling itself is not done in concert. We have not yet, however, examined the content of the words of folksong in order to see how it is related to the accompanying music.

Let us look first at the question of general mood or character. It is true, for example, that children's game songs sound different from ballads and have a different sort of word content than that of ballads. It is also true that folk hymns usually sound different from ballads, though they sometimes use the same tunes. The difference in sound is due not so much to a difference in the musical content, that is, the identity of the tune, but, rather, to a difference in singing style. For example, the hymn singing in Southern small towns that is done with the use of books that have especially shaped notes to convey different degrees of the scale—mi, fa, sol, la—is done by groups, in a very rhythmic style. Ballads are usually sung solo, in a way that tends to obscure the musical meter. Thus, the difference in musical character is often due more to a difference in performance practice than musical content.

We should also look at the character of songs—in the sense that some relate tragic stories, and others, stories that are happy or even comical. In other words, we should ask whether a comic text is usually sung to a tune that has elements of humor, whether a song with a "happy" ending has a happy-sounding tune, and whether a tragic story is accompanied by tragic music. In Anglo-American folksong, there seems to be little such correlation. Let us look at two tunes, as examples. The first, a song widely sung in Southern Ohio and Kentucky during the early twentieth century, is sung to a poem called "Lula Viers." It is a song with a definitely tragic story, which tells of the wanton murder of a girl by her lover, and his subsequent punishment. Like many ballads composed in the nineteenth and twentieth centuries in the United States, it tells a true story and ends with a moral. The second tune is "Our Goodman," an old English song with humorous words, once known widely in American folk communities and still sung.

Let us assume that these two tunes are really representative of their respective categories, the first of tragic songs, the second of funny ones. If we try to compare them in order to see whether the character of the words is reflected in the music, we come upon two serious problems. First, we must define for ourselves just what is humorous and what is tragic in music. Individual music lovers, especially those with some sophistication, may have very specific ideas on this subject. But let us take a rather wide view as a point of departure: Humor in music is expressed through the unexpected (that is, the sudden violation of an established pattern), through manifold repetition of a short musical motif, and through quick tempo; the tragic is expressed through dissonance and slow tempo. If we examine English and American folksongs along these lines, we find that there is a difference in average tempo between humorous and tragic songs. In other respects, however, there appears to be no significant difference, and the two examples we have cited certainly do not exhibit any significant stylistic differences. In other words, these two tunes do not appear to reflect the character of their accompanying texts.

Ex. 2. "Lula Viers," fifth stanza, from *Ohio Valley Ballads*, sung by Bruce Buckley (Folkways FP23/2).

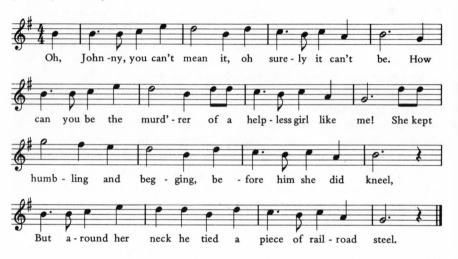

Oh, John-ny, you can't mean it, oh sure-ly it can't be. How can you be the murd'-rer of a help-less girl like me! She kept humb-ling and beg-ging, be-fore him she did kneel, But a-round her neck he tied a piece of rail-road steel.

Ex. 3. "Our Goodman," second stanza, from Jan Philip Schinhan, *The Music of the Ballads* (Durham, N. C.: Duke University Press, 1957), pp. 104–5.

2. Last night when I come home as drunk as I could be. There was a horse stand-in' in the sta-ble where my horse ought to be. 'Come here my lit-tle wife and ex-plain this thing to me: How come a horse stand-in' in the sta-ble where my horse ought to be?' 'You old fool, you cra-zy fool, Can't you nev-er see? It's noth-ing but a

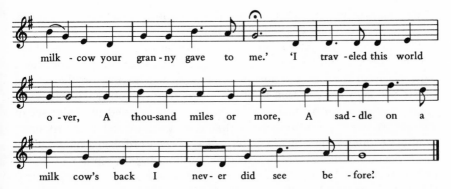

milk - cow your gran - ny gave to me.' 'I trav -eled this world o - ver, A thou-sand miles or more, A sad - dle on a milk cow's back I nev- er did see be - fore!

There is still the second problem to be resolved. Since the typical reader is not a member of a culture or subculture in which folksongs are sung as a matter of course, is it not possible that his (or the author's) criteria are irrelevant? And could it not be that a person who sings these songs might regard the tunes themselves as having very definitely a humorous or tragic character? In order to answer these questions, we would have to resort to field techniques, that is, to asking people who habitually sing these songs. This kind of questioning has been attempted, but it has been frustrated by the fact that folk singers have difficulty in separating in their minds the words and music of a song. Nevertheless, enough information has been elicited for us to be reasonably sure that the tunes themselves do not carry these connotations. The words, however, do carry them, and entire categories of music—song, fiddle playing, dance music—are also regarded as having some specific (though not easily articulated) character. But if a person asked one of the elderly men in Kentucky who knows these songs whether the tunes are themselves happy or sad, he would not get a very satisfactory answer.

Do Words and Music Express the Same Theme?

Is there then no way in which the meaning of the words is closely reflected in the music of American folksong? At the most obvious levels we seem to have drawn a blank, because individual words are certainly not emphasized, and neither is the overall mood of a song really reflected. There are, however, three ways in which we can establish the kind of relationship for which we have been looking: (1) by locating the expression of the character of a culture in its song; (2) by detecting similarities in the way in which different songs develop textual and musical meaning; and (3) by observing the development of a special sort of musical meaning through the interaction of musical and textual structure. All three are rather complicated concepts.

For the first one, let us refer to an idea presented in Chapter 3, based on the work of Alan Lomax, who believes that the music of a culture, or at least its favorite song style, reflects certain fundamental values and patterns of the culture; according to Lomax these are manifested in many aspects of music, particularly in the way the human voice is used in singing, in the way in which people who perform together relate to each other and to their audience, and in such things as the physical position and muscular set of a singer. In essence, Lomax believes that all of the most significant music in a culture expresses the same thing, regardless of the words being sung. Lomax also believes that in each culture, the folk music, being the music most accessible and acceptable to the largest body of people, is the best indicator of what is expressed. Lomax came to this conclusion partly because he noted that American folk singers from the British-derived sector of our culture tended to sound alike. They use a rather thin, nasal tone, they normally sing solo, and when they sing together, their voices don't blend well. There is a definite difference between men's and women's singing. Rhythm and meter are not of great importance, and rhythmic patterns are not adhered to very rigorously.

Even more indicative is the relationship of the Anglo-American folk singer to his audience. According to Lomax,

> "...the familiar pattern... is for the singer to sit quietly with his hands passive in his lap as he sings; his eyes are closed, or he gazes unseeingly over the heads of his listeners.... The listeners must remain silent and physically passive. Any movement on their part would interfere with the story. Any distraction would break the ballad singer's spell.... The...singer commands and dominates his audience during his performance."[2]

Lomax draws parallels with the symphony orchestra, and goes on to point out that this model for musical performance in analogous to the specialized, authoritarian approach to life in Western culture, in which the relationships among individuals always include the recognition of one who is in authority.

Does this general characterization of Anglo-American folk singing tell us something about the meaning of music? We would have to admit that the music of the folksongs expresses not meaning of the words themselves but, rather, something much more fundamental to the culture: the way in which people feel about themselves and each other. It complains (in its nasal, ornamented, sometimes searching sound) about the restriction that the culture places on individuals, about the emphasis on authority in relationships among people, about sexual restriction, about the lack of contact among the individual and his fellows. The words of folksongs express the same thing, but since words lend themselves to much finer gradation of meaning and

---

[2] Alan Lomax, "Song Structure and Social Structure," *Ethnology,* I (1961), 439–40.

much greater precision, the scope of their meaning can be much broader. Nevertheless, an examination of a large number of folksongs would show that the attitudes expressed in the music also occupy a substantial proportion of the texts. A complaining culture will have a complaining musical style, and a good many—but not all—of its folksongs will include words that express complaint. But on the other hand, speech, which deals largely with everyday matters, tends to cover up the expression of emotion. It is not surprising that in many cultures, complaints against the culture pattern, against rulers, against oppression and restriction of various sorts—things that a person would not dare express in speech—are tolerated when expressed in song. Thus, we may speculate that on the one hand, the music of folksong does not directly reflect the words because it expresses something much more basic; on the other hand, it reflects the words in the general sense that certain basic problems of the culture are articulated in each of the two forms of communication, though in different ways.

Afro-American folk music is in many ways related to that of the Anglo-Americans. Songs move back and forth between the two groups, and to some extent singing styles are shared. But there is, nevertheless, a great deal of difference; it is claimed that even in such almost universally known musics as rock, a trained listener can readily distinguish a black from a white singer. That this distinction is possible is almost certainly not related to heredity, but is the result of deeply ingrained cultural and musical patterning, which is due to the different musical heritages of the two groups. Afro-American culture, partly because of its latent African content, is different in content and style, and, thus, again following Lomax, we must assume that it would produce a different kind of musical sound and a different way of using the voice. It is characterized by emphasis on rhythm, good vocal blend in group singing, and much less of an authoritarian relationship between singer and audience, and also by greater freedom to explore various kinds of sounds. This may reflect a different sort of relationship among people, and different attitudes toward social life, sex, and work.

In a sense, then, the music of folksong reflects not the meaning of the words but, rather, the meaning of the culture. A second way in which words and music travel similar roads in folk music involves the way in which materials are selected for inclusion in the songs. If we compare English and American folk music with a body of song composed by sophisticated poets and composers—say, for example, the songs of nineteenth-century German and Austrian composers such as Schubert, Schumann, Brahms, and Hugo Wolf (who used poems by German literary masters such as Goethe, Schiller, and Heine for his texts)—we see that one of the distinguishing characteristics of folk music is its use of formulas. By this, we mean short but distinctive bits of music or groups of words that seem to travel from song to song. In songs of English origin, these formulas are frequently word groupings such as "milk-white steed," "lily-white hand," "jolly youth," "noble lord." They may be standardized beginnings, such as "come all ye lads and lasses," or "come all ye young people." Or they are poetic ways of expressing number, such as "he had daughters, one, two, three" instead of simply saying "three." These bits of text help to integrate each separate song into the whole repertory, they form a bridge between the individual creation and the entire body of song. In a sense, the folk composer-singer seems to be saying in these formulas, "This song has something special to say, but in a way it is also saying the same things that all of my songs and all of my people's songs say." Here, we see another manifestation of the point made in the previous section, that a folksong expressed not only its own content but also something very important and fundamental about its culture.

The music of folksongs also contains much that is similarly formulaic. The formulas may be analogous to the short, adjective-noun phrase formulas of the words. For example, there are characteristic interval-patterns that are used to begin songs, such as:

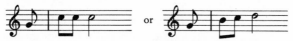

Also, the characteristic melodic contour, that is, the general upward and downward movement of the melody, is formulaic in nature. The most typical way for a melody in American folksong to move is in an arc-shaped pattern, with the second and third lines higher than the first and fourth. Of course, the rhythmic and metric patterns described at the beginning of this chapter also belong in the realm of formulas. Thus, the methods used to construct words and music are essentially the same, and the formulas used to develop verbal and musical content are essentially the same; this fact represents another way in which the words and music of folksong can be said to express the same thing and, thus, can be thought of as closely related.

However, there is also an important issue that seems to work at cross-purposes with the kind of analogous treatment of words and music just described. We have tried to show briefly that in certain ways words and music work together to express the same thing. But the same sort of statement can be made about the music dramas of Wagner and the songs of Schubert and Schumann, and we would have to admit that these composers did a much better job of uniting these two elements in song than did the folk composers. Are we simply to be satisfied to say that folk music does the same kinds of things that art music does, but that it does not do them as well, or that it stops short of accomplishing the same goals that art music achieves much more fully? This is, indeed, an acceptable answer, for, to be sure, the composers of art music are much better technicians of composition than the composers of folksong. But if we accept the fact that folk music expresses what an entire population wishes to express, we must also assume that the folk composers accomplish what they set out to do in a way that is satisfactory to the consumers of this music; otherwise, these consumers would force frequent and rapid change on the composers.

The point is that if we compare the words and the music of a folksong, we find that they are very different despite the similarities already noted. A ballad has words that narrate a story, a story that moves from simple narration of facts ("there was an old man in the north countree, and he had daughters, one, two, three") to the rendering of events of great stress and intensity ("as they were watching the ships come in, the oldest pushed the youngest in")—a story that has an ebb and flow of dramatic intensity, that uses dramatic and lyrical devices to move the listener. Its tune is a simple melody that is repeated, accompanying; uncritically as it were, quiet and stormy stanzas alike. Moreover, a ballad singer delivers all parts of his story with the same expression: he does not sing more excitedly when the story becomes dramatic; and he uses essentially the same singing style in dramatic and lyrical, tragic and comic ballads. This holds true even in the singing of modern folk singers who perform for an urban clientele, such as Bob Dylan or Pete Seeger, and it holds true even when the songs are composed specifically for the sophisticated listener, as was the case with Dylan's "The Times They Are A-Changing" and "With God on our Side."

One reason for this seeming disparity between the words and the music of a song, and between their respective emotional impacts, is the fact that in the Anglo-American folk culture the words of a song are considered more important. The tune exists as a vehicle for carrying the words, it definitely fulfills an accompanying role. Another reason is the fact that the contrast between verbal and musical meaning, the difference that one can occasionally find between the structural principles governing the development of the two, the obvious disparity between what the singer is saying and the way in which he is saying it, is itself significant. The contrast between the words and the music is itself a way of underlining the meaning of the words, and it provides an artistic effect that is a part of the entire style and is fully intended. The repetition of the stanzas and the unemotional tone of the singing style calls attention to the significance of the words and to their changing content.

Perhaps even more significant is another facet of this relationship. The cross-purposes at which the structures of the two lines, music and words, seem to work constitute a complex design whose points of tension and stress, alternating with areas in which there is agreement, are part of the essence of the style, much as the contrast and alternation between consonant and dissonant chords in a harmonic structure are the essential ingredients of harmonic design.

Let us look briefly at two songs that illustrate this last point. The first is an old English ballad, "The Gypsy Laddie," whose tune is unusual in its repertory, for it consists essentially of one musical motif:

Ex. 4. "The Gypsy Laddie," collected in Southern Indiana.

Lord Tho-mas he came home last night, in - quir-ing for his la - dy, The

an - swer that they gave to him, She's gone with the gyp-sy Da - vy

which appears in different forms: in its "main form" in lines 1 and 3, in somewhat varied form in line 2, and—in line 4—in the form of line 2, transposed down an octave. The four lines can thus be divided into groups, according to several different criteria. If we simply consider their identity, or tone content, we must group lines 1 and 3 together, in contrast with lines 2 and 4. If we consider melodic range, we see that the first three lines contrast with line 4. If we use the criterion of innovation, we see that lines 1, 2, and 4 include things that have not been done previously, but line 3 differs in that it is the only one that precisely repeats material that has already been presented. If we look at musical phraseology, we see that lines 1 and 2 together make up one unit, while lines 3 and 4 make up another. Thus, several kinds of grouping are possible.

Similarly, the words can be grouped in several ways. If we consider the content of the words without delving closely into their meaning, we see that the four lines are simply different—an ABCD structure. If we look more closely, however, various groupings develop. First, the stanza is readily divisible into two halves, one involving Lord Thomas, the other giving us information about his lady. The dramatic structure, however, sets the fourth line off from the rest, since it relates new and, for the listener, unexpected and unconventional information. The rhyme scheme is ABCB, thus uniting the second and fourth lines. In length, lines 1 and 3 and lines 2 and 4 are identical. The words are narrative, and eventually become highly dramatic; but the personality of the tune does not seem to reflect this mood. Even so, there are some parallels—for example, the setting off of the fourth line from the others.

This evident desire to have different currents moving through the structure of music and words, combined with the way the structures reflect the meanings, is shown in the various patterns in word-music relationships. Let us now turn to a style that offers quite a contrast to English and Anglo-American folksong, the folk music of the Czechs, in the western half of Czechoslovakia. It is perhaps a mistake to say that this repertory contrasts greatly with ours; there are similarities, such as the use of stanzas and strophic form, and the tendency to have four lines per stanza. But the differences loom.

In the first place, the accent structure of the Czech language is different from that of English. The first syllable of every word is accented. In English, the syllable to be stressed is not predictable, and the stress pattern may determine the meaning of a word (as in be*low* versus *bil*low, which are alike in pronunciation except for stress). Also, there is a resulting tendency for sentences in Czech to begin with stressed syllables; in English, because we use unstressed articles, prepositions, and prefixes, the tendency is for unstressed syllables to begin an utterance. One result of this is the tendency for English and American folksongs to begin on an unstressed musical beat—the upbeat or "pick up"—while Czech folksongs usually begin firmly on the downbeat. A second difference is due to the organization of Czech (and most other Eastern European) folk poetry, which is based on the number of syllables, not verse feet. In other words, what is important about the lines, "Lord Bateman was a noble lord" and "There was a youth and a jolly jolly youth," as far as rhythmic structure is concerned, is the fact that both have four stressed syllables that are more or less evenly spaced, and, thus, four feet of verse; this makes each of them susceptible to the same kind of musical treatment, despite the fact that the first has eight syllables, and the second, eleven. In the Czech folksong in Ex. 5, what is important is the fact that each line has seven syllables:

> Cerné oči jdete spát (Black eyes, go to sleep)
> Však musite rano vstat (For you must rise early in the morning)

(From Bruno Nettl and Ivo Moravcik, "Czech and Slovak Folk Songs Collected in Detroit," *Midwest Folklore* 5, no. 1 [Spring 1955], p. 44.)

Ex. 5. Segment of Czech folksong, "Černé oči."

The fact that there are also four words and, thus, four stressed syllables, in each line is not important. Notice also that the stresses are not spaced regularly. This kind of irregular placement of stresses can be seen even more clearly in the following lines of another Czech song:

> *Hrá*-ly *dud*-y u *Po*budy, *ja jsem je sly*šela
> (The bagpipes played in Pobudy)
> *Da*-va-li *mne za hrad*nika, *ja jsem ho ne*chtela
> (They were giving me to the gardener; I didn't want him)

(*Ibid.*, p. 40.)

Ex. 6. Segment of Czech folksong, "Hraly Dudy."

In line 1, the following syllables are stressed: 1, 2, 5, 6, 9, 10, 11, 12; and in the second line, 1, 4, 5, 6, 9, 10, 11, 12. But while English and American folksong composers usually make the stressed syllable of a verse-foot coincide with the stressed note of a musical measure Czech composers allow the stressed and unstressed syllables of a song text to fall where they may. It is true that in Czech folksongs there is some correlation—but not a very strong one—between the stresses in music and those in words, but the composers did not necessarily intend it to be that way. After all, if they really wish to make the stresses coincide, they could do so much more effectively and efficiently. Rather, this correlation is probably due to a similar patterning of words and music, possibly a result of the tendency for music and perhaps poetry to reflect basic values and patterns of the culture.

Let us look at the way words and music compare with each other in our first Czech song, "Černé oči." The tune is quite different from the English tunes we have examined because its lines vary in length; lines 1 and 4 are longer than lines 2 and 3. On the other hand, it is rather similar to "Lord Thomas" (or "The Gypsy Laddie"), examined above, in that its entire structure is based essentially on one musical idea, which is repeated and varied. The way in which the variation is accomplished is quite different. "Lord Thomas" takes the musical idea (line 1), changes its ending in line 2, repeats the original in line 3, and suddenly moves it down an octave in line 4. "Černé oči" presents the main idea (line 1), and repeats it, slightly changed, two tones higher, and the last part of it compressed, in line 2; line 3 is a transposition of line 2, down one tone; and line 4 is the some as line 1. Thus, while the last line of "Lord Thomas" moves to something radically new —within the context of the song—"Černé oči" ends by returning to the beginning.

A further comparison of the words of "Černé oči" with its music gives us the same kind of multi-directional movement that was found in the above discussion of "Lord Thomas." The text can be divided into two halves—line 1 and line 2 (a repetition of line 1), and line 3 and line 4 (a repetition of line 3). However, lines 1 and 3 are united in their presentation of new material, while lines 2 and 4 are both repetitions. All four lines have the same rhyme scheme. The two sentences differ in meaning, line 3 presenting a sort of conclusion drawn from the statement in line 1.

None of these ways of grouping the lines of text is reflected in the basic structure of the music. The musical lines can also be divided into groups, but by most criteria—length, content, repetition—we would divide lines 1 and 4 from lines 2 and 3, a grouping that we did not make in the lines of text. Here, then, we have a good illustration of the thesis given above, that contrast between verbal and musical meaning and between verbal and musical structure is itself a significant stylistic feature of many folksongs. A supporting bit of evidence is that the kind of pattern just described for one Czech folksong—the words consisting of two repeated lines, the music exhibiting a closed form in which the last line reiterates the first—is very widely used in Czech folk music. An examination of other folk music styles would provide examples that differ in detail but underscore the same general point.

Thus, while the words of folksong do not generally follow the music precisely and obviously, there are several ways in which words and music can be said to reflect the same meaning.

Words and Music in German Art Song

An extraordinary development of art song with piano accompaniment occurred in the German-speaking countries in the nineteenth century. Composers such as Schubert, Schumann, Wolf, and Brahms created a style of song so distinctive that it is known—in order to differentiate it from the art songs of other countries—by the German word for song, *Lied*. Living in the early romantic era, the creators of this genre were profoundly influenced by folksong and folklore, but their style was also derived from other models. However, the historical roots of German art song are not an issue here; we wish again to examine the relationship between music and words. These composers were faced with the same problems—musical expression of the meaning of the words, similarity or conflict between musical and textual structure, correlation between analogous elements of language and music—as the composers of folksongs, and they became much more involved in them. After all, folk composers solved many of these problems merely by resorting to traditional patterns and stereotypes; indeed, some of the problems, such as reflecting in the music specific ideas or events from the text, were simply ignored. There is little evidence, as we have already pointed out, that folk composers paid attention to the text-tune relationship in individual songs; nor do they seem to have attacked the problems for each song separately and individually.

To an extent, composers of Lieder also referred to stereotypes. The poems they used were frequently strophic; that is, each poem has several stanzas with the same form. The forms of the music can be roughly divided into two types, strophic and through-composed. A strophic song is one in which each stanza of text is set to the same music; a through-composed song provides special music for each part of the text and, ideally, none of the music is repeated. Actually, few songs follow these models precisely. Most strophic songs exhibit at least a tiny difference among the stanzas, due usually to the composer's desire to emphasize or illuminate some of the text's meaning. On the other hand, most through-composed songs exhibit some elements of strophic structure.

In the matter of setting individual words and lines, German Lieder presents no problem. That a stressed syllable must appear on a stressed note was taken for granted. In Lied style, however, a particular line of poetry might be set to an unlimited variety of rhythms, quite unlike the small number of acceptable rhythmic lines available to the English composer of folksong. The beginning of the poem "Erlkönig" by Goethe, which was set to music by many composers, is accompanied by various rhythmic schemes:

But the most interesting relationship to be studied in German art songs are those in which the meaning of the words, the moods, the ideas, and the implications of the text are reflected in the form and the content of the music. One of the most important differences between folksong and Lied is the presence in the latter of piano accompaniment, which does much more than provide a harmonic background; it is frequently used to musically express the ideas and events in the text. In many songs this is done through the persistent use of a short musical figure. In Schubert's "Erlkönig," the piano accompaniment is

dominated by this motif: 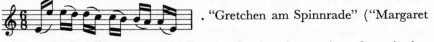 which underscores

the mysterious and supernatural atmosphere and the tremendous anxiety of the characters. His "Auf dem Wasser zu Singen" ("A Song to be Sung on the Water") uses a piano figure symbolic of a boat rocking on gentle waves:

 . "Gretchen am Spinnrade" ("Margaret

at the Spinning Wheel") uses a figure reflecting the turning of a spinning

wheel: . "Wehin," a song about a miller's

apprentice wandering along a rushing brook, has the gurgling and splashing of the brook in the piano accompaniment:  . And

"Die Forelle ("The Trout") uses an accompanying figure that represents the rapid swimming and sudden turns and leaps of the fish:

The use of a recurring figure of this sort is only one of many ways used by Lieder composers to underscore the ideas of the text.

To consider the more broadly formal relationships between words and music in art song, let us examine three songs: "Heidenröslein" and "Erlkönig" by Schubert and "Die beiden Grenadiere" by Schumann. "Heidenröslein," a poem by Goethe, is very much in the spirit of a folksong. It tells the story of a boy who sees a beautiful rose. He threatens to pluck it, and the rose replies by threatening to defend itself with its thorns. The boy plucks the rose and is wounded by the thorns. Each of the three stanzas has a refrain that has nothing to do with this miniature plot. In his musical setting, Schubert uses a strictly strophic form. He chooses to ignore the broader symbolism of the poem and, instead, underscores its folk-like nature by providing a simple, chordal and even guitar-like accompaniment. Passages for piano alone are minimal: there is only a two-measure postlude to each stanza, and this is simply a repetition of the singer's last line.

"Die beiden Grenadiere" ("The Two Grenadiers") is much more complex. The poem by Heine has four stanzas of four lines each, plus a short, two-line stanza in the middle. The text concerns two French soldiers in the Napoleonic wars; they were captured in Russia, but are now returning to France. When they arrive in Germany, they hear the rumor that Napoleon has been killed. Both wish to die, but one feels that he must go on living to support his wife and children; the second scorns his family and prepares to kill himself. The second half of the poem tells of his instructions to his comrade, who is to see that he is buried in France, in full military dress and with his weapons. Then, one day, he will hear his emperor riding over his grave and will rise from it to fight again.

The essentially somber mood of the text is reflected in a recurring piano

figure: [music notation] . The song begins in the minor mode, but as

the second soldier succumbs to his fantastic enthusiasm, it changes to major. Schumann obviously uses the two modes in this way because of the stereotyped qualities that are associated with them—sad for minor, optimistic and happy for major. In other ways, the song likewise progresses from the somber to the joyous, from depression to vigor, from the mood of a funeral march to that of a battle cry.

The form of the music, giving each musical line (the part to which a textual line of seven feet is set) one letter, is this:

AABC	The background of the story is told
ADDE	The soldiers express their sadness
AAF♭C	Second soldier determines to die; gives instructions for his burial
GG	Instructions for burying arms with him
HHIH	Vision of emperor returning and his rising from the grave

From this outline, one can see that this song is partially through-composed, but has strophic elements. Three of the sections begin with A, and the first and third subdivisions are almost alike. However, the progress of the story takes precedence over any tendency to proceed in a simple, strophic fashion. As long as the story is narrated, or as long as the soldiers discuss their fate in a rational manner, the music uses the materials presented near the beginning of the song. But as the monologue of the second soldier becomes increasingly fantastic, the music also changes; it ends with a literal quotation from the French national anthem, the "Marseillaise," and Schumann thereby follows the complete transformation of mood and content found in the poem.

Schumann is careful to keep the song musically unified, however. In addition to the piano figure that appears throughout, he begins the song with an intervallic motif (an ascending perfect fourth beginning on the anacrusis), which is also the beginning of the "Marseillaise," and which reappears throughout the song. Finally, he comments on the futility of the soldier's vision with a brief concluding piano passage that returns to the somber mood of the song's beginning.

Goethe's "Erlkönig" tells the story of a father who is hurrying through the countryside with his ill and delirious son. The boy sees visions of the Erlking, a fantastic figure (in German folklore, he was thought to carry off small children) who lures him with promises of games and fun. The child cries out, resisting the advances of the Erlking, and the father tries repeatedly to calm him. When the father arrives at an inn, he finds the boy dead. Except for introductory and closing stanzas, which are spoken by the narrator, the story takes the form of dialogue among the father, his son, and the Erlking.

Schubert's setting of the song suggests the main characteristics of these three. The unity of the composition is achieved by several devices: (1) the triplet figure mentioned above (p. 215) appears throughout; (2) the boy cries out in terror several times, each time accompanied by the same motif:

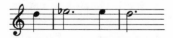

(3) the father's three attempts to quiet the boy are reflected in similar

musical materials:

On the other hand, the song is through-composed in the sense that no portion of any length reappears in its entirety. The juxtaposition of textual and musical content can be seen in the following table:

Text Stanza	Text Content	Main Musical Motif	Key	
1	Narrator tells of father and son riding.		Gm	
2	The son says he sees Erlking. Father says it's only fog.		Gm	Father in low register, son in high.
3	Erlking entices the boy.		B♭	Accompaniment waltz-like
4	The boy tells of Erlking's promises; Father says it's only the wind.		Gm	
5	Erlking tells of his daughters.		C	
6	Boy cries out that he sees the daughters. The father says it's only willows.		Am	
7	Erlking now threatens boy. Boy cries that Erlking has harmed him. Musical climax.		E♭	
8	Narrator concludes story.		Gm	Last line of song recitative style.

Schubert evidently makes great efforts to reflect the various levels of the text's meaning in his musical setting. Providing music of a different style for each character is the most obvious technique, but there are others. The climax of the text, which occurs in the seventh stanza, is accompanied by a musical climax. The increasing severity and insistence of the Erlking is indicated by the mounting intensity of the music he sings. The imperturbable father sings material of the same tempo and intensity throughout. The final line—the father finding his son dead and presumably carried off by the Erlking, a quite unexpected event—is sung with the use of recitative, a completely unexpected device, musically.

Strictly musical principles also contribute to the total effect. The tension generated by the accompaniment in triplets is relieved in stanzas 3 and 7 by the lighter and more melodious singing of the Erlking. There is a balance between the introduction of new thematic material and the recurrence of old. Stanzas 1, 2, 4, 6, and 8 are mainly in minor, alternating with other stanzas in major keys. The song progresses from a home key of G minor (in the edition for high voice) to B-flat major, C major, A minor, E-flat major, and eventually back to G minor, a circular pattern that complements the otherwise essentially alternating or rondo-like technique of presentation.

The Words and Music of Modern Folksong

At the beginning of this chapter, we pointed out that folk music in America today is quite different from what it was a hundred years ago. It has changed from a relatively isolated but extremely widespread phenomenon to a body of music that interacts constantly and in many ways with other kinds of music. And it changed from what may have been the most widely used kind of music in the nation to a kind of musical expression that various minorities consider to be their own. The contents of its words have also changed, and so, to an extent, has its musical style.

The music has, in fact, changed less than the words. If we examine the tunes used by Bob Dylan, Peter, Paul, and Mary, Joan Baez, the Byrds, Simon and Garfunkel, and Judy Collins, we see that they are not so very different from the tunes of "Lord Randall" and "Lula Viers." They frequently still have four lines, they use the same kinds of scales and melody patterns, they have a few typical rhythmic patterns that are at least related to those found in older folksong. There are also changes, of course. Folksongs in the modern, urban environment are sung by groups in harmony more frequently than by soloists. There is always musical accompaniment, whereas in earlier, rural times this happened only occasionally. Folk music today makes much more of the beat, and is more rhythmically complex. The singing style has become influenced by country and western, rock, and pop. Songs are actually written down, and very little of the old, traditional repertory is used—a fact that causes some to feel that folk music today is not really folk music. In some ways, indeed, it is not, but "it" has happened, the logical outcome of the establishment of mass media in the culture, beginning with print and continuing with recording, amplification, radio, television, and film.

The words of folk music have changed more, and this is no doubt due to the fact that for us today, "folk" and "folk music" mean something quite different from what these concepts meant in the past. Again, however, the situation today is a logical outcome of past events. In the distant past almost everyone was "the folk"; the folk were the majority of the population, and, thus, when an intellectual and economic elite developed, it was logical that folk music should be regarded as something low, uninteresting, uncreative, unimaginative. This attitude is still reflected in the twentieth century theory that the members of the folk community are unable to create something new; they only take over what is created by the elite in the cities and at the courts, and while using it, simplify and debase it. By the eighteenth century, however, folk music and the folk took on a different role in Western thought; the folk community was regarded as a haven of unspoiled purity, much as those in the world's simple cultures were considered the "noble savages." This view has come to the fore again in recent times, as concern with ecological and social problems begins to become an important factor in our lives. In the nineteenth century, a period of nationalism, the "folk" began to be the symbol of national tradition, of the nationally and culturally cohesive group, and the concept of folksong was one that reflected nationhood; and the words "folk song" became, in some languages, synonymous with "national song." Today, a period in which true, authentic folk music is sung only in isolated pockets of American culture, and when there is much concern with the rights and the separateness of minorities, folk music has become the music of special minority causes.

While the music of the folksong directly reflects the style of the old folk music, itself a downtrodden music, and while the modern folksong is a minority style within its combined rock-pop-jazz-country and western- soul culture, the words of folksongs present the views of the minorities. And there is a plethora of minorities.

First, there are the racial minorities—blacks, American Indians, Mexican-Americans—whose popular music contains many of their older folk traditions; it is interesting that members of these groups have become active in the folk music whose style is based on the Western (i.e., English and Anglo-American) folksong tradition. The words of their songs are in English, but they deal very frequently with the special problems, concerns, and feelings of their own group. A prime example of this kind of musician is Buffy Sainte-Marie, an American Indian.

Then there are the non-English speaking minorities, for whom the continuation and development of their European folk music traditions has been a special way of maintaining their national tradition in the face of modernization and Americanization. Ethnic groups such as Polish-Americans in Detroit, Czech-Americans in Chicago, and Mexican-Americans in the Southwest have taught their folksongs to their English-speaking children, believing that this form of expression could be maintained as a symbol of their special ethnicity, while social and economic life changed. (Chapter 4 contains a more substantial discussion of this trend.)

But most interesting, folk music in the English-derived style has become the music of minority viewpoints—the outrage against capitalist exploitation of the poor farmer (as in the songs of Woodie Guthrie), and support for the newly established labor unions during the Great Depression of the '30s; civil rights groups in the '50s ("We shall overcome"); the movement to end wars, especially the war in Vietnam during the '60s; and, more recently, the need to preserve our natural resources and to save our ecological system. The prime movers in espousing these causes, and in singing and hearing the songs concerned with them, have been minorities—the poor, the unskilled workers, the young, students, intellectuals.

Thus, folksong continues to exist, though in somewhat different form and with a different function from that of the past, in our contemporary urban culture. In style, its words and its music remain rather like those of the old folk songs. In the way they are composed, they resemble the broadside tradition of the nineteenth century, which made folksong responsive to the need for quick communication regarding news of local importance. In the details of musical style, it has moved in the direction of popular music, while retaining the essential elements of its rural predecessor. In the technical relationship of words and music, it continues the strophic and poetic practices of old English song. Its tunes do not reflect, any more accurately than they did in the old days of rural folk music, the words that are sung. But both the words and the music of folksong today express and symbolize something special and specific—the causes of minorities who are concerned about issues that attract only a few adherents. The minorities use folk music to speak to the rest of us.

BIBLIOGRAPHY

General information about folk music—its definition, characteristics, and major styles—is available in Bruno Nettl, *Folk and Traditional Music of the Western Continents,* 2nd ed. (Englewood Cliffs, N. J.: Prentice-Hall, 1973); English and American folk music are discussed in Chapters 4 and 10 of this book. More detail about the textual and musical forms of Anglo-American folksong is found in Chapters 7, 8, and 9 of Roger D. Abrahams and George Foss, *Anglo-American Folk Song Style* (Englewood Cliffs, N. J.: Prentice-Hall, 1969). Music and words of many of these songs are found in Bertrand H. Bronson, *The Traditional Tunes of the Child Ballads* (Princeton, N. J.: Princeton University Press, 1958–1972); Cecil J. Sharp, *English Folk Songs from the Southern Appalachians* (London: Oxford University Press, 1952); and Alan Lomax, *The Folk Songs of North America* (Garden City, N. Y.: Doubleday, 1960). Records that include some of the songs discussed here and others of the same type are Charles Seeger, ed., *Child Ballads Traditional in the United States*, (Library of Congress AAFS 57–58); and *Versions and Variants of Barbara Allen*, which makes possible a detailed comparison of versions of one song from the point of view of both words and music; and *Ohio Valley Ballads* sung by Bruce Buckley (Folkways 23/2), a record of American songs from ca. 1900. Material on the blues is available in Charles Keil, *Urban Blues* (Chicago: University of Chicago Press, 1966). The work of Alan Lomax referred to in this chapter is presented in his *Folk Song Style and Culture* (Washington, D. C.: American Association for the Advancement of Science, 1968) and "Song Structure and Social Structure," *Ethnology*, I (1962), 425–51. African tone languages and their relationship to music are discussed in George Herzog, "Speech-melody and Primitive Music," *Musical Quarterly*, XX, No. 4 (October, 1934), 452–66. Further discussion of Czech folk music is found in Nettl, *op. cit.*, pp. 80–81; and in Nettl and Ivo Moravcik, "Czech and Slovak Folk Songs Collected in Detroit," *Midwest Folklore*, V (1955), 40–48. Other facets of the relationship between language and music appear in Charles Boiles, "Tepehua Thought Songs," *Ethnomusicology*, XI (1967), 267–92.

Material on the relationship between words and music in art song can be found in Eric Sams, *The Songs of Robert Schumann* (New York: Norton, 1969); and Donald W. Ivey, *Song* (New York: Free Press, 1970).

Among the vast number of records that illustrate folk music in modern urban society, we mention only *The Times They Are A'Changing* by Bob Dylan (Columbia CS 8905); *Parsley, Sage, Rosemary and Thyme* by Simon and Garfunkel (Columbia CS 9363), and their *Bridge Over Troubled Water* (Columbia CS 9914); *Fifth Dimension* by The Byrds (Columbia CS 9349); *Illuminations* by Buffy Sainte-Marie (Vanguard VSD 79300); *The Mamas and the Papas Deliver* (Dunhill DS 50014). There is no way to give even a representative sampling of popular folk music records to illustrate the points made here. Readers may wish to refer to the *Rock Encyclopedia* by Lillian Roxon (New York: Grosset and Dunlap, 1969) for materials concerning the '50s and '60s. A historical view of the subject is Reginald Nettel, *A Social History of Traditional Song* (New York: A. M. Kelley, 1969).

8

The Performer as Creator:
Jazz Improvisation

RONALD BYRNSIDE

Improvisation and Fixed Music

An improvisational composition may be described, at least theoretically, as being composed and performed almost simultaneously; it is a nearly spontaneous musical creation that stands in contradistinction to a piece of fixed music, which is composed in its entirety before it is performed. The aim and result of an improvised piece is that it is unique—it can be created only once. It is not intended to be duplicated in future performances, and unless it is captured on recording disc or tape, it is lost to all except those who are present at the time of its creation.

Fixed music, on the other hand, aims at stability, and the performers of a piece of fixed music aim at a more or less precise re-creation of it each time they perform it. They are aided in this attempt either by some system of notation—which tries to fix the music on paper—or through aural transmission (folk musics, for example)—which tries to fix the music in the memory of those who come into contact with it. The piece, as the composer originally conceived it, may be altered in time. In the case of notated music, this is due to imprecisions in or variable interpretation of his notational symbols; with aurally transmitted musics, it may be due to the faulty memory

223

or even the caprice of the performer who does the transmitting. However, these kinds of alterations are mere accidents and are not representative of the idea of improvisation, for the intention of both the composer of fixed music and those who perform his work is to retain the music in its original state.

In so describing improvised and fixed musics we have established both the outer limits and the polarity of musical composition: the absolutely spontaneous and impermanent versus the rigorously premeditated and permanent. However, the history of musical composition reveals that these poles are largely theoretical, not real, and that purely improvisational pieces and utterly and permanently fixed pieces are rare. Thus, in considering improvisational musics we must remember that we are dealing with musics that are spontaneous only to one degree or another, but never wholly so.

The Bounds of Improvisation

The improviser works within certain limits, and only by understanding how and in what ways these limits bind the improviser can we develop an appreciation of what he does. The fleeting, impermanent nature of improvisational compositions has on occasion led to the faulty notion that the improviser is a sort of musical free agent who is bound by no conventions and guided by no logic or canon, and who creates music by allowing various and sundry bits of inspiration to "pop into his mind" and out of his voice or instrument at one and the same time. But this is not what he actually does. In making his music the improviser cannot escape his own musical habits, his previous musical experiences, his personal performance facility and compositional procedures. The music he creates while improvising is conditioned by these things, and is, thus, considerably more reflective than purely spontaneous in nature.

At the core of an improvisation there is a preconceived, premeditated musical idea and skeletal structure that, typically, is borrowed from some preexistent composition. This borrowed element may be nothing more than a formal structure and a sketchy harmonic outline, or it may consist of these things plus a specific pre-composed melody, or in some kinds of improvisational music it may consist only of melodic fragments and a very generalized formal design. In any case, this element, however detailed or sketchy it may be, provides a basis upon which the improviser composes his music. If a performer retains not only the essence but also most of the details of a given melody and changes it only in superficial ways, we will likely be disinclined to accept what he does as improvisational, because he is not really composing something new. More likely, we will recognize what he does as an ornamental or variational rendition of the borrowed tune.

Variation, Ornamentation, and the
Spirit of Improvisation

To varying degrees, the processes of variation, ornamentation, embellishment, and so forth can partake of the spirit of improvisation. In Chapter 1 it was suggested that from a certain point of view all music is variational, and that it is theoretically possible to understand all events in a given composition as variations of some central germinal idea, which is the piece in microcosmic form. But in the more ordinary sense of the term we understand variation as a process in which one or more segments of a composition are modifications of the initial section of the piece. We have seen this process in the classical theme with variations, and in other, related types of variational procedures. In such music the essence of improvisation is not present because, first, the variations are fixed, and, second, they are so regulated by the theme that they have life and make sense only by directly referring to that theme. Part of the charm and much of the purpose of such variations is to keep clearly before us the aural image of the theme, as if it were merely changing costumes with each succeeding variation.

On the other hand, there can be in such music something of the spirit of improvisation, something of the improvisational urge to compose anew rather than to merely duplicate. This urge can be pursued to the point where the theme is pushed almost, but never quite, out of our recollection.

Ornamentation and embellishment are variational processes that operate on a smaller, more localized level. If the term variation is used at the levels of the section or the phrase, then ornamentation is properly used at the level of the individual note. In some fixed musics ornamentation is precisely notated; and in others ornaments are notated as a series of shorthand-like symbols, or are not notated at all but are understood and performed by convention.

The Improviser as Composer

Before turning to some of the particulars of improvisational composition, let us compare in a general way the operations of the improviser-composer with those of the composer of fixed music. Thus far, we have discovered that the improviser is a creator of non-fixed and essentially non-duplicatable music, who composes with reference to some pre-planned idea and structure, which he borrows from another source.

The improviser's decision-making time differs from that of the composer of fixed music. In composing a piece of music, the latter ponders the nature, order, and interrelationships of the musical ideas with which he is working.

He weighs the merits of these ideas and their musical sense, as he molds and arranges them in what to him is presumably the perfect order. During this process one idea may begin to dominate others, and may thereby affect the shape and direction his composition takes—other ideas may be altered, or some of the original ideas may be eliminated or transformed into subordinate ideas. Such documents as Beethoven's musical sketchbooks clearly reveal that composers of fixed music often use a trial-and-error method in forming and placing ideas, and that they sometimes work with a single idea or set of ideas over an extended period. In short, the composition of such music may require considerable time.

The improviser's decision-making time is compressed to fractions of seconds. As he works with one small segment of his composition, he must simultaneously think, hear, and imagine what will follow this segment and what its relevance will be to preceding and subsequent moments of the piece. It is in the nature of his method of composing that his creative timing will be nearly synchronous with his playing of his instrument. The improviser cannot always know where his composition is going next. This does not necessarily mean that he is indecisive; it may be that as he explores and presents an idea, he discovers something in it that had not previously occurred to him while the idea was being formed in his mind—it may be something that, at that very instant, strikes him as a thing to be expanded and developed. Thus, his timing is further taxed: he must shift his ear, his mind, and his fingers way from the direction he had charted for them only a moment ago, and channel them into this new and unexpected path. He realizes simultaneously that this new and unexpected turn is accountable not only to itself, but to the whole composition as well. Serious risks are ever present in improvisational composition: a momentary lapse in concentration or a mistake in judgment can flaw the work. It is impossible for the improviser to go back and erase or redo a flaw. The ideas and their transformation into sound must be in order the first (and only) time.

Let us now turn our attention to the process and nature of improvisation as it is revaled in several different bodies of music. We shall focus primarily on certain fundamental aspects of jazz improvisation; then we shall branch out to examine briefly the process and uses of improvisation in certain styles of Western art music. Finally, we shall briefly examine the process in some non-Western musical traditions.

Improvisation in Jazz

Jazz crystallized into a distinct kind of music around the turn of this century, though its history extends back to an earlier time. When a comprehensive account of its origins appears, it may well reveal that the roots of this fascinating music are rather older and more diverse than is now generally accepted.

Jazz has undergone a series of stylistic changes in its relatively brief history, and under the general stylistic umbrella of jazz a number of particular styles have developed. This means that certain things that can be said about dixieland jazz are not true of the big band jazz of the '30s and '40s, or, for different reasons, of the bop and progressive jazz of the late '40s and early '50s, or, for still other reasons, of more recent jazz styles. Nevertheless, there have emerged a few characteristics of jazz in general that transcend stylistic boundaries. These characteristics can be separated into two categories (which are not mutually exclusive)—one concerning *what* is played in jazz, the other dealing with *how* it is played.

Most jazz pieces consist of expositions of some borrowed element and sections of improvisation that are composed within the framework of that element. By and large, the improvisational sections with their elements of variation and ornamentation of the borrowed element far outweigh any tendencies it may have toward the fixed state of pre-composed music. Indeed, improvisation is central to jazz. The fairly small body of borrowed and fixed pieces from which jazz compositions are made is severly limited in terms of musical complexity and variety. The borrowed element may be a popular song that has, in the great majority of cases, the formal structure AABA and a harmonic vocabulary consisting of simple triads and other chords that function in largely stereotyped and predictable ways. Or the borrowed element may be a blues, in which case the formal structure and harmonic language are even simpler and more predictable.

Jazz is essentially a cooperative music. Jazz singers and players can perform alone, but usually, jazz is performed by small ensembles (three to eight players), or by "big bands" (sixteen to twenty players). A rhythm section, usually consisting of piano, bass, drums, and optional guitar, forms a unit in both large and small ensembles. Each of the members of the rhythm section can perform solos, but the primary function of this unit is to articulate the beat and to provide the harmonic foundation for the entire ensemble. The other players perform solo improvisatory sections and arranged ensemble sections. For our purposes, the latter is either a notated or a pre-rehearsed section in which each player in the ensemble performs a prescribed fixed part. These fixed parts are composed by the arranger. Thus, while it is central to jazz, improvisation is not the only kind of musical activity found in it, rather, jazz encompasses a mixture of improvised and fixed sections of music.

At the general structural level, a great many jazz pieces follow the pattern illustrated below:

Brief introduction: Usually 4 to 8 bars, in which the beat, tempo, and key are established.

Exposition of the
borrowed element: Either pop song form:

A	A	B	A
8 bars	8 bars	8 bars	8 bars

or 12-bar blues form (sometimes 16-bar blues):

A	A(1)	B
4 bars	4 bars	4 bars

This section may or may not be arranged. In either case it ordinarily presents the borrowed element in a straightforward fashion. At the least it refers directly enough to the borrowed tune so that it is easily recognizable to anyone familiar with it.

Improvisations: A variable number of improvisatory sections, sometimes interspersed with short arranged sections. The solo sections, or choruses, are usually 16, 32, or 64 bars long if the borrowed element is a pop song, and either 12 or 24 bars long if it is a 12-bar blues. The solos may or may not refer directly to the borrowed melody.

Closing section: Final statement(s) of the borrowed tune. Like the exposition this section may or may not be arranged, but the borrowed melody is usually repeated in more or less its original form.

The recorded examples below illustrate this design or minor variations on it.

1. "Sunday" (written by Miller, Cohn, Stein, and Krueger); played by Gerry Mulligan, Ben Webster, and rhythm section on *The Jazz Round* (Verve VSPS–24, side I, and 4).

The piano opens with an 8-bar introduction. Then the saxes present one full chorus (32 bars) of the borrowed tune, which is ornamented, but clearly recognizable. This is followed by three choruses by Mulligan (baritone sax), then two choruses by the piano, then three choruses by Webster (tenor sax). Notice how the tune "Sunday" virtually disappears throughout these eight improvisatory solos. Each of the three soloists creates new music within the phrase structure and harmonic outline of the borrowed element. In the course of their improvisations the soloists make few and incidental references to the borrowed melody. These solos are followed by a 32-bar chorus, divided as follows: 8 bars—Mulligan; 8 bars—drums; 8 bars—Webster; 8 bars—drums. The piece concludes with a complete statement of the borrowed element. Again, the borrowed melody, though ornamented, is clearly recognizable. The tune "Sunday" is given below in its original form.

Ex. 1. "Sunday." Words & music by: Ned Miller, Chester Cohn Jules Stein, Benny Krueger. Copyright © 1926, Renewed 1953 Leo Feist Inc. Used By Permission.

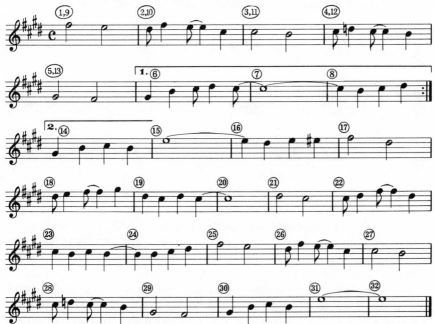

2. "Somebody Loves Me" (written by G. Gershwin, MacDonald, and DeSylva), played by Eddie Condon and his group on *Encyclopedia of Jazz on Records* (Decca DXF–140, Vol. III—"Jazz of the Forties," side 2, band 3).

There is no introductory section, but the borrowed element is presented twice in its entirety in the exposition section, and the melody is clearly recognizable. In the next section notice how the borrowed melody gives way to improvisatory melodic lines as the trumpet, baritone sax, clarinet, and trombone alternately create solos. In the short concluding section notice that only the first 8 bars of the borrowed melody are played. The borrowed tune "Somebody Loves Me" is presented below in its original form.

Ex. 2. "Somebody Loves Me" (B. G. De Sylva, Ballard MacDonald, George Gershwin). © 1924 New World Music Corporation. Copyright renewed. All Rights Reserved. Used by Permission of Warner Bros. Music.

The borrowed element, the overall formal structure illustrated on pages 227–228 and sections of improvisation constitute what is played in jazz (or at least most jazz, for there are exceptions to this generality). But to more clearly separate jazz from other kinds of music, it is necessary for us to acquaint ourselves with how these things are played in jazz, for a particular kind of performance practice is also central to jazz.

The term "swing" is sometimes used as a stylistic label for the big band jazz of the '30s and '40s—the so-called "swing era"—but it has a broader meaning when used to describe a certain performance practice typical of, and indeed unique to, all jazz. To swing the rhythm of a tune is to play it with a certain deliberate disregard for its indicated (notated) note values, and also to play it with certain accents and inflections that frequently run counter to the directions of the notation. More than any other factor it is the performer's swinging that prompts us to say, when we hear him play, that his performance is "jazzy." We sense this "jazziness" even when the performer is not improvising, but is merely playing the borrowed melody, as in the exposition sections described and outlined above.

In swinging a phrase that contains groups of even eighth notes or even quarter notes, the jazz performer tends to make them unequal. He accomplishes this by playing some of them as dotted eighth notes and some as sixteenth notes, as below.

Ex. 3. (A) Phrase of even eighth notes; (B) phrase with uneven eighth notes.

Or, and this is even more typical, he plays groups of even eighth or quarter notes in triplet fashion, as below.

Ex. 4. (A) Phrase of even quarter notes; (B) phrase of quarter-note triplets.

A good soloist does not adhere doggedly to either of these approaches. He will, rather, mix triplet figures with bursts of sixteenth and thirty-second notes, dotted notes, and even quarters or eighths. In any case, when swinging the jazz performer does not play the rhythm of the borrowed tune "straight" (as it is notated). Nor does he play the pitches of the borrowed tune "straight." The jazz performer will almost always add some extra pitches (ornamentation) or he may omit some of the given pitches, substituting rests or notes that are held longer.

Swing is also marked by frequent syncopation, that is, a temporary displacement of the normal accent pattern of a meter or an individual beat. A syncopation results in a shift of emphasis from the metrical downbeat to the metrical upbeat. This shift is normally achieved through either duration or conscious accent.

Ex. 5.

In Ex. 5, measure A illustrates the normal accent pattern of the 4/4 meter. In measure B the half note beginning beat two (a weak beat in normal 4/4) is held through beat three (a strong or secondary downbeat in normal 4/4), creating a syncopation, or temporary displacement of the normal downbeat-upbeat pattern of the 4/4 meter. In measure C the normal weak beats, two and four, are emphasized by being attacked more forcefully than the normal strong beats, one and three, thereby creating a syncopation.

In Ex. 6, note that syncopations are created by emphasizing the normally weak parts of individual beats. Here, the emphasis is created simply by making the weak (or last) parts of the beats longer than the normally strong (or first) parts of the beats.

Ex. 6. (A) Normal accentuation of beats in 4/4; (B, C, D) syncopated beats.

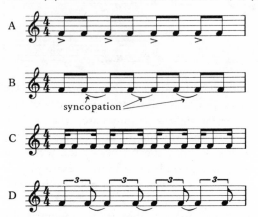

These notated examples do not indicate certain articulative and timbral qualities that are also characteristic of swing. For instance, notice below that Lester Young's swinging version of "Taking a Chance on Love" contains not only the triplet figures, syncopations, and melodic ornamentation discussed above, but also a tone quality—for the most part breathy, almost velvet-like— that is sometimes associated with swing. Notice, too, that several notes are not attacked in a clear, brittle way, but are approached in a sliding fashion. Some notes are attacked in a forceful, right-on-the-beat fashion; but after the attack, the sound becomes fuzzy, or the pitch is altered slightly, or the attacked note is ornamented. It is impossible to verbalize precisely about these inflections and the other techniques of swing discussed above, but in Ex. 7 several of them are marked with special signs (the key to which appears at the end of the example). The top line is Young's first chorus (which follows the opening piano chorus). The bottom line is the tune in its original form.

Ex. 7. "Taking a Chance on Love." Words by: John Latouche, Ted Fetter. Music by: Vernon Duke. Copyright © 1940, Renewed 1967 Miller Music Corporation. Used by permission. Played by Lester Young (tenor sax), Teddy Wilson (piano), with bass and drums, on *The Jazz Round* (Verve VSPS–24, side 2, band 2).

Key to special marks in the score:

>   = accented note

∧   = punched, crisp, right on the beat.

= note approached by slide.

= note attacked, the "swallowed."

= shuffled or lazy beat.

= fuzzy tone quality.

☆   = pinched sound.

= sound decays after attack.

The Improvisatory Solo

The so-called jazz "break" is a short, melodic passage played by a soloist at points when the accompanying ensemble is momentarily tacet (silent). Though the beat of the piece is felt during the break, it is not actually played by the rhythm section. The break, then, is a literal break in the otherwise relentless sounding of the beat, and an opportunity for the soloist to improvise with neither the fetters nor the assistance of the sounding beat.

At its best the break is an important introduction to, or in some cases an extension of, the main body of the soloist's improvisation, for it usually occurs at the end of one section and leads into the next. The superb improviser makes the break exciting by molding it so as to be continuous with the rest of the solo, and by creating the sensation that the beat is temporarily suspended. Moreover, the exciting break creates an internal rhythmic energy that seems to propel the music toward the reentrance of the sounding beat— we know the beat is about to return, and yet we are delightfully surprised when it does.

At its worst the break is mere filler, consisting of arpeggios or short scale passages that have no substantial musical value and no connection to the main body of the solo that follows. Also, such breaks are almost always rhythmically disappointing: they seem undesirable interruptions of the beat rather than exciting temporary suspensions of it.

Below is an annotated diagram of "Aunt Hagar's Blues" (written by W. C. Handy), played by King Oliver's Dixieland Syncopators, on *Encyclopedia of Jazz on Records* (Decca DXF–140, Vol. I—"Jazz of the Twenties," side 1, band 1), a piece containing several breaks.

4-bar introduction

Exposition of the borrowed element: 12-bar blues; ensemble with trumpet lead.

12-bar sax chorus: Contains two 1-bar breaks (bars 2 and 4). Neither of these breaks is very interesting: the first consists merely of three arpeggios; the second, a rapid, descending scale passage. Neither has any apparent connection with the rest of the solo that follows the breaks.

16-bar trumpet chorus: Bars 15 and 16 of this chorus constitute a clarinet break that leads into a clarinet chorus.

12-bar trombone chorus: Contains two 1-bar breaks (bars 2 and 4). These are more interesting, both melodically and rhythmically, than the sax breaks above. Bars 11 and 12 of this chorus make up a playful tuba break.

12-bar ensemble chorus: With trumpet lead, as in the original exposition.

Below is a similar diagram of the breaks in another piece on the same recording: "Wild Man Blues" (written by Armstrong and Morton), played by Johnny Dodd's Black Bottom Stompers with Louis Armstrong, (side 1, band 3).

8-bar introduction: Consists of two 2-bar trumpet breaks and a 4-bar ensemble section.

32-bar trumpet chorus: 2-bar breaks occur at bars 11–12, 15–16, 25–26, 27–28,
(this is a 16-bar blues)   and 31–32. Only the last of these seems a little weak; this
is due mainly to the fact that the sequential figure that
Armstrong plays in this break has become, in the course
of time, a worn-out cliché. The other breaks pop with
rhythmic excitement; each in its own way momentarily
conceals the location of the true beat. Further, each break
is marked by its own set of melodic figures, all of which
seem to grow from the body of the 32-bar chorus. In
addition, Armstrong offers us a variety of tone qualities in
these breaks.

32-bar clarinet chorus: Contains 2-bar breaks at bars 15–16, 25–26, and 27–28.
Again, these are satisfying because of their rhythmic
interest, melodic shape and continuity, and subtle variations in tone quality and dynamics.

The next cut on this same recording, "That's No Bargain," played by Red
Nichols and his Five Pennies, contains several obvious breaks—one each for
trumpet, guitar, sax, and drums.

Let us now turn our attention from the break or phrase ending to the
heart of the improvisational phrase. Improvisation is essentially linear. However, the improvised line cannot take the liberty of avoiding the accompanying harmonies by playing pitches that have no direct relationship to those
harmonies; if this were done, the music might lose its sense of direction.

In jazz the improvised melodic line and the chords from which it originates
are indissolubly bound together. The pitches that form the improvised line
are either members of the chords that accompany them, or they are dissonant pitches, subject to the laws of functional harmony that regulate
the use and placement of dissonances. In Ex. 8—the same song cited on
p. 229—notice that many of the pitches in the improvised trumpet line are
members of the basic triads and seventh chords accompanying it. The chord
tones are marked with an "x." In this example the improvised trumpet line
(and beginning in bar 16, the start of the improvised sax line) is on the top
staff. The basic chords of the original (borrowed) song are on the lower
staff.

Ex. 8. "Somebody Loves Me" (B. G. De Sylva, Ballard MacDonald, George Gershwin).
© 1924 New World Music Corporation. Copyright renewed. All Rights Reserved. Used
by Permission of Warner Bros. Music.

Coleman Hawkins's version of "How Deep Is the Ocean" (written by Irving Berlin), in *Encyclopedia of Jazz on Records* (Decca DXF–140, Vol. III—"Jazz of the Forties," side 1, band 4), concludes with an extended unaccompanied solo. Here, we begin to enter the realm of the cadenza which we shall discuss on p. 244.

This improvised line—reproduced in Ex. 9—is much more intricate and undoubtedly much more interesting than the improvised trumpet line in Ex. 8. Here, the playing of the soloist—Coleman Hawkins—is not dominated by arpeggios. Rather, Hawkins uses the chords of the borrowed song as a backdrop for an elaborate, many-faceted improvisation consisting of a skillful and musically arresting web of melodic turns, scalar passages, arpeggiated figures, and leaps; though he uses all of these techniques in accordance with the principles of functional harmony, there remain numerous and tasteful dissonances. Notice, too, that Hawkins does not merely "noodle" around the borrowed tune; in true improviser-composer fashion he develops the whole 16-bar section from a very small collection of germinal ideas. In addition to the attractive shape of the line he creates, he seems to contrast activity and relaxation, using bursts of quick notes (triplet sixteenths, groups of six and of four sixteenths, and so forth) on the one hand, and longer notes (halves, quarters, and some eighths) on the other. Notice that sometimes the relaxing longer notes land on the metrically strong beats, and at other times the more active, quick note groups are given this privilege; thus, the inherent force of the downbeat is alternately characterized by sensations of relaxation and activity. All of this is accomplished within the context of swing, as it was discussed earlier.

This solo is illustrated below.

Ex. 9. "How Deep Is the Ocean."

For our last recorded example, we return to the Mulligan-Webster rendition of "Sunday," cited on p. 229. Mulligan's break, followed by his first chorus and the beginning of his second chorus, is shown in Ex. 10. Ex. 14 contains the last bar of Mulligan's third chorus (the "lead-in" to the first piano chorus) and the beginning of that piano chorus. Ex. 15 contains the opening measures of Webster's first chorus.

Ex. 10. "Sunday."

In examining these improvisations one discovers that each is very carefully organized and is built around a small set of compact germinal ideas. Although this music is improvised, it is clearly not the product of chance or accident.

Mulligan's first chorus centers on the note G♯ and on arpeggiated figures containing G♯. The unfolding emphasis on this note begins in the very first bar of the chorus:

Ex. 11.

These three statements of G♯ linger in our memory through seven beats of rest. Mulligan's activity resumes in the second half of bar 3. Notice the emphasis on G♯ in that bar, and again in bar 5 where both the lower and the upper octave of G♯ are presented. Also introduced in bar 5 is the arpeggiated figure with which Mulligan works throughout this chorus:

Ex. 12.

The "X"s over the G♯ (bar 5), G natural (bar 6), and F♯ (bar 7) indicate the path of a descending chromatic line. This line (and diatonic versions of it) is another idea that becomes an integral part of the chorus. This descending scalar figure always begins on G♯—again we note that Mulligan uses that pitch as a focal point. Notice the focal placement of G♯ in bar 9 (on the metrical downbeat). Notice also in bar 10 the scalar descent from G♯ to F♯ to E (a diatonic version of the idea mentioned above). The Xs over the G♯ (bar 13), F♯ (bar 14), and E (bar 15) once more outline this figure.

The features of the first half of this chorus continue to dominate the second half (bars 17–32), where the central importance of G♯, the short, descending scale lines beginning on G♯, and the arpeggios that feature G♯ are clearly evident. (See Ex. 10.) Note how the descending scalar idea is stretched over four bars; G♯ (bar 17), G natural (bar 18), F♯ (bar 19), E (bar 20); and then compressed to less than two bars: G♯ (bar 21), F♯ (bar 21), E (bar 22). Near the end of bar 24, and continuing through bar 25, Mulligan works with a half-step figure, G to G♯ (again, G♯!). This is echoed in the whole-step figure (of bar 26), C♯ to B. All of these half- and whole-step figures anticipate the leading idea of the first part of Mulligan's second chorus, the first two bars of which are:

Ex. 13.

Thus, Mulligan not only develops continuity within a single chorus, he also creates continuity between one chorus and the next, for the idea begun at the end of the first chorus becomes the central idea in the second chorus. This musical continuity is carried a step further, from soloist to soloist. Compare the last bar (the "lead-in" bar) of Mulligan's third chorus with the opening of the first piano chorus, and notice how the X-marked notes in the former are repeated in the first bar of the piano chorus. The pianist seizes upon Mulligan's last utterance, repeats it, adds to it something of his own, and uses that as his initial idea. The idea stated in bars 1 and 2 is echoed in a variant form in bars 3 and 4, and again in bars 5 and 6.

Ex. 14.

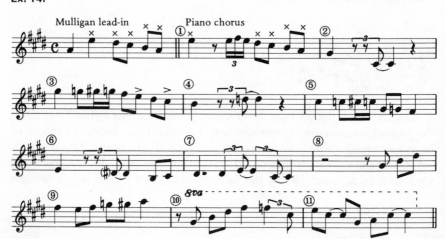

The opening of Webster's first chorus also demonstrates how the jazz improviser develops small ideas and fragments by repeating but constantly varying them. Notice how the essence of the first seven bars of Webster's chorus is contained in the very first bar, and observe that bars 3, 4, 6, and 7 are variations of bar 1.

Webster's second idea, of which only bars 9 to 11 are given here, is reminiscent of the opening of Mulligan's second chorus.

Ex. 15.

The careful listener will discover that the remainder of this solo, and, in fact, all the remaining solo portions are made in the manner outlined above.

A wider acquaintance with jazz can only lead one to a deeper appreciation of the marvels and excitement of jazz improvisation. The two albums from which the examples in this chapter are drawn provide dozens of fine improvisatory soles, played in a variety of jazz styles by ensembles ranging from small groups to big bands. The first, *The Jazz Round,* presents eight very well-known jazz performers, each doing two different numbers; each number combines one soloist with a second soloist and/or a group. As a whole, the recording provides us with the opportunity to enjoy the musical interactions of performers representing different eras and styles. The second album, *Encyclopedia of Jazz on Records,* is a good, comprehensive, and relatively inexpensive anthology of jazz and jazz styles from the '20s to the '50s.

Improvisation and Western Art Music

It was suggested earlier that musical traditions that rely upon notation do so in an effort to fix the music, to retain it in the state in which the composer originally conceived it. Notation has, therefore, a tendency to thwart improvisation—it is by its very nature inimical to improvisation. Notational systems exhibiting varying degrees of completeness and precision have been used in some of the world's art musics, and a striving for complete, precise notation has been one of the dominant concerns in Western art music since the Middle Ages. This urge to indicate to performers as precisely as possible what-is to be played (or sung), when it is to be played, and at what speed and in what manner it is to be played leaves little room for improvisation. But notation need not completely destroy the spirit of improvisation; in fact, it has not done so in Western art music, though in some eras improvisation has been more plentiful and more important than in others.

In the Classical concerto improvisation is considerably restricted, in the sense that improvisatory sections (which we shall discuss below) are surrounded by fixed music. As we have seen, jazz depends upon improvisation for its very life, though jazz pieces can never quite be totally improvised. The reverse of this holds true for the Classical concerto, which depends upon a state of fixedness for its life and, indeed, its perpetuation, though, as we shall see, there are within this music pockets of improvisation.

In jazz the borrowed and arranged (fixed) elements are necessary but secondary to the improvised elements; they serve as a backdrop for the improviser. In the Classical concerto improvisation is permitted to enter the music at certain prescribed points, but is never permitted to dominate the music.

In the Classical concerto improvisation is restricted to particular sections called cadenzas. Typically, a cadenza is played near the end of both the first movement and the third (and concluding) movement of a concerto. Some cadenzas were pre-composed and notated, but the performer had the option of improvising his own cadenza within certain limits. These short improvisational sections are bounded by pre-composed, explicitly notated music; thus, improvisation is not permitted to stray beyond its regulated boundaries, nor to intrude on the rest of the music.

The composer of a concerto would often not pre-compose and notate the music for the cadenzas, but would instead leave it to the performer—and often in the Classical era, the performer was none other than the composer— to improvise for an appropriate length of time, in a manner consistent with the style of the rest of the composition. In improvising the cadenza, the performer could elect to vary, develop, or embellish materials that had been introduced in the main body of the movement. Or, he could improvise in a freer way, using only the skeletal aspects, not the detail of some previously stated passage as a base. However, in many cases the cadenza was used more as a platform for sheer virtuosic display.

Cadenzas were written for all of Mozart's piano concertos. Some of these were notated by Mozart himself, some by various nineteenth- and twentieth-century piano virtuosis. But some performers do not play these fixed cadenzas, preferring instead to keep alive this tradition of improvising the cadenzas.

The cadenzas that Mozart is known to have improvised when he played his concertos in public may not have resembled very closely the notated cadenzas that have been preserved and attributed to this composer. It is likely that the latter were intended for Mozart's students, not for himself. Doubtless, he would not have needed them, and perhaps he would not have used them even if they had been in front of him when he performed. If this were in fact the case, it would be an indication not only of Mozart's technical prowess as a performer, but also of his ability to improvise and his profound interest in the process of improvisation.

In discussing his Piano Concerto in D Major (K. 175) Mozart said: "Whenever I play this concerto I play whatever occurs to me at the moment." Of course, the members of the accompanying orchestra played from notated parts, and, thus, the ideas that Mozart allowed to "occur to him at the moment" would have been severely regulated by what they were playing. Nevertheless, and with the above limitations in mind, we are struck by the fact that on this occasion, and others as well, Mozart spoke as an improviser.

If we can believe the testimony of several of Mozart's contemporaries, then we must conclude that Mozart was an extraordinary improviser, and that some of his most impressive efforts as a composer may well have been created (and, lamentably, lost to us forever) in this manner. One of these contemporaries said:

> In my youth I had opportunities of hearing and admiring many distinguished virtuosi...but I cannot describe my amazement and delight in hearing the great and immortal W.A. Mozart play variations and improvisations on the pianoforte. ... It was to me like the gift of new senses of sight and hearing. The bold flights of his imagination into the highest regions, and again, down to the very depths of the abyss, caused the greatest masters of music to be lost in amazement and delight.[1]

Another said:

> If I dared to pray the Almighty to grant me one more earthly joy it would be that I might once again hear Mozart improvise; those who have not heard him can form no idea of his extraordinary performances.[2]

And another:

> What they most admire is his (Mozart's) playing out of his head whatever is laid before him, a fugue subject, or other theme.[3]

---

1 Ambros Rieder, *Recollections,* quoted in Otto Jahn, *Life of Mozart,* Vol. II (New York: Cooper Square Publishers, 1891), p. 439. Quoted with permission of Cooper Square Publishers.
2 *Ibid.*
3 *Ibid.,* Vol. I, p. 386.

Improvisation flourished in the Baroque art music. In fact, improvisation, together with variation and ornamentation, constitute the central, dominant force in this music. Again, due to their impermanent nature, we cannot experience firsthand the improvisations of the acknowledged Baroque masters of the art, such as J.S. Bach, G.F. Handel, and Domenico Scarlatti. But we can at least approach the experience by examining some of the fixed music that has survived from this era; we can do this because it is clear that in many cases the notated score represents only part of the music that was actually performed—the rest, which was not necessarily reflected in the notation, was played nevertheless and was an integral part of the composition. Some of this latter music was improvisatory.

A fundamental characteristic of almost all Baroque music was the employment of a partially improvisatory system known as basso continuo or thorough bass. The thorough bass, which was normally played by a keyboard instrument and one or more other instruments, consisted of a notated bass line and a series of numerical symbols placed above or below the notes of this line. The numbers indicated what harmonies were to be played in conjunction with the bass notes—they were a kind of shorthand for written-out chords. This in itself is not improvisatory. However, these symbols were a mere shadow of what was actually played by the performers: they were expected to improvise musical lines, using these suggested chords as a basis and, of course, operating in accordance with the laws of functional harmony. There is a very substantial difference between what we see notated in many modern editions of Baroque pieces and how those pieces actually sounded, for what does not appear is these editions are the improvisatory parts. It must be remembered, however, that the basso-continuo instruments functioned largely as a harmonic pad, atop which were the fixed (notated) solo lines (though the solo lines themselves were subject to frequent and extensive variation and ornamentation). Ultimately, then, a Baroque composition might be a mixture of fixed and quasi-improvisatory elements. But, unlike the Classical music discussed above—where improvisation was restricted to certain sections of the music that were bordered by other sections of fixed music—this Baroque music was both improvisational and fixed simultaneously and continuously. That is, in Baroque music improvisation was not partitioned off but, rather, ran throughout the music.

Closely related to the thorough bass is another Baroque technique, the ground bass or basso ostinato (also discussed in Chapter 1). The Baroque ground bass frequently functioned as a fixed melody (which carried with it some fixed harmonic implications), on top of which a series of melodic or harmonic variations was constructed. Hear, for instance, Claudio Monteverdi's *Zefiro torna e di soavi* (the score of which is found in *Tutte le Opera di Claudio Monteverdi*, edited by G. Francesco Malipiero [Asola, 1926–42]). Note the series of melodic inventions and variations above the basso ostinato:

Ex. 16. Monteverdi: *Zefiro torna e di soavi*, beginning.

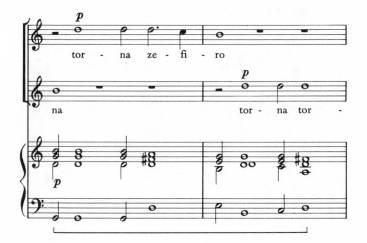

Although we are dealing entirely with fixed music in this instance, the fixed ground bass was very frequently the underpinning of improvised parts.

A seventeenth-century English composer and music theorist, Christopher Simpson, explained how the ground bass was used in conjunction with an improvisatory process called divisions or discant. In his treatise, *The Division Viol* (Part III, p. 27), Simpson wrote:

> A ground, subject, or bass is pricked down in two several [separate] papers; one for him who is to play the ground upon an organ, harpsichord, or what other instrument may be apt for that purpose; the other for him that plays upon the viol, who, having the said ground before his eyes, as his theme or subject, plays such variety of Descant or Division in accordance thereto, as his skill and present invention do then suggest unto him.

The "present invention" is, of course, the improvisatory element, the shape and direction of which are governed by the harmonies implied by or otherwise associated with the ground bass. Once more, this is a Baroque musical style in which fixed and improvisatory elements operated in tandem.

Improvisation of a sort occupies other forms of Baroque music, such as the *da capo* aria from middle-to-late Baroque opera seria. The third section of this three-part, ABA form was frequently not a literal repetition of the first A section, but, rather, was subject to the improvisatory, virtuosic manipulations of the singer.

Improvisation is also found in earlier periods of Western art music; it occupies a position of some importance in certain nineteenth-century music; and it has been central to a considerable quantity of avant-garde music since about 1950.

Improvisation in Some Non-Western Musics

Improvisation is important in several non-Western musical systems. Since most non-Western music does not use notation, it is sometimes assumed that all of it is in some sense improvised. This view, however, is quite erroneous. Non-Western cultures differ greatly in their attitudes toward composition and performance, but all of them have pieces of fixed music. The fact remains, though, that we can discuss the concept of improvisation in non-Western music at several levels.

In some cultures, precision in performance is regarded as important. In certain tribal cultures, for instance, a ceremony may be rendered invalid if the accompanying song is not performed accurately. In other cultures, a performer is encouraged to change a song as he repeats it, or to develop his own version of it; this is done, broadly speaking, through improvisation.

A number of non-Western cultures have developed improvisation in a systematic fashion. Most prominent among these are the high cultures of the Middle East, India, and Indonesia. The most highly developed of these systems is that of India.

In Indian music there are several specific types of improvisation, classified essentially by the rhythmic structure of the style of music being performed. In the music of Northern India the freest kind of improvisation is called *alap*; it has no meter, and its rhythm is sometimes compared to the rhythm of speech. But the performer of an *alap* is bound by many rules. Particularly important are the rules of the raga he has chosen to perform, for these govern the tones that he may use, the relative importance of each tone, and the way in which each tone is normally approached. Moreover, he is usually expected to center his performance on one important tone at a time, presenting them in ascending order. Thus, while he improvises, he must work within a rigidly prescribed system.

Other types of North Indian improvisation are *jor*, which has a "beat" but no metric organization, being essentially a succession of single downbeats; *jhala*, which is like *jor* only quicker; and *gat*, which is set to a *tala*. The latter is accompanied by a set of two drums—the *tabla*—and the improvisation often involves a kind of musical competition between the players of the *sitar* (or other melodic instrument) and the *tabla*.

In South Indian music there are similar forms. The South Indian singer performs *alapana* (very much like the *alap*) and *tanam* (analogous to *jor*). While these forms are based on the *raga* and its principles alone, there are improvisatory forms based upon fixed compositions. *Niraval*, for example, appropriates a line from a composed song and repeats it with improvised variations, interpolating original passages. As with *niraval, svara kalpana* refers only occasionally to the appropriated line; this form consists largely of rapid passages that incorporate the Indian equivalents of our do-re-mi-fa sequence, and exhibits the virtuosity of the singer.

In Arabic music the basis of improvisation is the *maqam,* a concept similar to the *raga,* which consists of a scale of notes and some typical melodic motifs that the performer may incorporate in his performance. Generally speaking, the Arabic improviser is less bound by rules than his Indian counterpart. Nevertheless, analysis of Arabic improvisations reveals that Arabic musicians work very much within the limits of a self-imposed system. The more one is acquainted with an individual improviser, the more clearly predictable his music becomes.

The same is true of Persian musicians, who work within a system called the *dastgahs.* They must memorize precisely a large body of music, and their improvisations are, in effect, performances and interpretations of what they have learned. However, Persian musicians do not usually consider themselves as improvisers upon a model; rather, they view themselves as interpreters of fixed compositions. And because each musician has his own way of performing the *dastgahs,* each exhibits very specific, characteristic ways of playing or singing.

Indian and Middle Eastern musics are essentially soloistic. Melody accompanied by drum, or by a second melodic instrument echoing the main soloist is as far as they go in developing an ensemble. True group improvisation is found, however, in the *gamelan* music of Java and Bali. Here, a large orchestra (*gamelan*) is the performing ensemble. Some of the many instruments perform a fixed tune, while others improvise variations that are performed simultaneously with the main melody. Again, the improvisations are highly predictable, governed as they are by tradition.

Thus, there is much improvisation in non-Western music, but it is subject to rules, both articulated and unspoken, just as the composition of fixed pieces is.

During the twentieth century, the systems just described have of course been affected by aspects of modernization and by Western musical thought and practice. Just what these effects may be has not been studied in detail, but perhaps two of them are of special interest: (1) fixed pieces are becoming more fixed, and, thus, the distinction between composition (in the ordinary sense) and improvisation is becoming greater; (2) because of their exposure to many different styles, and because conservative attitudes toward all aspects of life are being replaced by more liberal views, improvisers seem willing to go beyond the limitations of the system and strike out in new directions. This, of course, causes some upheaval in the Asian musical world. Sometimes the children of musicians who have modernized their styles try to revert to more conservative models. And conservative musicians may react unfavorably to innovation. But there is no doubt that the improvisatory systems of East and West have begun to affect one another substantially; this may be seen in the experimentation of jazz musicians with Indian instruments and the *raga* concept, and in the willingness of some Indian musicians to try their hand at Middle Eastern and even jazz styles of improvisation.

BIBLIOGRAPHY

The literature on improvisation is relatively small. The following items are useful discussions of various aspects of the nature, history, and performance of jazz, and some include valuable discographies.

BLESH, RUDI, *Shining Trumpets*. New York: Knopf, 1946.

HODER, ANDRÉ, *Jazz: its Evolution and Essence*. New York: Grove Press, 1956.

JONES, LEROI, *Black Music*. New York: William Morrow & Co., 1967.

SARGEANT, WINTHROP, *Jazz: Hot and Hybrid*. New York: Dutton, 1946.

SCHULLER, GUNTHER, *Early Jazz*, Vol. 1. New York: Oxford University Press, 1968.

STEARNS, MARSHALL, *The Story of Jazz*. New York: Oxford University Press, 1958, 1970.

TIRRO, FRANK, "The Silent Theme Tradition in Jazz," *Musical Quarterly*, LIII, No. 3 (1967), 313–34.

The following items discuss improvisation primarily in the context of Western art music.

ARNOLD, FRANCK, *The Art of Accompaniment from a Thorough-Bass as Practiced in the XVIIth & XVIIIth Centuries*. London: Holland Press, 1961.

BLOM, ERIC, ed., *Grove's Dictionary of Music and Musicians*. London: Macmillan & Co., Ltd., 1954. See the article entitled "Extemporization."

FERRAND, ERNST, *Improvisation in Nine Centuries of Western Music*. Cologne: A. Volk Verlag, 1961.

SIMPSON, CHRISTOPHER, *The Division Viol; or the Art of Playing ex tempore Upon a Ground Bass*. London: J. Curwen, 1955.

9

Technology and Music:
The Effect of the Phonograph

CHARLES HAMM

Music is constantly changing. Historical events, political and military maneuvers that bring several cultures into contact or conflict with one another, changing intellectual currents within a culture—these and other things can contribute to changes in musical styles and languages. But these changes can also come about because of technological developments that alter the course of a given culture and also the arts within it. Scientists and craftsmen who are not involved with music can do things that have no initial connection with music, but which may eventually have a profound effect on this art.

The question of technology and music will be investigated in this chapter by means of a discussion of a scientific discovery—the invention and development of the phonograph—that had a profound effect on the music of Western Europe and America, and eventually the entire world. First, the history of the phonograph will be traced, then the effects of this invention on the course of music will be discussed, and finally some general comments will be made about the effect that scientific advances may have had on music.

As is so often the case with inventions, the idea of the phonograph hatched in the minds of several individuals, evidently unknown to each other, almost simultaneously. Charles Cros, a Frenchman, was the first to conceive of a method to capture and reproduce sound. His ideas, contained in a paper written April 18, 1877, were first mentioned publicly in the fall of that year in an article written by a clergyman interested in new scientific inventions; that article also contained the first use of the term "phonograph." But M. Cros never built a machine, although his plan for the phonograph was viable. The first workable phonograph was built by the American inventor, Thomas Edison. He conceived the phonograph, apparently with no knowledge of Cros' work, as a result of his attempt to capture and reproduce telegraph signals. He noticed that paper tape with indentions representing Morse code dots and dashes, when drawn through his machine at high speed, made a "light musical, rhythmic sound, resembling human talk heard indistinctly." This observation led him to attempt to record telephone messages. His notebooks indicate that by the summer of 1877, he had experimented with a stylus that cut modulatory patterns in a hard substance in response to varying sounds—the basic method of making records to this day.

Later that year, Edison had perfected his invention to the point that when he shouted the words, "Mary had a little lamb,..." into a recording horn, something resembling the original could be heard when the tinfoil cylinder was played back. Edison later said of this occasion: "I was never so taken aback in my life." This fascinating new invention was very soon commercialized by the Edison Speaking Phonograph Company. Its entertainment value was tapped almost immediately, and audiences across the United States were astonished by its ability to speak in many languages, to imitate animals, and to reproduce cornettist Jules Levy's version, first plain and then highly embellished, of "Yankee Doodle"—perhaps the first demonstration of the phonograph's potential to reproduce music.

However, there were very serious problems with tonal quality; this, in addition to Edison's new and all-consuming interest in developing a light bulb, doomed the "talking machine" to a decade of commercial neglect after its initial success. Continuing research by others did, however, yield some improvements during those years. By 1888 the device was sophisticated enough for an attempt to be made to record classical music; in that year the twelve-year-old prodigy Josef Hofmann became the first classical artist to cut a cylinder. Hans von Bülow, the famous German conductor and pianist, recorded a Chopin mazurka very shortly thereafter. He is said to have been so astonished upon hearing the playback that he fainted dead away. The Crystal Palace in London was the scene of an attempt to record a large ensemble in the same year. The event was the annual Handel festival and the music was from his oratorio *Israel in Egypt*; London newspapers reported that the music was recorded with "perfect accuracy."

In spite of this enthusiasm for the fidelity of the phonograph, the results were very poor indeed, at least by modern-day standards. Many technical problems were still to be solved, foremost among these, the cylinder itself. The material for the Edison phonograph cylinder was tinfoil, which was inscribed with the modulations of the recording stylus as the cylinder was turned by hand and later by electric motor. The tinfoil cylinder was subject to rapid wear, and after being played back only a few times its grooves (cut in an up-and-down manner—the so-called "hill-and-dale" method—as opposed to the lateral modulation of today) would be almost totally destroyed. The development of the wax cylinder, which reduced surface noises, only partially alleviated the problem. Mechanical reproduction was done by directing sound vibrations into a horn that caused a diaphragm attached to the cutting stylus to move by sympathetic vibration. But this method could reproduce only a narrow band of mid-range frequencies. These technical problems, in addition to a time limit of only two minutes per cylinder, tended to discourage the recording of much serious music in these early years.

But in the 1890s the talking machine began to flourish as a form of popular entertainment, not in the home (for costs were much too prohibitive) but as "nickel-in-the-slot machines," the precursors of the present-day jukebox. John Philip Sousa and his U.S. Marine Band were among the busiest of the early recording artists, making many recordings of marches and other band pieces. Another popular artist was John Y. Atlee, a virtuoso whistler. But there was a dearth of classical recordings. The 1891 Columbia catalogue listed an arrangement of an aria from Verdi's *Il Trovatore* as its only item of "serious" music.

A technical development responsible for giving the young industry a new impetus was the perfection of the laterally-cut disc, still basic to the modern recording industry. It was developed and marketed in the mid 1890s by Emile Berliner, who called it the "gramophone." The cylinder did not go out of use immediately (in fact, it lingered on as long as 1929 in the Thomas A. Edison, Inc. catalogues), but actually continued to grow in use in the first decade of the twentieth century. In fact, the cylinder was used to record the only major collection of classical music made in America during the early history of the phonograph record. This was the work of Gianni Bettini, who invented a higher quality method of recording and was able to persuade top Italian operatic singers and other stars to record for him. His collection included performances by Yvette Guilbert, Pol Plançon, Frances Saville, and many other singers of the day. Sarah Bernhardt did a dramatic reading for him, and a Bettini recording of Mark Twain is the first known recording of this famous American. Some of Bettini's recordings were private, and not for sale, but most were available on special order at prices of up to six dollars per two-minute cylinder—this at a time when most companies sold their products for fifty cents each.

By 1900 the repertory of recorded art music in both the U.S. and Europe (where Pathé in France and other companies elsewhere had a larger percentage of classical music among their commercial offerings) consisted mostly of arias and other selections from opera. There were practically no attempts to record orchestral music; the reason for this was technical limitations. The voice, with piano accompaniment, was all that the recording horn of that day could handle. An orchestra, with its complex acoustics, was simply beyond the capabilities of recording techniques of the time.

Enrico Caruso, the man who was to be responsible for making recorded classical music fashionable and profitable, cut his first cylinder in the winter of 1901. In March, 1902, he made a series of discs in Milan that are probably the first completely successful recordings in terms of sound quality. Caruso's success was due to some extent to the physical characteristics of his tenor voice, very strong and rich in overtones, which effectively masked the surface noise on these early discs.

This year—1902—and the next (when twelve-inch, four-minute 78-rpm discs were introduced) marked the beginning of the modern recording era. It became possible to select from a wide variety of music styles and artists, pay a reasonable price, and expect to receive a quality product. The use of both sides of the disc, begun in 1904, made the record a better bargain, and successful attempts to record orchestral accompaniments that same year made it possible for the record to be a more satisfying musical product. The disc was also acquiring a cultural position of its own, which occasionally bordered on snobbery. By 1905 many important vocal artists (Patti, Lehmann, Battistini, and others) and composer-performers (Debussy) had recorded in the studios of the leading record companies. This led to the view that the phonograph record was a cultural instrument capable of involvement with "serious" music. "If you Believe in Music, You Need a Victor-Victrola!" ran a favorite typical advertisement of the Victor Talking Machine Company.

The three most important record manufacturers in America were Victor, Columbia, and Edison. Columbia temporarily discontinued its line of classical music after 1903, when it discovered that such recordings seldom showed a profit. Edison likewise was involved with other types of music, so Victor had a virtual monopoly on the market, which lasted until World War II. The collaboration of Caruso with Victor signalled the beginning of a most fruitful period for both. From February, 1906, when he recorded some operatic arias accompanied by orchestra, until his death in 1921, Caruso earned over two million dollars from his recordings. Victor also profited financially from this partnership, but probably benefited even more from the prestige that accompanied it. Prestige and classical music were linked in the minds of many people, and because Caruso's reputation was so great, his association with Victor elevated this company's status. There is no way of knowing exactly how many non-classical recordings Victor's impressive array of "Red Seal Label" artists were indirectly responsible for selling; but the facts show that Vietor dominated the overall industry during its years of superiority in the classical field, with a catalogue that was otherwise not much different from either Columbia's or, later, Decca's.

Thomas A. Edison, Inc., formed the third corner of the recording industry. Almost from the very beginning, when he showed little interest in the cultural and entertainment potential of his invention. Edison was the most conservative of the three. He continued to make cylinder phonographs and recordings although the general trend in the industry was toward the disc. His products appealed and were sold to "the good old 'ragtime-coon songs–Sousa-Herbert-monologues–sentimental ballads' crowd," as an Edison house organ put it.

A dichotomy was thus established: the disc was directed at one general class and the cylinder at another. Thus, Edison's belated attempt in 1906 to introduce recordings of opera was inevitably doomed to failure; the potential customers for such fare owned incompatible disc-playback equipment. Edison realized his mistake, stopped recording this sort of music, and continued to manufacture cylinders appealing to his "crowd" until 1929. He made a last futile effort to enter the disc market in 1913, but this venture had little impact; thereafter, the inventor's influence steadily waned in the industry that he had founded, and his company folded in 1929.

Vocal music continued to make up the bulk of the recorded classical repertoire. In 1915 Victor could offer the buyer six different versions of the "Toreador Song" from Bizet's *Carmen,* but only the slow movements from Beethoven's Fifth Symphony and Sixth Symphony, from the entire output of this composer. Despite advances in recording technique, limitations of mechanical sound reproduction still hindered the industry. The sound had to be directed to a single recording horn, and often the volume and complexity of an orchestra would simply overload the acoustical capabilities of the system. Efforts to overcome these problems included the Stroh violin with its built-in sound horn that could be aimed directly at the recording horn; or the use of fewer instruments—often, only six violins were in an orchestra used to record classical music.

In Europe, solo piano recordings were popular from the early 1900s, with Backhaus, Paderewski, Pachmann, and others making recordings. Only in the 1910s did such fare find an audience in America. In addition to pianists, other famous European virtuosi of the day (Joseph Szigeti, Jan Kubelik, Josef Joachim, and others) were recorded.

By 1901 European companies had issued more or less complete versions of some of the most popular operas; nothing of the sort was attempted in America until much later. Recordings of orchestral music also reflected a greater European appetite for the classics; one could find some complete Beethoven symphonies, conducted by Arthur Nikisch and other well-known leaders, in European record stores by the mid 1910s.

Although the 1910s in America were not golden years for recordings of classical music, they were bonanza years for the recording industry as a whole. Dollar sales of records reached a peak not surpassed for almost thirty years. Largely responsible for this was the enthusiasm in the country during those years for the Turkey Trot, the One-Step, the Tango, the Boston, and other dances.

A pattern was established in those years: popular music was the money-maker, the commodity that made it possible for record companies to expand their listing of classical music, almost as a prestige-seeking public service. The dance-band craze also led to the first discs by the Original Jazz Band. Released in 1917, these were the first recorded examples of the music that was to play such a prominent role in American musical life in the decades to come.

The recording industry continued to improve the quality and variety of its classical repertoire in the '20s. For example, the first recording of an orchestral piece by J. S. Bach, the *Brandenburg* Concerto No. 3, was made in 1925. But recordings of classical music still suffered from the limitations of the 168–2,000 Hz. acoustical range imposed by the recording and playback equipment of the time (compared to the 20–20,000 Hz. range of modern recordings). Despite this handicap, the record companies (particularly European ones) continued to introduce new and often complete recordings of items in the standard concert repertoire.

Two German companies had issued separate versions of the complete Beethoven symphonies by 1925. Mahler's mammoth Second Symphony was recorded, and other works by such Romantic composers as Bruckner, Berlioz, Tchaikovsky, and Richard Strauss were issued in uncut versions. Many of these were still unavailable to American consumers, who had to be content with a plethora of jazz and dance records.

The important year 1925 saw the first application of electrodynamics to the recording process and a resulting increase in sound quality. Both recording and playback methods had been mechanical until that time, but in that year Bell Laboratories marketed (with Victor) the Orthophonic Victrola—a playback system using an electromagnetic pickup and speaker system—and the recording process utilized the newly developed electrical microphone. These developments made possible recordings of greater clarity that had greater dynamic range and a new sense of "presence." The first successful recording using this method, though a milestone, was not designed to demonstrate its value for classical music; it was Columbia's recording of "John Peel," sung by 850 voices, with "Adeste Fideles" on the reverse side using a chorus of approximately 4,850!

In the period between these developments and the depression years of the '30s more classical music was recorded and released. The Beethoven death centenary in 1927 prompted many new electrical recordings of his works, including all the symphonies and many of the quartets. Schubert's death centenary the following year produced a similar boom for his music. Wagner's *Tristan und Isolde* was released almost uncut (thirty-eight sides!), and Bach's B Minor Mass was issued, complete, on thirty-four sides.

The depression years hit the entertainment-oriented record industry especially hard. During the worst years of this period, sales were about four percent of what they had been earlier. Despite this, RCA Victor introduced a startling innovation in September, 1931, the "long-playing" record. A performance by Stokowski of Beethoven's Fifth Symphony was put on the two sides of one new long-playing record, as opposed to the five or six sides needed on 78-rpm discs. This was accomplished by doubling the number of grooves per inch and lowering the turntable speed to 33 1/3 rpm. The venture was doomed to failure at this time by the economic depression, by the loss of quality (a compromise for convenience), and by RCA Victor's failure to introduce an inexpensive new turntable for the new speed.

The record industry eventually began to climb out of the economic doldrums; a new company, Decca, almost overnight captured a large share of the market by dropping the price of the "bread-and-butter" dance record from seventy-five to thirty-five cents per disc. Technology continued to make improvements in quality: the expansion of the frequency response down to 30 Hz. in 1934 made possible the first recording of Richard Strauss' *Also Sprach Zarathustra,* with its famous opening 30 Hz. organ pedal point.

Various societies dedicated to the recording of a composer's complete output were active during these years, most of them among the less economically depressed Europeans. The Hugo Wolf Song Society was founded in 1931. Arthur Schnabel was commissioned by the Beethoven Sonata Society in 1932 to begin recording the complete Beethoven sonatas; this mammoth task was completed in 1939. Song cycles, quartets, preludes and fugues, and other works never before recorded were released under the auspices of similar societies.

Most classical recordings were still made in Europe. But a significant change began in 1936 when RCA Victor scored a coup by getting Arturo Toscanini to record for them. This relationship, which was to last seventeen years, was responsible for again bringing the American public into contact with recorded art music. Columbia further stimulated the classical market in 1940 by signing many of the top American artists and orchestras to exclusive recording contracts and promoting their recordings enthusiastically. Furthermore, they dropped their price from four dollars to one dollar for each 78-rpm disc. Almost overnight, Americans had access to inexpensive but good classical recordings by American musicians. The consumer responded by making 1941 an extremely good year for the industry, with all signs pointing to even better things. Record companies responded in turn by expanding the available repertory. During these years Schoenberg, Ives, Dufay, Josquin, and other "esoteric" composers appeared in the catalogues, very often in first recordings. But the outbreak of World War II and a strike of studio musicians in 1942–43 again depressed sales.

Events during the war years led to further technological advances. Magnetic tape and greater frequency response bands, originally developed for military use and paid for by Department of War research and development contracts, were later exploited commercially. Sales jumped dramatically after the war: twice as many discs sold in 1946 as any previous year, and an upward climb continued until June, 1948.

As a result of research and development begun during the war, Columbia was able to introduce its Long-Playing Record (the LP) in June, 1948. Unlike Victor in 1931, Columbia had perfected the new system before putting it on the market, and it also simultaneously introduced an inexpensive 33 1/3-rpm turntable. The advantages of the LP were impressive: in playing time, one LP (at $4.85) equalled five conventional 78-rpm discs ($7.25); the quality of sound was higher because of improvements in cutting methods; and greater convenience in handling and storage was obvious. However, RCA Victor introduced records later that year at another speed, 45 rpm. The result was a "Battle of the Speeds" to determine which would become standard. Two years of bitter competition led to an eventual compromise whereby 33 1/3-rpm discs were used for classical music and other albums, and 45s for single popular selections. Sales slumped during the several years of uncertainty in which customers waited to see the outcome before committing themselves to equipment that might become obsolete. Even after the matter was resolved, the public needed time to update their playback systems, and the manufacturers needed time to convert their catalogues to LP format and rerecord older items to take advantage of improvements in sound quality. It was not until 1955 that sales reached the volume of pre-LP days, and it took even longer for catalogues to become as complete.

The recorded repertoire continued to enlarge upon the standard concert fare of these early days of the LP. Bartók's complete string quartets were recorded in 1949, and pieces by Berg, Stravinsky, Webern, Schoenberg, and other major contemporary composers were being issued, as well as several works by such earlier composers as Palestrina. The standard repertoire was not being ignored, however. Toscanini's famous recording of the complete Beethoven symphonies was issued, the first "complete Beethoven" by a single conductor.

Technical developments have continued since the introduction of the LP, mostly along the lines of greater apparent physical dimension of sound. Audio Fidelity, Inc., announced the stereo LP in early 1958. The extra "presence" of two-channel sound captured the listener's imagination so much that ten years later, records were released only in this format. Quadraphonic sound, discussed in the late '60s, became a commercial reality in the early '70s.

The economic history of the recording industry since the mid '50s, when it righted itself after the shock of the LP, reveals that total sales will push toward two billion dollars in the mid '70s. Almost every year has shown a substantial increase in sales. Marketing procedures have changed so much that the listener now prefers to buy recordings at discount prices from a self-service bin at the supermarket or discount record center, instead of paying higher prices at a retail record store, as was formerly the case.

The recorded repertoire has both broadened and deepened. It has become profitable both for one new recording to offer a piece new to the repertoire, and for another to be the twenty-fourth available version of the *Nutcracker* Suite. Stereo has added the dimension of space; some producers, such as John Culshaw, have exploited its possibilities in personal ways to the point that their recordings carry their personal stamp, much as many movie director's films exhibit an individual style. Prosperity has allowed the recording of many works that may not realize a profit, as well as colossal tasks such as the complete recording of Wagner's *Der Ring des Nibelungen* and all of the Mahler symphonies. Many first recordings of both new and old music were among the approximately seven thousand new classical releases in the decade of the '60s, the most fruitful decade for the recorded repertoire in the history of the phonograph record.

Since monaural sound was compatible with stereophonic equipment from the very first, there was little significant change in catalogues with the coming of stereo. Thus, the conversion to stereo occurred painlessly with no loss of repertoire. A similar compatibility exists with quadraphonic sound and stereo playback equipment. The future of the recording industry appears bright economically, and prospects seem good for a constantly expanding repertory.

The phonograph record was a completely new element in musical life, eventually reaching and changing every aspect of it. Audiences, performers, critics and historians, educators, even composers—all were touched in some way by this new invention.

Music is a nonverbal, temporal art. There is no such thing as a musical artifact or object. Manuscripts, instruments, printed scores are not the pieces of musical art. One cannot go to a museum to see a piece of music, or erect a piece of music in the town square, or sit down and read a good piece of music—unless one has the rare gift to "hear" music by looking at a score, and then it is only the single person who hears it inside his own head. Because of this, music has been less aware of its history than any other art. Until quite recently, most musicians knew little or nothing of the actual music of earlier centuries. Palestrina was the only composer from before the seventeenth century to maintain even a subliminal level of interest in the consciousness of musicians throughout much of the nineteenth century. Many later composers knew nothing of the music of Monteverdi, Schütz, Vivaldi, or even Johann Sebastian Bach. There was simply no opportunity to hear this music.

Musical life revolved around contemporary music, and opportunities to hear performances were limited. Even where there were weekly or nightly concerts, only a relatively small number of compositions could be performed and heard. Furthermore, these pieces were almost invariably by popular contemporary composers. Thus, any musician's exposure to music was severely limited by this sort of musical life.

The comparison with the situation today is startling. We have, in the twentieth century, an unprecedented awareness and knowledge of an incredible range of music, gained in large part from hearing this music on the phonograph. Today, in a single afternoon, a listener can hear the music of Gesualdo, a gamelan orchestra, Ditters von Dittersdorf, Dufay, the Papago Indians, Mendelssohn, and Stephen Foster.

The exposure to a diversity of styles (a "horizontal" effect) has had a profound effect on musical life since the advent of the phonograph, as has also the "vertical" effect (or, depth within a single style, period, or genre). Today, a person can not only choose from a wide variety of pieces, he can also repeat any or all of them as many times as his patience or interest will allow. Anyone can now listen to Beethoven's Ninth Symphony more times in one day than most nineteenth-century musicians were able to do in a lifetime of concert-going.

Among the first areas of classical music to be explored by recordings were the Medieval and Renaissance periods. A pioneer in the recording of this early music was *L'Anthologie Sonore,* a joint French-American venture that resulted in a representative sample of Medieval and Renaissance music. These recordings were not aimed at a large segment of even the classical music market but were intended for a new minority of musically knowledgeable listeners. From this modest beginning in the '30s, the repertoire of early music has continued to grow, though it is still perhaps the most neglected in terms of the number of recorded compositions.

Lacunae are gradually being filled by musical organizations (such as the New York Pro Musica) whose function and reputation is based entirely upon performing early music. Major anthologies and collections, such as the *History of Music in Sound,* are adding to the repertory of music from these periods, and there is now considerable interest in this music, a growing audience for it, and more and more performers (professional and amateur) of it.

In order to have a valid view of history—musical history or any other kind —it is necessary to have information that is as complete as possible. Interest in the music of the Medieval and Renaissance periods is an important step toward an understanding of the entire musical past. The phonograph record has been an invaluable tool in helping us move toward a continually more complete picture of this past.

The LP, with its potential to make available extended works in an inexpensive and convenient form, has helped music historians to deal with music of the nineteenth century in a way that would otherwise have been impossible. This century saw the creation of works on a larger scale, in terms of both length of composition and size of performing groups, than at any earlier point in history. Recent interest in the music of such composers as Mahler and Berlioz has been precipitated at least in part by the availability of works that had not been recorded before. Mahler's Second Symphony had been available on 78-rpm discs, but it cost twenty-two dollars and took up eleven discs. Today, it is recorded on only two discs and can be bought for about five dollars at a discount house. This situation has made Mahler's music readily available to a much wider public than before, and all of his compositions are now available for both the public and the scholar. Berlioz was known only by performances and recordings of a mere handful of the many pieces he wrote. Today, almost all of his works are available on LPs, and he is not only a more popular composer with concert audiences, he is also much better understood by musical scholars because they have been able, through the phonograph record, to know and judge his output from the point of view of how it sounds rather than how it looks on paper.

Baroque music can also be seen in a better perspective now. Many composers of this period wrote an enormous number of compositions, and only a tiny fraction of their output could be heard before the perfection of the LP. But now enough works by such men as Telemann and Vivaldi are available to permit a fairer evaluation of these men as composers. And even such a famous composer as J. S. Bach can be evaluated and understood more clearly, now that more than ten times as many of his cantatas have been recorded since the invention of the LP.

As the phonograph has made available more and more music from the past, our understanding of the history of music has expanded and deepened, and this process will undoubtedly continue as the recorded repertory continues to grow.

What has been the effect of the phonograph on performers and audiences? There were predictions almost from the beginning that phonograph records would be the death of live music, that no one who owned or could buy a disc of a given composition would pay to go to a concert to hear that piece, that the home would replace the concert hall as the place to listen to classical music. Surprisingly, there was a growth in concert audiences paralleling the growth of the recorded repertoire. So many factors complicate the picture that it is difficult to contend, unequivocally, that the recording industry has promoted this growth of audience size. The percentage of the record market devoted to classical music has shrunk from a high of nearly forty percent after World War II to somewhere near five percent recently. However, the total sales during this period increased so dramatically that this drop in percentage does not represent a drop in volume. In interpreting this statistic one must remember the nature of the recorded repertoire which, as pointed out above, changed as drastically as did the percentages. To the record-buying public of pre-LP days, "classical" very often meant four-minute overtures, arias, opera highlights, short piano pieces, and the like. Many of these short pieces featured "hit" artists such as Stokowski, Rachmaninoff, and Caruso—individuals whose reputations rivaled those of popular music artists. "Classical music" and "popular music" were in some ways the same. The LP ended the four-minutes-per-side limitation and the star system based on the $1.35 Red Seal Label disc. The demise of the popular-classical "star" brought an end to massive public support for "classical" music. But as the repertoire changed and expanded, the record buyer became less of a dilettante and more knowledgeable. Width was lost, but depth was gained. Classical music sales came to be maintained by serious, knowledgeable listeners.

Various surveys tell us that these listeners, rather than being totally dedicated to the record, are also concert-goers, perhaps in search of the extra dimension that live music offers. Their presence alone does not explain the tripling of the sum spent for admissions to the performing arts since the last world war. During the same time span admissions to spectator sports rose only slightly, and are now considerably less per year than admissions to the performing arts. Since these "spectator sports dollars" vary in proportion to leisure time and free money, the increase in the amount of money spent for the performing arts is probably a function of something other than available free time.

The increase in audiences for classical music reflects and is a result of an increase in the number of performing organizations. The number of civic and community orchestras, for example, has multiplied threefold since the last war, roughly the same increase as that in attendance. Is there, then, a relationship between more performing groups and larger audiences for classical music and the development of the recording? The answer is undoubtedly positive. The recording bred musical knowledge, and the resulting interest in and love for music must be responsible for filling concert halls in cities and towns across this country for the last quarter century.

The increased interest in classical music in this country is reflected by the growth of existing music schools and the creation of new ones. These produce professional musicians who either become performers or teach others to become competent amateur musicians. These amateurs are the backbone of school and community performing organizations, whose number doubled between 1950 and 1963 and has increased at an even faster rate since. Students do not enter a professional music school without a prior knowledge of and love for classical music—and large numbers of them acquired this from listening to records.

There has been a curious but direct relationship between the history of the phonograph record and performers' repertory. In the early decades of the industry, orchestras were contracted to record what they played, and they all played much the same standard, eighteenth- or nineteenth-century German-Austrian repertory. With the increased sophistication of the listener-buyer of postwar days came a demand for something other than standard concert fare. After the introduction and success of the LP, the producer's philosophy became: "You record what *we* want you to record." This attitude led to potential success for artists and musical organizations willing and able to record music outside the standard concert repertoire (such as the New York Pro Musica), and for performers who were primarily recording artists, not concert artists (Glenn Gould, for example). The resulting diversification of concert and record programming affected all levels of performing musical society. Confidence in doing something excitingly different or even in knowing that an interpretation of the "standard" Beethoven Fifth does not have to be like Furtwängler's or Toscanini's was a result of the new philosophy, and in turn resulted in the greater variety that one is apt to find in concerts today.

The quality and even the general nature of performance have changed since the advent of the phonograph record. The infinite repeatability of a single recorded performance has forced an exhaustive revamping of performance standards and practices. Recordings are actually responsible for influencing live performance and promoting a higher level of musical technique. The mistake that may be unnoticeable and unimportant in live performance becomes unbearable upon repeated playings of a record. The performer is always under pressure before live audiences to equal the quality of recordings. The standard for performances today has become technical perfection—a minimum of mistakes, precise rhythms, and an avoidance of mannerisms. Most performers today pursue this goal, not necessarily to sell records—the majority of them still do not make recordings—but as the prevailing ideal of performance.

The contrast between the performer trained in pre-recording days and today's performer is startling; Bach by Wanda Landowska and Bach by Glenn Gould are two different Bachs. Nicholas Harnoncourt and the Vienna Concentus Musicus have become successful at recording Baroque music largely because of their unmannered, precise, authentic treatment of the score. The clavichord has been revived because of the demand for authenticity and also because its original milieu, the salon, is duplicated by the living room, bedroom, den, study, or wherever record listening is done in the home today.

The performer on a record is faceless; his personality will intrude only within the rather narrow limits of the laws of performance practice. The educated listener is not particularly interested in the idiosyncrasies of the performer and will not tolerate an uneven or inaccurate interpretation. Audiences in pre-recording days, particularly in much of the nineteenth century, went to see a given performer, a personality, a face. Accurate and authentic performance was often not a prime requirement. But the recording has changed all this..

Professional musical activity has not collapsed in the twentieth century because of the phonograph, as some predicted. Quite the contrary. There are larger and much better informed audiences for classical music than ever before in the history of the country. The number of performing groups, both professional and amateur, has increased many times over. The number of students preparing for professional careers has grown enormously, as has the number of schools offering instruction in music. Musicians today play a far greater range of compositions, with better technique and a better sense of historical styles, than ever before. And the phonograph record has played an important role in all of these developments and expansions.

The effect on composers has been much more mixed and complex. They have, of course, benefited from the general vitality and growth of music in the country, and from the possibility of having their own compositions recorded, but some aspects of a recording-dominated musical life have not been altogether beneficial.

Until the mid '30s, almost the only contemporary music available on records was that of such successful operatic composers as Puccini. By 1938, however, The *Gramophone Shop Encyclopedia of Recorded Music* was describing Arnold Schoenberg as "perhaps the most significant composer of our times" and listing complete versions of his *Gurrelieder* (twenty-seven sides) and *Verklärte Nacht*. The same catalogue spoke of Charles Ives as "perhaps the most original and characteristically 'American' composer this country has produced," but only some eight minutes of his music was commercially available. Stravinsky was important enough to have two full pages dedicated to recordings of his music. By the beginning of the '40s there were some recordings of pieces by Bartók, Berg, Hindemith, and almost all of the important composers of the early decades of the century, and as this generation of composers became better known, their recorded repertory grew.

The late '40s saw many recordings of such new works as Gian Carlo Menotti's *The Medium* and *The Telephone*, Leonard Bernstein's *Jeremiah* Symphony, John Cage's *Three Dances for Two Prepared Pianos*, Edgar Varèse's *Octandre*, and other pieces representing a younger group of composers. The recording of new works continues to the present day, even though the industry is often unwilling to gamble on unknown names and qualities. Several notable independent efforts have been made to overcome the inertia of the industry and to enlarge the repertory of contemporary music. Composers Recording, Inc., is dedicated to recording only contemporary composers, and the Louisville Symphony Orchestra has built its reputation largely on an ambitious series of recordings of contemporary music issued under the Louisville label. However, a summation of a recent year's "New Listings" in the monthly *Schwann's Long-Playing Record Catalog* showed almost as many new recordings of Mozart as of all twentieth-century composers combined. More significantly, after one subtracts the recordings of such old and now-established men as Stravinsky, Prokofiev, Bartók, and Schoenberg, the figures reveal an almost general disregard of new contemporary music.

In previous centuries, musical activity centered in whatever compositions were currently most in favor—always contemporary. Twentieth-century composers must compete for attention with music from the five or six previous centuries. This situation is unique to the present century; the phonograph record has played a major role in making musicians and audiences aware of and familiar with music of the past. To the extent that this situation makes it difficult for a composer to have his music performed, listened to, understood, and accepted, the recording industry has been his enemy.

Nevertheless, the twentieth-century composer has benefited in many ways from the phonograph. A composer's reputation is now based at least in part on his representation in the *Schwann Catalog*. Competitions for new works may include as part of the prize a recording session and the commercial release of the recording. Nonesuch Records commissioned Morton Subotnick to write *Silver Apples of the Moon,* which was subsequently released on its label as part of the commission. These are but a few examples of composers being directly influenced and rewarded by the recording.

Electronic music owes its birth and much of its history to the technology of the recording. The famous RCA Synthesizer was built by a recording company with the hope that it could be developed to the point where it could replace live sound sources. This machine is the father both of electronic music and of much of the later sophisticated equipment that has drawn on the electronic equipment, knowledge, and techniques of the recording industry.

Compositions that use magnetic tape sources are indebted to recording technology. The Beatles constructed *Sergeant Pepper's Lonely Hearts Club Band* along almost classical structural lines, using tape to add sounds over other sounds and to erase unwanted sounds. John Cage uses the technology of the phonograph as a sound source in his composition for magnetic photograph pickup cartridges entitled *Cartridge Music.* Many other composers of both classical and popular music are maintaining that the recording and its unique qualities, rather than being a limitation on the creative process, can become an integral part of the conception and creation of a new piece of music.

Developments in contemporary music sometimes parallel those in the sister arts of painting, sculpture, theater, and literature. Marshall McLuhan has said that some of the changes in these arts—changes from the realism of previous centuries to the abstract, expressionistic nature of the present—have resulted from the various new forms of media communications. As he puts it,

The painter could no longer depict a world that had been photographed. He turned, instead, to reveal the inner process of creativity in expressionism and in abstract art. Likewise, the novelist could no longer describe objects or happenings for readers who already knew what was happening by photo, press, film, and radio. The poet and novelist turned to those inward gestures of the mind by which we achieve insight and by which we make ourselves and our world.[1]

Music, by nature more abstract and therefore less subject to laws and structures based on natural objects and speech patterns than the plastic and verbal arts, has captured time and exists in space—through the recording. As an object, it can now be examined and criticized as a "thing"; we often speak now of "albums" and "recordings" rather than "music." The avant-garde of the present sometimes reacts against much the same realism as it did in the other arts, attempting to create works that depend for their effectiveness not merely on sound, but on visual and theatrical aspects that cannot be captured on a recording.

The phonograph record has enabled us to deal with and understand the music of the past in a way never before possible in the history of music. It has been less successful in dealing with contemporary music, perhaps because the present is not yet part of history. It is ironic that this contemporary technological creation has resulted in increased interest in and knowledge of the past, at the expense of the present—at least as far as composition is concerned.

New methods of education for both personal understanding of music and group instruction are possible because of the phonograph record. Radio broadcasts of classical music in the '30s greatly expanded the audience for this music, but these were merely extensions of concert-hall listening. It was difficult to become familiar with a wide range of works or even single compositions because there was still no chance to hear these works often enough to know them well. With the availability of an increasing number of recordings of complete classical works, however, thus making it possible to hear a work an infinite number of times, it became possible to achieve an understanding of a piece of music without having seen a single note of it. The possibility of an exclusively aural comprehension of music now existed.

Students in music courses are now played recordings that demonstrate styles, ideas, and techniques of whatever type of music is being discussed, and they have the opportunity to hear these works as many times as they wish. This is still a relatively new educational experience, but there is already evidence of both positive and negative results. Students taught by sound rather than written music react more strongly to nuances of sound and to differences among individual interpretations. Their sense of the nature and variety of tone color is more highly developed. However, the structural ele-

---

[1] Marshall McLuhan, *Understanding Media: The Extensions of Man* (New York: Signet Books, The New American Library, 1964), p. 246.

ments of music are less well understood. Technical aspects of music that can be demonstrated and understood more clearly when the music is seen on paper are less easily recognized.

Outside of class there is a new breed of music-listener, the record "buff." He has an enormous knowledge of the literature of music, can recognize, discuss, and compare different performers and performances, but he does not read music and has little understanding of technical matters.

In summary, musical life in America developed in quite different directions in the twentieth century from those it had taken before. There was an unprecedented rise of interest in classical music, a great increase in the number of people who played it and listened to it, an increase in the number of performing organizations, an expansion of the number of schools offering music instruction. There was an ever-increasing knowledge of the history of music, on the part of both performers and listeners. Performers became better, technically and stylistically. Composers benefited from the growing number of performers and musically knowledgeable listeners, but as the percentage of performance time given to music of the past increased, they found themselves in competition with composers from earlier centuries—a situation never before known in the history of Western music. Technical understanding of music grew, but along side this was another type of understanding—that of the listener who knew a great deal about music by ear, from listening, but who was not a musician himself, and perhaps did not even read music.

The phonograph record was a central factor in all of this.

Other technological developments in the past have had a similarly profound effect on the course of music history. The invention of printing, for example, eventually altered the course of music, though its effect was not immediate. It was not until 1501 that the Italian printer Petrucci perfected a satisfactory method of printing polyphonic music accurately and relatively cheaply. Until this time, music had been performed from and circulated by manuscripts, which were extremely time-consuming and expensive to produce. Petrucci; his Italian contemporaries Gardane, Scott, and Antico; such French printers as Attaignant and LeRoy & Ballard; and then a number of Germans and Englishmen—the prints of these men were not used to perform from at first, but were means whereby music could be circulated more easily and widely than before. A royal court in Krakow or Toledo or in England, the musical director of a cathedral in Cambrai or Regensburg or Vienna or Reggio Emilio, a prince in Denmark or Hungary or Germany, could purchase one or more prints containing a large number of pieces and have these copied into manuscripts, from which they would be sung.

Lute music could be played directly from prints, and as the character of music changed in the early seventeenth century with instrumental and solo music replacing music for large choral groups, the performers could read directly from the printed music. The first effect of printing on music had been to make possible a wider dissemination of music; the second effect was to make music available in a much cheaper and more accessible form to larger and steadily increasing numbers of performers. Western music had been developing from an oral tradition in the early Christian era to a written tradition with modest beginnings in Medieval times. But even throughout the Renaissance period, oral traditions were an important part of this music; and it was not until printing took root, providing the means for the mass reproduction of music, and it was not until the economics of Western music reached the point where thousands of people had the money to purchase this music that the greatest effect of printing on music was felt, in the eighteenth and nineteenth centuries.

Throughout the history of Western music, the technology of instrument building has had an effect on how music was performed and written. The availability of a keyboard instrument with a completely chromatic scale prompted composers to write passages they could and would not otherwise have done; the more sonorous and easily played stringed instruments built in the Baroque period contributed to the flood of compositions for strings characteristic of this time; wind instruments with completely accurate and usable chromatic scales and brass instruments with valves (making it possible for them to play full chromatic scales also) changed the character of orchestral sound in the late eighteenth and nineteenth centuries; electronic music could not have been written in recent decades if instruments capable of producing electronic sounds had not been developed.

Music is a complex and sensitive art, responding to changes of various sorts—including technological developments.

SUGGESTED READING LIST

GELATT, ROLAND, *The Fabulous Phonograph: From Edison to Stereo.* New York: Appleton-Century-Crofts, 1966.

HARRISON, NEIL F., *Report on the Record Business.* New York, 1947.

McLUHAN, MARSHALL, *Understanding Media: The Extensions of Man.* New York: The New American Library, 1964.

TOFFLER, ALVIN, *The Culture Consumers: A Study of Art and Affluence in America.* New York: St. Martin's Press, 1964.